Mometrix
TEST PREPARATION

DSST®

Math for Liberal Arts Exam Secrets Study Guide

Dear Future Exam Success Story

First of all, **THANK YOU** for purchasing Mometrix study materials!

Second, congratulations! You are one of the few determined test-takers who are committed to doing whatever it takes to excel on your exam. **You have come to the right place.** We developed these study materials with one goal in mind: to deliver you the information you need in a format that's concise and easy to use.

In addition to optimizing your guide for the content of the test, we've outlined our recommended steps for breaking down the preparation process into small, attainable goals so you can make sure you stay on track.

We've also analyzed the entire test-taking process, identifying the most common pitfalls and showing how you can overcome them and be ready for any curveball the test throws you.

Standardized testing is one of the biggest obstacles on your road to success, which only increases the importance of doing well in the high-pressure, high-stakes environment of test day. Your results on this test could have a significant impact on your future, and this guide provides the information and practical advice to help you achieve your full potential on test day.

Your success is our success

We would love to hear from you! If you would like to share the story of your exam success or if you have any questions or comments in regard to our products, please contact us at **800-673-8175** or **support@mometrix.com**.

Thanks again for your business and we wish you continued success!

Sincerely,
The Mometrix Test Preparation Team

Need more help? Check out our flashcards at:
http://MometrixFlashcards.com/DSST

Written and edited by the Mometrix Exam Secrets Test Prep Team
Printed in the United States of America

TABLE OF CONTENTS

Introduction

Thank you for purchasing this resource! You have made the choice to prepare yourself for a test that could have a huge impact on your future, and this guide is designed to help you be fully ready for test day. Obviously, it's important to have a solid understanding of the test material, but you also need to be prepared for the unique environment and stressors of the test, so that you can perform to the best of your abilities.

For this purpose, the first section that appears in this guide is the **Secret Keys**. We've devoted countless hours to meticulously researching what works and what doesn't, and we've boiled down our findings to the five most impactful steps you can take to improve your performance on the test. We start at the beginning with study planning and move through the preparation process, all the way to the testing strategies that will help you get the most out of what you know when you're finally sitting in front of the test.

We recommend that you start preparing for your test as far in advance as possible. However, if you've bought this guide as a last-minute study resource and only have a few days before your test, we recommend that you skip over the first two Secret Keys since they address a long-term study plan.

If you struggle with **test anxiety**, we strongly encourage you to check out our recommendations for how you can overcome it. Test anxiety is a formidable foe, but it can be beaten, and we want to make sure you have the tools you need to defeat it.

Secret Key #1 – Plan Big, Study Small

There's a lot riding on your performance. If you want to ace this test, you're going to need to keep your skills sharp and the material fresh in your mind. You need a plan that lets you review everything you need to know while still fitting in your schedule. We'll break this strategy down into three categories.

Information Organization

Start with the information you already have: the official test outline. From this, you can make a complete list of all the concepts you need to cover before the test. Organize these concepts into groups that can be studied together, and create a list of any related vocabulary you need to learn so you can brush up on any difficult terms. You'll want to keep this vocabulary list handy once you actually start studying since you may need to add to it along the way.

Time Management

Once you have your set of study concepts, decide how to spread them out over the time you have left before the test. Break your study plan into small, clear goals so you have a manageable task for each day and know exactly what you're doing. Then just focus on one small step at a time. When you manage your time this way, you don't need to spend hours at a time studying. Studying a small block of content for a short period each day helps you retain information better and avoid stressing over how much you have left to do. You can relax knowing that you have a plan to cover everything in time. In order for this strategy to be effective though, you have to start studying early and stick to your schedule. Avoid the exhaustion and futility that comes from last-minute cramming!

Study Environment

The environment you study in has a big impact on your learning. Studying in a coffee shop, while probably more enjoyable, is not likely to be as fruitful as studying in a quiet room. It's important to keep distractions to a minimum. You're only planning to study for a short block of time, so make the most of it. Don't pause to check your phone or get up to find a snack. It's also important to **avoid multitasking**. Research has consistently shown that multitasking will make your studying dramatically less effective. Your study area should also be comfortable and well-lit so you don't have the distraction of straining your eyes or sitting on an uncomfortable chair.

The time of day you study is also important. You want to be rested and alert. Don't wait until just before bedtime. Study when you'll be most likely to comprehend and remember. Even better, if you know what time of day your test will be, set that time aside for study. That way your brain will be used to working on that subject at that specific time and you'll have a better chance of recalling information.

Finally, it can be helpful to team up with others who are studying for the same test. Your actual studying should be done in as isolated an environment as possible, but the work of organizing the information and setting up the study plan can be divided up. In between study sessions, you can discuss with your teammates the concepts that you're all studying and quiz each other on the details. Just be sure that your teammates are as serious about the test as you are. If you find that your study time is being replaced with social time, you might need to find a new team.

Secret Key #2 – Make Your Studying Count

You're devoting a lot of time and effort to preparing for this test, so you want to be absolutely certain it will pay off. This means doing more than just reading the content and hoping you can remember it on test day. It's important to make every minute of study count. There are two main areas you can focus on to make your studying count.

Retention

It doesn't matter how much time you study if you can't remember the material. You need to make sure you are retaining the concepts. To check your retention of the information you're learning, try recalling it at later times with minimal prompting. Try carrying around flashcards and glance at one or two from time to time or ask a friend who's also studying for the test to quiz you.

To enhance your retention, look for ways to put the information into practice so that you can apply it rather than simply recalling it. If you're using the information in practical ways, it will be much easier to remember. Similarly, it helps to solidify a concept in your mind if you're not only reading it to yourself but also explaining it to someone else. Ask a friend to let you teach them about a concept you're a little shaky on (or speak aloud to an imaginary audience if necessary). As you try to summarize, define, give examples, and answer your friend's questions, you'll understand the concepts better and they will stay with you longer. Finally, step back for a big picture view and ask yourself how each piece of information fits with the whole subject. When you link the different concepts together and see them working together as a whole, it's easier to remember the individual components.

Finally, practice showing your work on any multi-step problems, even if you're just studying. Writing out each step you take to solve a problem will help solidify the process in your mind, and you'll be more likely to remember it during the test.

Modality

Modality simply refers to the means or method by which you study. Choosing a study modality that fits your own individual learning style is crucial. No two people learn best in exactly the same way, so it's important to know your strengths and use them to your advantage.

For example, if you learn best by visualization, focus on visualizing a concept in your mind and draw an image or a diagram. Try color-coding your notes, illustrating them, or creating symbols that will trigger your mind to recall a learned concept. If you learn best by hearing or discussing information, find a study partner who learns the same way or read aloud to yourself. Think about how to put the information in your own words. Imagine that you are giving a lecture on the topic and record yourself so you can listen to it later.

For any learning style, flashcards can be helpful. Organize the information so you can take advantage of spare moments to review. Underline key words or phrases. Use different colors for different categories. Mnemonic devices (such as creating a short list in which every item starts with the same letter) can also help with retention. Find what works best for you and use it to store the information in your mind most effectively and easily.

Secret Key #3 – Practice the Right Way

Your success on test day depends not only on how many hours you put into preparing, but also on whether you prepared the right way. It's good to check along the way to see if your studying is paying off. One of the most effective ways to do this is by taking practice tests to evaluate your progress. Practice tests are useful because they show exactly where you need to improve. Every time you take a practice test, pay special attention to these three groups of questions:

- The questions you got wrong
- The questions you had to guess on, even if you guessed right
- The questions you found difficult or slow to work through

This will show you exactly what your weak areas are, and where you need to devote more study time. Ask yourself why each of these questions gave you trouble. Was it because you didn't understand the material? Was it because you didn't remember the vocabulary? Do you need more repetitions on this type of question to build speed and confidence? Dig into those questions and figure out how you can strengthen your weak areas as you go back to review the material.

Additionally, many practice tests have a section explaining the answer choices. It can be tempting to read the explanation and think that you now have a good understanding of the concept. However, an explanation likely only covers part of the question's broader context. Even if the explanation makes perfect sense, **go back and investigate** every concept related to the question until you're positive you have a thorough understanding.

As you go along, keep in mind that the practice test is just that: practice. Memorizing these questions and answers will not be very helpful on the actual test because it is unlikely to have any of the same exact questions. If you only know the right answers to the sample questions, you won't be prepared for the real thing. **Study the concepts** until you understand them fully, and then you'll be able to answer any question that shows up on the test.

It's important to wait on the practice tests until you're ready. If you take a test on your first day of study, you may be overwhelmed by the amount of material covered and how much you need to learn. Work up to it gradually.

On test day, you'll need to be prepared for answering questions, managing your time, and using the test-taking strategies you've learned. It's a lot to balance, like a mental marathon that will have a big impact on your future. Like training for a marathon, you'll need to start slowly and work your way up. When test day arrives, you'll be ready.

Start with the strategies you've read in the first two Secret Keys—plan your course and study in the way that works best for you. If you have time, consider using multiple study resources to get different approaches to the same concepts. It can be helpful to see difficult concepts from more than one angle. Then find a good source for practice tests. Many times, the test website will suggest potential study resources or provide sample tests.

Practice Test Strategy

If you're able to find at least three practice tests, we recommend this strategy:

Untimed and Open-Book Practice

Take the first test with no time constraints and with your notes and study guide handy. Take your time and focus on applying the strategies you've learned.

Timed and Open-Book Practice

Take the second practice test open-book as well, but set a timer and practice pacing yourself to finish in time.

Timed and Closed-Book Practice

Take any other practice tests as if it were test day. Set a timer and put away your study materials. Sit at a table or desk in a quiet room, imagine yourself at the testing center, and answer questions as quickly and accurately as possible.

Keep repeating timed and closed-book tests on a regular basis until you run out of practice tests or it's time for the actual test. Your mind will be ready for the schedule and stress of test day, and you'll be able to focus on recalling the material you've learned.

Secret Key #4 – Pace Yourself

Once you're fully prepared for the material on the test, your biggest challenge on test day will be managing your time. Just knowing that the clock is ticking can make you panic even if you have plenty of time left. Work on pacing yourself so you can build confidence against the time constraints of the exam. Pacing is a difficult skill to master, especially in a high-pressure environment, so **practice is vital**.

Set time expectations for your pace based on how much time is available. For example, if a section has 60 questions and the time limit is 30 minutes, you know you have to average 30 seconds or less per question in order to answer them all. Although 30 seconds is the hard limit, set 25 seconds per question as your goal, so you reserve extra time to spend on harder questions. When you budget extra time for the harder questions, you no longer have any reason to stress when those questions take longer to answer.

Don't let this time expectation distract you from working through the test at a calm, steady pace, but keep it in mind so you don't spend too much time on any one question. Recognize that taking extra time on one question you don't understand may keep you from answering two that you do understand later in the test. If your time limit for a question is up and you're still not sure of the answer, mark it and move on, and come back to it later if the time and the test format allow. If the testing format doesn't allow you to return to earlier questions, just make an educated guess; then put it out of your mind and move on.

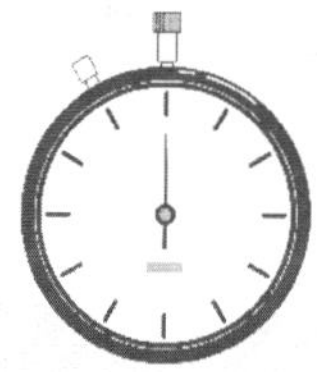

On the easier questions, be careful not to rush. It may seem wise to hurry through them so you have more time for the challenging ones, but it's not worth missing one if you know the concept and just didn't take the time to read the question fully. Work efficiently but make sure you understand the question and have looked at all of the answer choices, since more than one may seem right at first.

Even if you're paying attention to the time, you may find yourself a little behind at some point. You should speed up to get back on track, but do so wisely. Don't panic; just take a few seconds less on each question until you're caught up. Don't guess without thinking, but do look through the answer choices and eliminate any you know are wrong. If you can get down to two choices, it is often worthwhile to guess from those. Once you've chosen an answer, move on and don't dwell on any that you skipped or had to hurry through. If a question was taking too long, chances are it was one of the harder ones, so you weren't as likely to get it right anyway.

On the other hand, if you find yourself getting ahead of schedule, it may be beneficial to slow down a little. The more quickly you work, the more likely you are to make a careless mistake that will affect your score. You've budgeted time for each question, so don't be afraid to spend that time. Practice an efficient but careful pace to get the most out of the time you have.

Secret Key #5 – Have a Plan for Guessing

When you're taking the test, you may find yourself stuck on a question. Some of the answer choices seem better than others, but you don't see the one answer choice that is obviously correct. What do you do?

The scenario described above is very common, yet most test takers have not effectively prepared for it. Developing and practicing a plan for guessing may be one of the single most effective uses of your time as you get ready for the exam.

In developing your plan for guessing, there are three questions to address:

- When should you start the guessing process?
- How should you narrow down the choices?
- Which answer should you choose?

When to Start the Guessing Process

Unless your plan for guessing is to select C every time (which, despite its merits, is not what we recommend), you need to leave yourself enough time to apply your answer elimination strategies. Since you have a limited amount of time for each question, that means that if you're going to give yourself the best shot at guessing correctly, you have to decide quickly whether or not you will guess.

Of course, the best-case scenario is that you don't have to guess at all, so first, see if you can answer the question based on your knowledge of the subject and basic reasoning skills. Focus on the key words in the question and try to jog your memory of related topics. Give yourself a chance to bring the knowledge to mind, but once you realize that you don't have (or you can't access) the knowledge you need to answer the question, it's time to start the guessing process.

It's almost always better to start the guessing process too early than too late. It only takes a few seconds to remember something and answer the question from knowledge. Carefully eliminating wrong answer choices takes longer. Plus, going through the process of eliminating answer choices can actually help jog your memory.

Summary: Start the guessing process as soon as you decide that you can't answer the question based on your knowledge.

How to Narrow Down the Choices

The next chapter in this book (**Test-Taking Strategies**) includes a wide range of strategies for how to approach questions and how to look for answer choices to eliminate. You will definitely want to read those carefully, practice them, and figure out which ones work best for you. Here though, we're going to address a mindset rather than a particular strategy.

Your odds of guessing an answer correctly depend on how many options you are choosing from.

Number of options left	5	4	3	2	1
Odds of guessing correctly	20%	25%	33%	50%	100%

You can see from this chart just how valuable it is to be able to eliminate incorrect answers and make an educated guess, but there are two things that many test takers do that cause them to miss out on the benefits of guessing:

- Accidentally eliminating the correct answer
- Selecting an answer based on an impression

We'll look at the first one here, and the second one in the next section.

To avoid accidentally eliminating the correct answer, we recommend a thought exercise called **the $5 challenge**. In this challenge, you only eliminate an answer choice from contention if you are willing to bet $5 on it being wrong. Why $5? Five dollars is a small but not insignificant amount of money. It's an amount you could afford to lose but wouldn't want to throw away. And while losing $5 once might not hurt too much, doing it twenty times will set you back $100. In the same way, each small decision you make—eliminating a choice here, guessing on a question there—won't by itself impact your score very much, but when you put them all together, they can make a big difference. By holding each answer choice elimination decision to a higher standard, you can reduce the risk of accidentally eliminating the correct answer.

The $5 challenge can also be applied in a positive sense: If you are willing to bet $5 that an answer choice *is* correct, go ahead and mark it as correct.

Summary: Only eliminate an answer choice if you are willing to bet $5 that it is wrong.

Which Answer to Choose

You're taking the test. You've run into a hard question and decided you'll have to guess. You've eliminated all the answer choices you're willing to bet $5 on. Now you have to pick an answer. Why do we even need to talk about this? Why can't you just pick whichever one you feel like when the time comes?

The answer to these questions is that if you don't come into the test with a plan, you'll rely on your impression to select an answer choice, and if you do that, you risk falling into a trap. The test writers know that everyone who takes their test will be guessing on some of the questions, so they intentionally write wrong answer choices to seem plausible. You still have to pick an answer though, and if the wrong answer choices are designed to look right, how can you ever be sure that you're not falling for their trap? The best solution we've found to this dilemma is to take the decision out of your hands entirely. Here is the process we recommend:

Once you've eliminated any choices that you are confident (willing to bet $5) are wrong, select the first remaining choice as your answer.

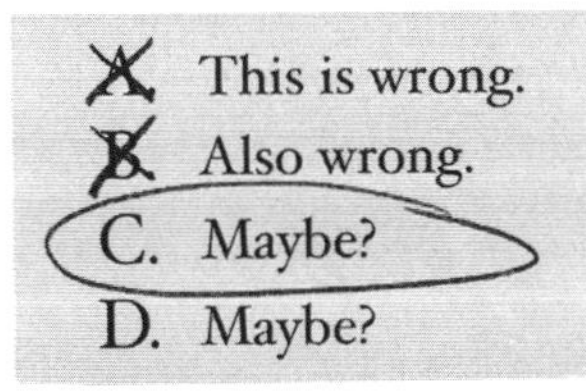

Whether you choose to select the first remaining choice, the second, or the last, the important thing is that you use some preselected standard. Using this approach guarantees that you will not be enticed into selecting an answer choice that looks right, because you are not basing your decision on how the answer choices look.

This is not meant to make you question your knowledge. Instead, it is to help you recognize the difference between your knowledge and your impressions. There's a huge difference between thinking an answer is right because of what you know, and thinking an answer is right because it looks or sounds like it should be right.

Summary: To ensure that your selection is appropriately random, make a predetermined selection from among all answer choices you have not eliminated.

Test-Taking Strategies

This section contains a list of test-taking strategies that you may find helpful as you work through the test. By taking what you know and applying logical thought, you can maximize your chances of answering any question correctly!

It is very important to realize that every question is different and every person is different: no single strategy will work on every question, and no single strategy will work for every person. That's why we've included all of them here, so you can try them out and determine which ones work best for different types of questions and which ones work best for you.

Question Strategies

✓ Read Carefully

Read the question and the answer choices carefully. Don't miss the question because you misread the terms. You have plenty of time to read each question thoroughly and make sure you understand what is being asked. Yet a happy medium must be attained, so don't waste too much time. You must read carefully and efficiently.

✓ Contextual Clues

Look for contextual clues. If the question includes a word you are not familiar with, look at the immediate context for some indication of what the word might mean. Contextual clues can often give you all the information you need to decipher the meaning of an unfamiliar word. Even if you can't determine the meaning, you may be able to narrow down the possibilities enough to make a solid guess at the answer to the question.

✓ Prefixes

If you're having trouble with a word in the question or answer choices, try dissecting it. Take advantage of every clue that the word might include. Prefixes can be a huge help. Usually, they allow you to determine a basic meaning. *Pre-* means before, *post-* means after, *pro-* is positive, *de-* is negative. From prefixes, you can get an idea of the general meaning of the word and try to put it into context.

✓ Hedge Words

Watch out for critical hedge words, such as *likely, may, can, often, almost, mostly, usually, generally, rarely*, and *sometimes*. Question writers insert these hedge phrases to cover every possibility. Often an answer choice will be wrong simply because it leaves no room for exception. Be on guard for answer choices that have definitive words such as *exactly* and *always*.

✓ Switchback Words

Stay alert for *switchbacks*. These are the words and phrases frequently used to alert you to shifts in thought. The most common switchback words are *but, although*, and *however*. Others include *nevertheless, on the other hand, even though, while, in spite of, despite*, and *regardless of*. Switchback words are important to catch because they can change the direction of the question or an answer choice.

✓ FACE VALUE

When in doubt, use common sense. Accept the situation in the problem at face value. Don't read too much into it. These problems will not require you to make wild assumptions. If you have to go beyond creativity and warp time or space in order to have an answer choice fit the question, then you should move on and consider the other answer choices. These are normal problems rooted in reality. The applicable relationship or explanation may not be readily apparent, but it is there for you to figure out. Use your common sense to interpret anything that isn't clear.

Answer Choice Strategies

✓ ANSWER SELECTION

The most thorough way to pick an answer choice is to identify and eliminate wrong answers until only one is left, then confirm it is the correct answer. Sometimes an answer choice may immediately seem right, but be careful. The test writers will usually put more than one reasonable answer choice on each question, so take a second to read all of them and make sure that the other choices are not equally obvious. As long as you have time left, it is better to read every answer choice than to pick the first one that looks right without checking the others.

✓ ANSWER CHOICE FAMILIES

An answer choice family consists of two (in rare cases, three) answer choices that are very similar in construction and cannot all be true at the same time. If you see two answer choices that are direct opposites or parallels, one of them is usually the correct answer. For instance, if one answer choice says that quantity x increases and another either says that quantity x decreases (opposite) or says that quantity y increases (parallel), then those answer choices would fall into the same family. An answer choice that doesn't match the construction of the answer choice family is more likely to be incorrect. Most questions will not have answer choice families, but when they do appear, you should be prepared to recognize them.

✓ ELIMINATE ANSWERS

Eliminate answer choices as soon as you realize they are wrong, but make sure you consider all possibilities. If you are eliminating answer choices and realize that the last one you are left with is also wrong, don't panic. Start over and consider each choice again. There may be something you missed the first time that you will realize on the second pass.

✓ AVOID FACT TRAPS

Don't be distracted by an answer choice that is factually true but doesn't answer the question. You are looking for the choice that answers the question. Stay focused on what the question is asking for so you don't accidentally pick an answer that is true but incorrect. Always go back to the question and make sure the answer choice you've selected actually answers the question and is not merely a true statement.

✓ EXTREME STATEMENTS

In general, you should avoid answers that put forth extreme actions as standard practice or proclaim controversial ideas as established fact. An answer choice that states the "process should be used in certain situations, if..." is much more likely to be correct than one that states the "process should be discontinued completely." The first is a calm rational statement and doesn't even make a definitive, uncompromising stance, using a hedge word *if* to provide wiggle room, whereas the second choice is far more extreme.

⊘ Benchmark

As you read through the answer choices and you come across one that seems to answer the question well, mentally select that answer choice. This is not your final answer, but it's the one that will help you evaluate the other answer choices. The one that you selected is your benchmark or standard for judging each of the other answer choices. Every other answer choice must be compared to your benchmark. That choice is correct until proven otherwise by another answer choice beating it. If you find a better answer, then that one becomes your new benchmark. Once you've decided that no other choice answers the question as well as your benchmark, you have your final answer.

⊘ Predict the Answer

Before you even start looking at the answer choices, it is often best to try to predict the answer. When you come up with the answer on your own, it is easier to avoid distractions and traps because you will know exactly what to look for. The right answer choice is unlikely to be word-for-word what you came up with, but it should be a close match. Even if you are confident that you have the right answer, you should still take the time to read each option before moving on.

General Strategies

⊘ Tough Questions

If you are stumped on a problem or it appears too hard or too difficult, don't waste time. Move on! Remember though, if you can quickly check for obviously incorrect answer choices, your chances of guessing correctly are greatly improved. Before you completely give up, at least try to knock out a couple of possible answers. Eliminate what you can and then guess at the remaining answer choices before moving on.

⊘ Check Your Work

Since you will probably not know every term listed and the answer to every question, it is important that you get credit for the ones that you do know. Don't miss any questions through careless mistakes. If at all possible, try to take a second to look back over your answer selection and make sure you've selected the correct answer choice and haven't made a costly careless mistake (such as marking an answer choice that you didn't mean to mark). This quick double check should more than pay for itself in caught mistakes for the time it costs.

⊘ Pace Yourself

It's easy to be overwhelmed when you're looking at a page full of questions; your mind is confused and full of random thoughts, and the clock is ticking down faster than you would like. Calm down and maintain the pace that you have set for yourself. Especially as you get down to the last few minutes of the test, don't let the small numbers on the clock make you panic. As long as you are on track by monitoring your pace, you are guaranteed to have time for each question.

⊘ Don't Rush

It is very easy to make errors when you are in a hurry. Maintaining a fast pace in answering questions is pointless if it makes you miss questions that you would have gotten right otherwise. Test writers like to include distracting information and wrong answers that seem right. Taking a little extra time to avoid careless mistakes can make all the difference in your test score. Find a pace that allows you to be confident in the answers that you select.

✓ KEEP MOVING

Panicking will not help you pass the test, so do your best to stay calm and keep moving. Taking deep breaths and going through the answer elimination steps you practiced can help to break through a stress barrier and keep your pace.

Final Notes

The combination of a solid foundation of content knowledge and the confidence that comes from practicing your plan for applying that knowledge is the key to maximizing your performance on test day. As your foundation of content knowledge is built up and strengthened, you'll find that the strategies included in this chapter become more and more effective in helping you quickly sift through the distractions and traps of the test to isolate the correct answer.

Now that you're preparing to move forward into the test content chapters of this book, be sure to keep your goal in mind. As you read, think about how you will be able to apply this information on the test. If you've already seen sample questions for the test and you have an idea of the question format and style, try to come up with questions of your own that you can answer based on what you're reading. This will give you valuable practice applying your knowledge in the same ways you can expect to on test day.

Good luck and good studying!

Real Number Systems

Real Numbers

Numbers and Their Classifications

There are several different kinds of numbers. When you learn to count as a child, you start with **natural numbers**. You may know them as counting numbers. These numbers begin with 1, 2, 3, and so on. **whole numbers** are all natural numbers and zero. **integers** are all whole numbers and their related negative values (...$-2, -1, 0, 1, 2$...). Fractions with an integer in the numerator and a non-zero integer in the denominator are called **rational numbers**.

Numbers such as pi (π) that do not end or repeat and cannot be given as a fraction are known as **irrational numbers**. Any number that has the imaginary number i, where $i^2 = -1$ and $i = \sqrt{-1}$ is known as a **complex number**. All natural numbers, whole numbers, integers, rational numbers, and irrational numbers are **real numbers**. Complex numbers are not real numbers.

Aside from the number 1, all natural numbers are known as prime or composite. **prime numbers** are natural numbers that are greater than 1 and have factors that are 1 and itself (e.g., 3). On the other hand, **composite numbers** are natural numbers that are greater than 1 and are not prime numbers. The number 1 is a special case because it is not a prime number or composite number.

Numbers are the basic building blocks of mathematics. These terms show some elements of numbers:

Integers – The set of positive and negative numbers. This set includes zero. Integers do not include fractions $\left(\frac{1}{3}\right)$, decimals (0.56), or mixed numbers $\left(7\frac{3}{4}\right)$.

Even number – Any integer that can be divided by 2 without a remainder. For example: 2, 4, 6, 8, 10, etc.

Odd number – Any integer that cannot be divided evenly by 2. For example: 3, 5, 7, 9, and so on.

Decimal number – a number that uses a decimal point to show the part of the number that is less than one. Example: 1.234.

Decimal point – a symbol used to separate the ones place from the tenths place in decimals. This symbol is used to separate dollars from cents in currency.

Decimal place – the position of a number to the right of the decimal point. In the decimal 0.123, the 1 is in the first place to the right of the decimal point, which is the tenths place, and is equivalent to $\frac{1}{10}$. The 2 is in the second place, which is the hundredths place, and is equivalent to $\frac{2}{100}$. The 3 is in the third place, which is the thousandths place, and is equivalent to $\frac{3}{1000}$. So, the decimal is the same as: $0.123 = \frac{1}{10} + \frac{2}{100} + \frac{3}{1000}$

Review Video: Classification of Numbers
Visit mometrix.com/academy and enter code: 461071

Review Video: Rational and Irrational Numbers
Visit mometrix.com/academy and enter code: 280645

THE NUMBER LINE

A number line is a graph with marks at regular intervals to indicate values. Essentially, since the intervals are all the same, this graph shows the distance between numbers. A number line can be used to demonstrate the relationship between any value, including zero, negatives, positives, fractions, and more.

EXAMPLE

Name each point on the number line below:

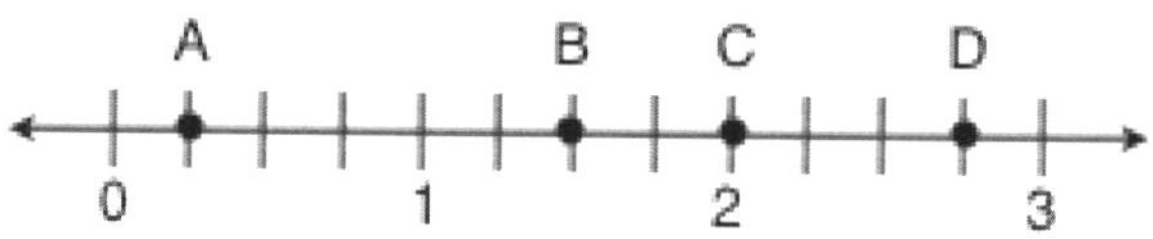

Use the dashed lines on the number line to identify each point. Each dashed line between two whole numbers is $\frac{1}{4}$. The line halfway between two numbers is $\frac{1}{2}$.

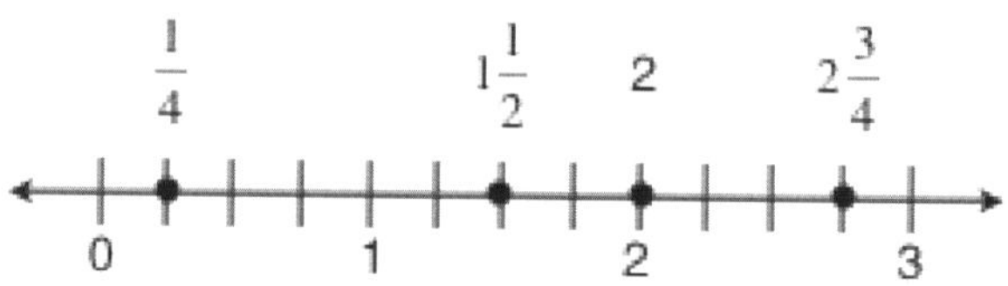

Review Video: The Number Line
Visit mometrix.com/academy and enter code: 816439

ABSOLUTE VALUE

A precursor to working with negative numbers is understanding what **absolute values** are. A number's absolute value is simply the distance away from zero a number is on the number line. The absolute value of a number is always positive and is written $|x|$.

EXAMPLE

Show that $|3| = |-3|$.

The absolute value of 3, written as $|3|$, is 3 because the distance between 0 and 3 on a number line is three units. Likewise, the absolute value of -3, written as $|-3|$, is 3 because the distance between 0 and -3 on a number line is three units. So, $|3| = |-3|$.

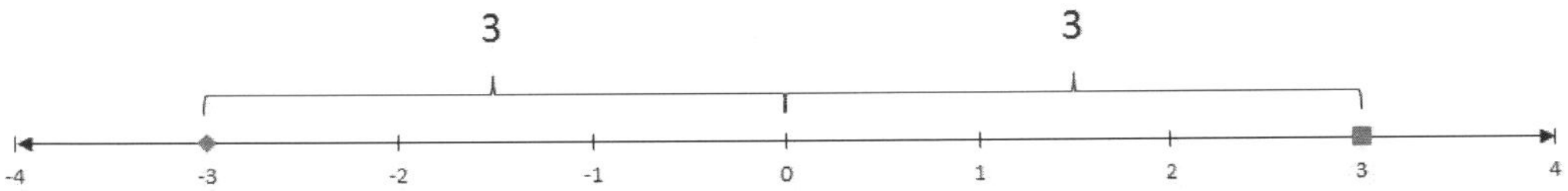

Review Video: Absolute Value
Visit mometrix.com/academy and enter code: 314669

Writing Numbers in Word Form

Write each number in words:

- 29: twenty-nine
- 478: four hundred seventy-eight
- 98,542: ninety-eight thousand five hundred forty-two
- 302, 876: three hundred two thousand eight hundred seventy-six

Write each decimal in words:

- 0.06: six hundredths
- 6.0: six
- 0.009: nine thousandths
- 0.901: nine hundred one-thousandths

Percentages

Percentages can be thought of as fractions that are based on a whole of 100; that is, one whole is equal to 100%. The word percent means "per hundred." Fractions can be expressed as a percentage by finding equivalent fractions with a denominator of 100. For example: $\frac{7}{10} = \frac{70}{100} = 70\%$.

To express a *percentage as a fraction*, divide the percentage number by 100 and reduce the fraction to its simplest possible terms. For example: $60\% = \frac{60}{100} = \frac{3}{5}$.

Decimal Illustration

Use a model to represent the decimal: 0.24.

The decimal 0.24 is twenty-four hundredths. One possible model to represent this fraction is to draw 100 pennies, since each penny is worth one-hundredth of a dollar. Draw one hundred circles to represent one hundred pennies. Shade 24 of the pennies to represent the decimal twenty-four hundredths.

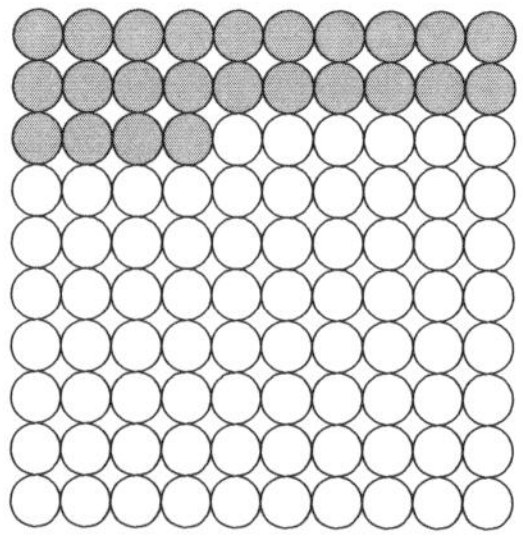

Review Video: Decimals
Visit mometrix.com/academy and enter code: 837268

Fractions

A **fraction** is a number that is expressed as one integer written above another integer, with a dividing line between them $\left(\frac{x}{y}\right)$. It represents the **quotient** of the two numbers "x divided by y." It can also be thought of as x out of y equal parts.

The top number of a fraction is called the **numerator**, and it represents the number of parts under consideration. The 1 in $\frac{1}{4}$ means that 1 part out of the whole is being considered in the calculation. The bottom number of a fraction is called the **denominator**, and it represents the total number of equal parts. The 4 in $\frac{1}{4}$ means that the whole consists of 4 equal parts. A fraction cannot have a denominator of zero; this is referred to as "*undefined.*"

Fractions can be manipulated, without changing the value of the fraction, by multiplying or dividing (but not adding or subtracting) both the numerator and denominator by the same number. If you divide both numbers by a common factor, you are **reducing** or simplifying the fraction. Two fractions that have the same value but are expressed differently are known as **equivalent fractions**. For example, $\frac{2}{10}, \frac{3}{15}, \frac{4}{20}$, and $\frac{5}{25}$ are all equivalent fractions. They can also all be reduced or simplified to $\frac{1}{5}$.

When two fractions are manipulated so that they have the same denominator, this is known as finding a **common denominator**. The number chosen to be that common denominator should be the least common multiple of the two original denominators. Example: $\frac{3}{4}$ and $\frac{5}{6}$; the least common multiple of 4 and 6 is 12. Manipulating to achieve the common denominator: $\frac{3}{4} = \frac{9}{12}; \frac{5}{6} = \frac{10}{12}$.

Proper Fractions and Mixed Numbers

A fraction whose denominator is greater than its numerator is known as a **proper fraction**, while a fraction whose numerator is greater than its denominator is known as an **improper fraction**. Proper fractions have values *less than one* and improper fractions have values *greater than one.*

A **mixed number** is a number that contains both an integer and a fraction. Any improper fraction can be rewritten as a mixed number.
Example: $\frac{8}{3} = \frac{6}{3} + \frac{2}{3} = 2 + \frac{2}{3} = 2\frac{2}{3}$.

Similarly, any mixed number can be rewritten as an improper fraction.
Example: $1\frac{3}{5} = 1 + \frac{3}{5} = \frac{5}{5} + \frac{3}{5} = \frac{8}{5}$.

Review Video: Proper and Improper Fractions and Mixed Numbers
Visit mometrix.com/academy and enter code: 211077

Review Video: Overview of Fractions
Visit mometrix.com/academy and enter code: 262335

Common Denominators with Fractions

When two fractions are manipulated so that they have the same denominator, this is known as finding a **common denominator**. The number chosen to be that common denominator should be the **least common multiple** of the two original denominators. Example: $\frac{3}{4}$ and $\frac{5}{6}$; the least common multiple of 4 and 6 is 12. Manipulating to achieve the common denominator: $\frac{3}{4} = \frac{9}{12}; \frac{5}{6} = \frac{10}{12}$.

Operations with Fractions

Adding and Subtracting Fractions

If two fractions have a common denominator, they can be added or subtracted simply by adding or subtracting the two numerators and retaining the same denominator.
Example: $\frac{1}{2} + \frac{1}{4} = \frac{2}{4} + \frac{1}{4} = \frac{3}{4}$

If the two fractions do not already have the same denominator, one or both of them must be manipulated to achieve a common denominator before they can be added or subtracted.

Review Video: Adding and Subtracting Fractions
Visit mometrix.com/academy and enter code: 378080

Multiplying Fractions

Two fractions can be multiplied by multiplying the two numerators to find the new numerator and the two denominators to find the new denominator.

Example: $\frac{1}{3} \times \frac{2}{3} = \frac{1 \times 2}{3 \times 3} = \frac{2}{9}$

Dividing Fractions

Two fractions can be divided by flipping the numerator and denominator of the second fraction and then proceeding as though it were a multiplication.

Example: $\frac{2}{3} \div \frac{3}{4} = \frac{2}{3} \times \frac{4}{3} = \frac{8}{9}$

Review Video: Multiplying and Dividing Fractions
Visit mometrix.com/academy and enter code: 473632

Simplifying Expressions with Fractions

Example 1

How to simplify: $\frac{2/5}{4/7}$

Dividing a fraction by a fraction may appear tricky, but it's not if you write out your steps carefully. Follow these steps to divide a fraction by a fraction.

Rewrite the problem as a multiplication problem. Dividing by a fraction is the same as multiplying by its **reciprocal**, also known as its **multiplicative inverse**. The product of a number and its reciprocal is 1. Because $\frac{4}{7}$ times $\frac{7}{4}$ is 1, these numbers are reciprocals. Note that reciprocals can be found by simply interchanging the numerators and denominators. So, rewriting the problem as a multiplication problem gives $\frac{2}{5} \times \frac{7}{4}$.

Perform multiplication of the fractions by multiplying the numerators by each other and the denominators by each other. In other words, multiply across the top and then multiply across the bottom.

$$\frac{2}{5} \times \frac{7}{4} = \frac{2 \times 7}{5 \times 4} = \frac{14}{20}$$

Make sure the fraction is reduced to lowest terms. Both 14 and 20 can be divided by 2.

$$\frac{14}{20} = \frac{14 \div 2}{20 \div 2} = \frac{7}{10}$$

Example 2

How to simplify: $\frac{1}{4} + \frac{3}{6}$

Fractions with common denominators can be easily added or subtracted. Recall that the denominator is the bottom number in the fraction and that the numerator is the top number in the fraction.

The denominators of $\frac{1}{4}$ and $\frac{3}{6}$ are 4 and 6, respectively. The lowest common denominator of 4 and 6 is 12 because 12 is the least common multiple of 4 (multiples 4, 8, 12, 16, ...) and 6 (multiples 6, 12, 18, 24, ...). Convert each fraction to its equivalent with the newly found common denominator of 12.

$$\frac{1 \times 3}{4 \times 3} = \frac{3}{12}; \frac{3 \times 2}{6 \times 2} = \frac{6}{12}$$

Now that the fractions have the same denominator, you can add them.

$$\frac{3}{12} + \frac{6}{12} = \frac{9}{12}$$

Be sure to write your answer in lowest terms. Both 9 and 12 can be divided by 3, so the answer is $\frac{3}{4}$.

Example 3

How to simplify: $\frac{7}{8} - \frac{8}{16}$

The denominators of $\frac{7}{8}$ and $\frac{8}{16}$ are 8 and 16, respectively. The lowest common denominator of 8 and 16 is 16 because 16 is the least common multiple of 8 (multiples 8, 16, 24 ...) and 16 (multiples 16, 32, 48, ...). Convert each fraction to its equivalent with the newly found common denominator of 16.

$$\frac{7 \times 2}{8 \times 2} = \frac{14}{16}; \frac{8 \times 1}{16 \times 1} = \frac{8}{16}$$

Now that the fractions have the same denominator, you can subtract them.

$$\frac{14}{16} - \frac{8}{16} = \frac{6}{16}$$

Be sure to write your answer in lowest terms. Both 6 and 16 can be divided by 2, so the answer is $\frac{3}{8}$.

Example 4

How to simplify: $\frac{1}{2} + \left(3\left(\frac{3}{4}\right) - 2\right) + 4$

When simplifying expressions, first perform operations within groups. Within the set of parentheses are multiplication and subtraction operations. Perform the multiplication first to get $\frac{1}{2} + \left(\frac{9}{4} - 2\right) + 4$. Then, subtract two to obtain $\frac{1}{2} + \frac{1}{4} + 4$. Finally, perform addition from left to right:

$$\frac{1}{2} + \frac{1}{4} + 4 = \frac{2}{4} + \frac{1}{4} + \frac{16}{4} = \frac{19}{4}$$

Converting Percentages, Fractions, and Decimals

Converting decimals to percentages and percentages to decimals is as simple as moving the decimal point. To *convert from a decimal to a percentage*, move the decimal point **two places to the right**. To *convert from a percentage to a decimal*, move it **two places to the left**. Examples include:

$$0.23 = 23\%;\ 5.34 = 534\%;\ 0.007 = 0.7\%;\ 700\%\ 7.00;\ 86\% = 0.86; 0.15\% = 0.0015$$

It may be helpful to remember that the percentage number will always be larger than the equivalent decimal number.

Example 1

Convert 15% to both a fraction and a decimal.

Write the percentage over 100 because percent means "per one hundred." So, 15% can be written as $\frac{15}{100}$. Fractions should be written in the simplest form, which means that the numbers in the numerator and denominator should be reduced if possible. Both 15 and 100 can be divided by 5:

$$\frac{15 \div 5}{100 \div 5} = \frac{3}{20}$$

As before, write the percentage over 100 because percent means "per one hundred." So, 15% can be written as $\frac{15}{100}$. Dividing a number by a power of ten (10, 100, 1000, etc.) is the same as moving the decimal point to the left by the same number of spaces that there are zeros in the divisor. Since 100 has 2 zeros, move the decimal point two places to the left: $15\% = 0.15$

In other words, when converting from a percentage to a decimal, drop the percent sign and move the decimal point two places to the left.

EXAMPLE 2

Write 24.36% as a fraction and then as a decimal. Explain how you made these conversions.

24.36% written as a fraction is $\frac{24.36}{100}$, or $\frac{2436}{10,000}$, which reduces to $\frac{609}{2500}$. 24.36% written as a decimal is 0.2436. Recall that dividing by 100 moves the decimal two places to the left.

> **Review Video: Converting Percentages to Decimals and Fractions**
> Visit mometrix.com/academy and enter code: 287297

EXAMPLE 3

Convert $\frac{4}{5}$ to a decimal and to a percentage.

To convert a fraction to a decimal, simply divide the numerator by the denominator in the fraction. The numerator is the top number in the fraction and the denominator is the bottom number in a fraction. So $\frac{4}{5} = 4 \div 5 = 0.80 = 0.8$.

Percent means "per hundred." $\frac{4 \times 20}{5 \times 20} = \frac{80}{100} = 80\%$.

EXAMPLE 4

Convert $3\frac{2}{5}$ to a decimal and to a percentage.

The mixed number $3\frac{2}{5}$ has a whole number and a fractional part. The fractional part $\frac{2}{5}$ can be written as a decimal by dividing 5 into 2, which gives 0.4. Adding the whole to the part gives 3.4. Alternatively, note that $3\frac{2}{5} = 3\frac{4}{10} = 3.4$

To change a decimal to a percentage, multiply it by 100.

$3.4(100) = 340\%$. Notice that this percentage is greater than 100%. This makes sense because the original mixed number $3\frac{2}{5}$ is greater than 1.

> **Review Video: Converting Fractions to Percentages and Decimals**
> Visit mometrix.com/academy and enter code: 306233

REAL WORLD PROBLEMS WITH PERCENTAGES

A percentage problem can be presented three main ways: (1) Find what percentage of some number another number is. Example: What percentage of 40 is 8? (2) Find what number is some percentage of a given number. Example: What number is 20% of 40? (3) Find what number another number is a given percentage of. Example: What number is 8 20% of?

The three components in all of these cases are the same: a **whole** (W), a **part** (P), and a **percentage** (%). These are related by the equation: $P = W \times \%$. This is the form of the equation you would use to solve problems of type (2). To solve types (1) and (3), you would use these two forms:

$$\% = P/W \text{ and } W = P/\%$$

The thing that frequently makes percentage problems difficult is that they are most often also word problems, so a large part of solving them is figuring out which quantities are what. Example: In a school cafeteria, 7 students choose pizza, 9 choose hamburgers, and 4 choose tacos. Find the percentage that chooses tacos. To find the whole, you must first add all of the parts: $7 + 9 + 4 = 20$. The percentage can then be found by dividing the part by the whole ($\% = \frac{P}{W}$):

$$\frac{4}{20} = \frac{20}{100} = 20\%$$

Review Video: Converting Decimals to Fractions and Percentages
Visit mometrix.com/academy and enter code: 986765

Review Video: Converting Decimals, Improper Fractions, and Mixed Numbers
Visit mometrix.com/academy and enter code: 696924

Example 1

What is 30% of 120?

The word "of" indicates multiplication, so 30% of 120 is found by multiplying 30% by 120. First, change 30% to a fraction or decimal. Recall "percent" means per hundred, so $30\% = \frac{30}{100} = 0.30$. 120 times 0.3 is 36.

Example 2

What is 150% of 20?

150% of 20 is found by multiplying 150% by 20. First, change 150% to a fraction or decimal. Recall that "percent" means per hundred, so $150\% = \frac{150}{100} = 1.50$. So, $(1.50)(20) = 30$. Notice that 30 is greater than the original number of 20. This makes sense because you are finding a number that is more than 100% of the original number.

Example 3

What is 14.5% of 96?

Change 14.5% to a decimal before multiplying. $0.145 \times 96 = 13.92$. Notice that 13.92 is much smaller than the original number of 96. This makes sense because you are finding a small percentage of the original number.

Example 4

According to a survey, about 82% of engineers were highly satisfied with their job. If 145 engineers were surveyed, how many reported that they were highly satisfied?

$$82\% \text{ of } 145 = 0.82 \times 145 = 118.9$$

Because you can't have 0.9 of a person, we must round up to say that 119 engineers reported that they were highly satisfied with their jobs.

Example 5

On Monday, Lucy spent 5 hours observing sales, 3 hours working on advertising, and 4 hours doing paperwork. On Tuesday, she spent 4 hours observing sales, 6 hours working on advertising, and 2 hours doing paperwork. What was the percent change for time spent on each task between the two days?

The three tasks are observing sales, working on advertising, and doing paperwork. To find the amount of change, compare the first amount with the second amount for each task. Then, write this difference as a percentage compared to the initial amount.

Amount of change for observing sales: 5 hours − 4 hours = 1 hour.

The percent of change is $\frac{\text{amount of change}}{\text{original amount}} \times 100\%$.

$$\frac{1\text{ hour}}{5\text{ hours}} \times 100\% = 20\%$$

Lucy spent 20% less time observing sales on Tuesday than she did on Monday.

Amount of change for working on advertising: 6 hours − 3 hours = 3 hours

The percent of change is:

$$\frac{3\text{ hours}}{3\text{ hours}} \times 100\% = 100\%$$

Lucy spent 100% more time working on advertising on Tuesday than she did on Monday.

Amount of change for doing paperwork: 4 hours − 2 hours = 2 hours.

The percent of change is

$$\frac{2\text{ hours}}{4\text{ hours}} \times 100\% = 50\%$$

Lucy spent 50% less time working on paperwork on Tuesday than she did on Monday.

Example 6

A patient was given 40 mg of a certain medicine. Later, the patient's dosage was increased to 45 mg. What was the percent change in his medication?

To find the percent change, first compare the original and new amounts. The original amount was 40 mg, and the increased amount is 45 mg, so the dosage of medication was increased by 5 mg (45 − 40 = 5). Note, however, that the question asks not by how much the dosage changed but by what percentage it changed. Percent change = $\frac{\text{new amount}-\text{original amount}}{\text{original amount}} \times 100\%$.

$$\frac{45\text{ mg} - 40\text{ mg}}{40\text{ mg}} \times 100\% = \frac{5}{40} \times 100\% = 0.125 \times 100\% = 12.5\%$$

The percent change is 12.5%. Since the result is positive, this is an increase.

Real World Problems with Rational Numbers

Example 1

A woman's age is thirteen more than half of 60. How old is the woman?

"More than" indicates addition, and "of" indicates multiplication. The expression can be written as $\frac{1}{2}(60) + 13$. So, the woman's age is equal to: $\frac{1}{2}(60) + 13 = 30 + 13 = 43$

Example 2

A patient was given pain medicine at a dosage of 0.22 grams. The patient's dosage was then increased to 0.80 grams. By how much was the patient's dosage increased?

The first step is to determine what operation (addition, subtraction, multiplication, or division) the problem requires. Notice the keywords and phrases "by how much" and "increased." "Increased" means that you go from a smaller amount to a larger amount. This change can be found by subtracting the smaller amount from the larger amount: 0.80 grams − 0.22 grams = 0.58 grams

Remember to line up the decimal when subtracting.

$$\begin{array}{r} 0.80 \\ -\ 0.22 \\ \hline 0.58 \end{array}$$

Example 3

At a hotel, $\frac{3}{4}$ of the 100 rooms are occupied today. Yesterday, $\frac{4}{5}$ of the 100 rooms were occupied. On which day were more of the rooms occupied and by how much more?

First, find the number of rooms occupied each day. To do so, multiply the fraction of rooms occupied by the number of rooms available: Number occupied = Fraction occupied × Total number

Today: $\frac{3}{4} \times 100 = 75$
Yesterday: $\frac{4}{5} \times 100 = 80$

The difference in the number of rooms occupied is $80 - 75 = 5$ rooms. Therefore, five more rooms were occupied yesterday than today.

Example 4

At a school, 40% of the teachers teach English. If 20 teachers teach English, how many teachers work at the school?

To answer this problem, first think about the number of teachers that work at the school. Will it be more or less than the number of teachers who work in a specific department such as English? More teachers work at the school, so the number you find to answer this question will be greater than 20.

40% of the teachers are English teachers. "Of" indicates multiplication, and words like "is" and "are" indicate equivalence. Translating the problem into a mathematical sentence gives $40\% \times t = 20$, where t represents the total number of teachers. Solving for t gives $t = \frac{20}{40\%} = \frac{20}{0.40} = 50$. Fifty teachers work at the school.

EXAMPLE 5

A patient was given blood pressure medicine at a dosage of 2 grams. The patient's dosage was then decreased to 0.45 grams. By how much was the patient's dosage decreased?

The decrease is represented by the difference between the two amounts:

$$2 \text{ grams} - 0.45 \text{ grams} = 1.55 \text{ grams}.$$

Remember to line up the decimal point before subtracting.

$$\begin{array}{r} 2.00 \\ -\ 0.45 \\ \hline 1.55 \end{array}$$

EXAMPLE 6

Two weeks ago, $\frac{2}{3}$ of the 60 customers at a skate shop were male. Last week, $\frac{3}{6}$ of the 80 customers were male. During which week were there more male customers?

First, you need to find the number of male customers that were in the skate shop each week. You are given this amount in terms of fractions. To find the actual number of male customers, multiply the fraction of male customers by the number of customers in the store.

Two weeks ago: Actual number of male customers $= \frac{2}{3} \times 60 = \frac{2\times60}{3\times1} = \frac{120}{3} = 40$

Last week: Actual number of male customers $= \frac{3}{6} \times 80 = \frac{3\times80}{6\times1} = \frac{240}{6} = 40$

The number of male customers was the same both weeks.

Operations and Properties

Four Basic Mathematical Operations

Addition increases the value of one quantity by the value of another quantity. Example: $8 + 9 = 17$. The result is called the **sum**. With addition, the order does not matter. $4 + 2 = 2 + 4$.
Subtraction is the opposite operation to addition; it decreases the value of one quantity by the value of another quantity. Example: $6 - 4 = 2$; $17 - 8 = 9$. The result is called the **difference**. Note that with subtraction, the order does matter. $6 - 4 \neq 4 - 6$.
Multiplication can be thought of as repeated addition. One number tells how many times to add the other number to itself. Example: 3×2 (three times two) $= 2 + 2 + 2 = 6$. With multiplication, the order does not matter. $2 \times 3 = 3 \times 2$ or $3 + 3 = 2 + 2 + 2$.
Division is the opposite operation to multiplication; one number tells us how many parts to divide the other number into. Example: $20 \div 4 = 5$; if 20 is split into 4 equal parts, each part is 5. With division, the order of the numbers does matter. $20 \div 4 \neq 4 \div 20$.

Review Video: Mathematical Operations
Visit mometrix.com/academy and enter code: 208095

Subtraction with Regrouping

Example 1

Demonstrate how to subtract 189 from 525 using regrouping.

First, set up the subtraction problem:

$$\begin{array}{r} 525 \\ -\ 189 \\ \hline \end{array}$$

Notice that the numbers in the ones and tens columns of 525 are smaller than the numbers in the ones and tens columns of 189. This means you will need to use regrouping to perform subtraction. To subtract 9 from 5 in the ones column you will need to borrow from the 2 in the tens columns:

$$\begin{array}{rrrr} & 5 & 1 & 15 \\ - & 1 & 8 & 9 \\ \hline & & & 6 \end{array}$$

To subtract 8 from 1 in the tens column, borrow from the 5 in the hundreds column:

$$\begin{array}{rrrr} & 4 & 11 & 15 \\ - & 1 & 8 & 9 \\ \hline & & 3 & 6 \end{array}$$

Last, subtract the 1 from the 4 in the hundreds column:

$$\begin{array}{rrrr} & 4 & 11 & 15 \\ - & 1 & 8 & 9 \\ \hline & 3 & 3 & 6 \end{array}$$

Example 2

Demonstrate how to subtract 477 from 620 using regrouping.

First, set up the subtraction problem:

$$\begin{array}{r} 620 \\ -\ 477 \\ \hline \end{array}$$

Notice that the numbers in the ones and tens columns of 620 are smaller than the numbers in the ones and tens columns of 477. This means you will need to use regrouping to perform subtraction. To subtract 7 from 0 in the ones column you will need to borrow from the 2 in the tens column.

$$\begin{array}{rrrr} & 6 & 1 & 10 \\ - & 4 & 7 & 7 \\ \hline & & & 3 \end{array}$$

To subtract 7 from the 1 that is still in the tens column, borrow from the 6 in the hundreds column.

$$\begin{array}{rrrr} & 5 & 11 & 10 \\ - & 4 & 7 & 7 \\ \hline & & 4 & 3 \end{array}$$

Lastly, subtract 4 from the 5 remaining in the hundreds column to get:

$$\begin{array}{rrrr} & 5 & 11 & 10 \\ - & 4 & 7 & 7 \\ \hline & 1 & 4 & 3 \end{array}$$

Properties of Mathematical Operations

Commutative property – The product is the same regardless of the order of factors. For example:

$$2 \times 5 = 5 \times 2$$

Associative property – The product is the same regardless of grouping. For example:

$$(2 \times 5) \times 3 = 2 \times (5 \times 3)$$

Distributive property – Multiplying a sum by a number is the same as multiplying each addend by the number and then adding the products. For example:

$$2 \times (3 + 4) = (2 \times 3) + (2 \times 4) = 14$$

Zero property – The sum of a number and 0 is that number. In multiplication, the product of a number and 0 is 0. For example:

$$3 + 0 = 3 \text{ and } 3 \times 0 = 0$$

Operations with Positive and Negative Numbers

Addition

When adding signed numbers, if the signs are the same simply add the absolute values of the addends and apply the original sign to the sum. For example, $(+4) + (+8) = +12$ and $(-4) + (-8) = -12$. When the original signs are different, take the absolute values of the addends and subtract the smaller value from the larger value, then apply the original sign of the larger value to the difference. For instance, $(+4) + (-8) = -4$ and $(-4) + (+8) = +4$.

Subtraction

For subtracting signed numbers, change the sign of the number after the minus symbol and then follow the same rules used for addition. For example, $(+4) - (+8) = (+4) + (-8) = -4$.

MULTIPLICATION

If the signs are the same the product is positive when multiplying signed numbers. For example, $(+4) \times (+8) = +32$ and $(-4) \times (-8) = +32$. If the signs are opposite, the product is negative. For example, $(+4) \times (-8) = -32$ and $(-4) \times (+8) = -32$. When more than two factors are multiplied together, the sign of the product is determined by how many negative factors are present. If there are an odd number of negative factors then the product is negative, whereas an even number of negative factors indicates a positive product. For instance, $(+4) \times (-8) \times (-2) = +64$ and $(-4) \times (-8) \times (-2) = -64$.

DIVISION

The rules for dividing signed numbers are similar to multiplying signed numbers. If the dividend and divisor have the same sign, the quotient is positive. If the dividend and divisor have opposite signs, the quotient is negative. For example, $(-4) \div (+8) = -0.5$.

OPERATIONS WITH DECIMALS

ADDING AND SUBTRACTING DECIMALS

When adding and subtracting decimals, the decimal points must always be aligned. Adding decimals is just like adding regular whole numbers. Example: $4.5 + 2 = 6.5$.

If the problem-solver does not properly align the decimal points, an incorrect answer of 4.7 may result. An easy way to add decimals is to align all of the decimal points in a vertical column visually. This will allow you to see exactly where the decimal should be placed in the final answer. Begin adding from right to left. Add each column in turn, making sure to carry the number to the left if a column adds up to more than 9. The same rules apply to the subtraction of decimals.

Review Video: Adding and Subtracting Decimals
Visit mometrix.com/academy and enter code: 381101

MULTIPLYING DECIMALS

A simple multiplication problem has two components: a **multiplicand** and a **multiplier**. When multiplying decimals, work as though the numbers were whole rather than decimals. Once the final product is calculated, count the number of places to the right of the decimal in both the multiplicand and the multiplier. Then, count that number of places from the right of the product and place the decimal in that position.

For example, 12.3×2.56 has three places to the right of the respective decimals. Multiply 123×256 to get 31488. Now, beginning on the right, count three places to the left and insert the decimal. The final product will be 31.488.

Review Video: How to Multiply Decimals
Visit mometrix.com/academy and enter code: 731574

DIVIDING DECIMALS

Every division problem has a **divisor** and a **dividend**. The dividend is the number that is being divided. In the problem $14 \div 7$, 14 is the dividend and 7 is the divisor. In a division problem with decimals, the divisor must be converted into a whole number. Begin by moving the decimal in the divisor to the right until a whole number is created. Next, move the decimal in the dividend the same number of spaces to the right. For example, 4.9 into 24.5 would become 49 into 245. The decimal was moved one space to the right to create a whole number in the divisor, and then the same was done for the dividend. Once the whole numbers are created, the problem is carried out normally: $245 \div 49 = 5$.

Review Video: Dividing Decimals
Visit mometrix.com/academy and enter code: 560690

Parentheses

Parentheses are used to designate which operations should be done first when there are multiple operations. Example: $4 - (2 + 1) = 1$; the parentheses tell us that we must add 2 and 1, and then subtract the sum from 4, rather than subtracting 2 from 4 and then adding 1 (this would give us an answer of 3).

Review Video: Mathematical Parentheses
Visit mometrix.com/academy and enter code: 978600

Order of Operations

The **order of operations** is a set of rules that dictates the order in which we must perform each operation in an expression so that we will evaluate it accurately. If we have an expression that includes multiple different operations, the order of operations tells us which operations to do first. The most common mnemonic for the order of operations is **PEMDAS**, or "Please Excuse My Dear Aunt Sally." PEMDAS stands for parentheses, exponents, multiplication, division, addition, and subtraction. It is important to understand that multiplication and division have equal precedence, as do addition and subtraction, so those pairs of operations are simply worked from left to right in order. For example, evaluate the expression $5 + 20 \div 4 \times (2 + 3) - 6$ using the correct order of operations.

P	Perform the operations inside the parentheses	$5 + 20 \div 4 \times 5 - 6$
E	There are no exponents to simplify	
MD	Perform multiplication and division from left to right	$5 + 5 \times 5 - 6$ $5 + 25 - 6$
AS	Perform addition and subtraction from left to right	$30 - 6$ 24

Review Video: Order of Operations
Visit mometrix.com/academy and enter code: 259675

Factors and Greatest Common Factor

Factors are numbers that are multiplied together to obtain a **product**. For example, in the equation $2 \times 3 = 6$, the numbers 2 and 3 are factors. A **prime number** has only two factors (1 and itself), but other numbers can have many factors.

A **common factor** is a number that divides exactly into two or more other numbers. For example, the factors of 12 are 1, 2, 3, 4, 6, and 12, while the factors of 15 are 1, 3, 5, and 15. The common factors of 12 and 15 are 1 and 3.

A **prime factor** is also a prime number. Therefore, the prime factors of 12 are 2 and 3. For 15, the prime factors are 3 and 5.

The **greatest common factor** (**GCF**) is the largest number that is a factor of two or more numbers. For example, the factors of 15 are 1, 3, 5, and 15; the factors of 35 are 1, 5, 7, and 35. Therefore, the greatest common factor of 15 and 35 is 5.

Review Video: Factors
Visit mometrix.com/academy and enter code: 920086

Review Video: Greatest Common Factor and Least Common Multiple
Visit mometrix.com/academy and enter code: 838699

Multiples and Least Common Multiple

The least common multiple (**LCM**) is the smallest number that is a multiple of two or more numbers. For example, the multiples of 3 include 3, 6, 9, 12, 15, etc.; the multiples of 5 include 5, 10, 15, 20, etc. Therefore, the least common multiple of 3 and 5 is 15.

Review Video: Multiples
Visit mometrix.com/academy and enter code: 626738

Systems of Numeration

Place Value

Write the place value of each digit in the following number: 14,059.826

1: ten-thousands
4: thousands
0: hundreds
5: tens
9: ones
8: tenths
2: hundredths
6: thousandths

Review Video: Place Value
Visit mometrix.com/academy and enter code: 205433

Base 10 Expanded Form

The base 10 expanded form of a number is the number written out as a sum of multiples of powers of 10, according to place value (coefficients must be less than 10). For example, 5,234 in expanded form is 5,000+200+30+4. Sometimes the term is used interchangeably with **expanded notation**, in which the powers of 10 and the coefficients are written as separate factors. In expanded notation, 5,234 is: $5 \times 1000 + 2 \times 100 + 3 \times 10 + 4 \times 1$. Expanded notation also applies to decimal numbers. For example, 21.32 in expanded notation is: $2 \times 10 + 1 \times 1 + 3 \times \frac{1}{10} + 2 \times \frac{1}{100}$

Although **base 10 expanded form** is not used often, it is important to understand because it explains the base 10 form that we use to represent numbers. The standard positional notation is essentially the expanded form without writing out each numeral as a power of ten. Each number is in a place corresponding to its power of ten, with zeroes as placeholders for any "missing" powers. For example, 3,025 is equal to $3 \times 1000 + 0 \times 100 + 2 \times 10 + 5 \times 1$. An understanding of this system also helps in understanding how other mathematical operations, such as multiplication and addition, work.

Binary Numbering System

The binary numbering is based on powers of a number and is a base-2 system, based on multiples of two rather than ten, as in the most commonly used decimal system. Binary works in a manner similar to the decimal system, but uses just two symbols that can be used to represent numerical values: 0 and 1. When counting in the binary system, begin in the ones place with 0 and go up to 1. Because there are only those two symbols, in order to represent a higher value, a "1" must be used in the "twos" place, since there is no symbol that can be used in the binary system for 2. Thus, Binary counting would look something like this: 000, 001, 010, 011, 100, 101, 110, etc.

Binary to Decimal Conversion

The decimal numbering system, a numbering system constructed on multiples of ten, is most commonly used in everyday life. It is also called base-10. Binary numbering is based on multiples of two rather than ten. To convert a binary number to a decimal number, multiply each digit in the binary number by 2^p, where p is the number of places the digit is to the left of the final digit. In other words, the last digit is multiplied by $2^0 = 1$, the digit one space to the left is multiplied by

$2^1 = 2$, the digit two spaces to the left is multiplied by $2^2 = 4$, etc. Once this is done, take the sum of all of these products to find the equivalent decimal number.

Decimal to Binary Conversion

To convert a decimal to the binary numbering system, create a table and first subtract the largest possible power of two, and keep subtracting the next largest possible power from the remainder, marking 1s in each column where this is possible and 0s where it is not. For example, if converting 104 from decimal to binary, the largest power of two that is less than 104 is $2^6 = 64$. This means that it will be a 7-digit binary number, beginning with a 1. Subtract and move on to the next power of 2: $104 - 64 = 40$. The next smallest power of two is $2^5 = 32$. This is less than the remaining number of 40, so the second digit in the binary number is also a 1. Subtract and move on to the next power of 2: $40 - 32 = 8$. The next smallest power of two is $2^4 = 16$. This is larger than the remaining number, so the third digit is a 0. $2^3 = 8$ is exactly equal to the remaining number, so the fourth digit is a 1 and we know that the remaining digits, representing 2^2, 2^1, and 2^0, will all be 0. Thus, 104 converted from decimal to binary is 1101000

Another method of converting from decimal to binary involves constructing a table with three columns: division expression, quotient, and remainder, and then using division to find the conversion. First, take the decimal number and divide it by 2. Put the division expression in the upper left-most cell of the table. Take the quotient of the division and put it in the second cell of the row, then place the remainder, either 0 or 1, in the last cell of the row. For each successive row, put the quotient from the previous row in the left-most column and divide it by two, then place the new quotient in the second cell of the row and put the remainder in the last cell of the row. The last row will always be: 1 0 1. The 1s and 0s in the remainder column from the bottom to the top equal the binary number. Using our example of 104:

104	52	0
52	26	0
26	13	0
13	6	1
6	3	0
3	1	1
1	0	1

Counting from bottom to top, we read the binary number to be 1101000.

Roman Numerals

In ancient Rome, a system of **numerals** was devised that is still occasionally used today. The system consists of 7 letters to represent numbers: I = 1, V = 5, X = 10, L = 50, C = 100, D = 500, and M = 1,000. To represent numbers between these 7 main numbers, a system of addition and subtraction was devised. Generally, for a string of letters, the values of the letters are added. For example, $XVI = 10 + 5 + 1 = 16$. As long as the numbers are all arranged in order from greatest to least, this is all you have to do. There are a handful of exceptions where you must subtract one number from another. The following letter pairs are the exceptions that you must be on the lookout for:

- IV = 5 − 1 = 4
- IX = 10 − 1 = 9

- XL = 50 − 10 = 40
- XC = 100 − 10 = 90
- CD = 500 − 100 = 400
- CM = 1000 − 100 = 900

If one of these letter pairs appears, it should be treated as a single unit worth the value indicated, calculated by subtracting the first of the pair from the second. The rest of the string of letters is summed as usual. For example: MCMLXXI = 1000 + 900 + 50 + 10 + 10 + 1 = 1971.

Exponents

An **exponent** is a superscript number placed next to another number at the top right. It indicates how many times the base number is to be multiplied by itself. Exponents provide a shorthand way to write what would be a longer mathematical expression, for example: $2^4 = 2 \times 2 \times 2 \times 2$. A number with an exponent of 2 is said to be "squared," while a number with an exponent of 3 is said to be "cubed." The value of a number raised to an exponent is called its power. So 8^4 is read as "8 to the 4th power," or "8 raised to the power of 4."

The properties of exponents are as follows:

Property	Description
$a^1 = a$	Any number to the power of 1 is equal to itself
$1^n = 1$	The number 1 raised to any power is equal to 1
$a^0 = 1$	Any number raised to the power of 0 is equal to 1
$a^n \times a^m = a^{n+m}$	Add exponents to multiply powers of the same base number
$a^n \div a^m = a^{n-m}$	Subtract exponents to divide powers of the same base number
$(a^n)^m = a^{n \times m}$	When a power is raised to a power, the exponents are multiplied
$(a \times b)^n = a^n \times b^n$ $(a \div b)^n = a^n \div b^n$	Multiplication and division operations inside parentheses can be raised to a power. This is the same as each term being raised to that power.
$a^{-n} = \frac{1}{a^n}$	A negative exponent is the same as the reciprocal of a positive exponent

Note that exponents do not have to be integers. Fractional or decimal exponents follow all the rules above as well. Example: $5^{\frac{1}{4}} \times 5^{\frac{3}{4}} = 5^{\frac{1}{4}+\frac{3}{4}} = 5^1 = 5$.

> **Review Video: Exponents**
> Visit mometrix.com/academy and enter code: 600998
>
> **Review Video: Properties of Exponents**
> Visit mometrix.com/academy and enter code: 532558

Example

Simplify $(2x^4)^2(xy)^4 \times 4y^3$ using the laws of exponents.

According the order of operations, the first step in simplifying expressions is to evaluate within the parentheses. Moving from left to right, the first set of parentheses contains a power raised to a power. The rules of exponents state that when a power is raised to a power, you *multiply* the exponents. Since $4 \times 2 = 8$, $(2x^4)^2$ can be written as $4x^8$. The second set of parentheses raises a product to a power. The rules of exponents state that you raise every value within the parentheses to the given power. Therefore, $(xy)^4$ can be written as x^4y^4. Combining these terms with the last term gives you, $4x^8 \times x^4y^4 \times 4y^3$. In this expression, there are powers with the same base. The rules of exponents state that you *add* powers with the same base, while multiplying the coefficients. You can group the expression as $(4x^8 \times x^4) \times (y^4 \times 4y^3)$ to organize the values with the same base. Then, using this rule add the exponents. The result is $4x^{12} \times 4y^7$, or $16y^{12}y^7$.

Roots

A **root**, such as a square root, is another way of writing a fractional exponent. Instead of using a superscript, roots use the radical symbol ($\sqrt{\ }$) to indicate the operation. A radical will have a number underneath the bar, and may sometimes have a number in the upper left: $\sqrt[n]{a}$, read as "the nth root of a." The relationship between radical notation and exponent notation can be described by this equation: $\sqrt[n]{a} = a^{\frac{1}{n}}$. The two special cases of $n = 2$ and $n = 3$ are called square roots and cube roots. If there is no number to the upper left, it is understood to be a square root ($n = 2$). Nearly all of the roots you encounter will be square roots. A square root is the same as a number raised to the one-half power. When we say that a is the square root of b ($a = \sqrt{b}$), we mean that a multiplied by itself equals b: ($a \times a = b$).

A **perfect square** is a number that has an integer for its square root. There are 10 perfect squares from 1 to 100: 1, 4, 9, 16, 25, 36, 49, 64, 81, 100 (the squares of integers 1 through 10).

Review Video: Roots
Visit mometrix.com/academy and enter code: 795655

Review Video: Perfect Squares and Square Roots
Visit mometrix.com/academy and enter code: 648063

Scientific Notation

Scientific notation is a way of writing large numbers in a shorter form. The form $a \times 10^n$ is used in scientific notation, where a is greater than or equal to 1 but less than 10, and n is the number of places the decimal must move to get from the original number to a. Example: The number 230,400,000 is cumbersome to write. To write the value in scientific notation, place a decimal point between the first and second numbers, and include all digits through the last non-zero digit ($a = 2.304$). To find the appropriate power of 10, count the number of places the decimal point had to move ($n = 8$). The number is positive if the decimal moved to the left, and negative if it moved to the right. We can then write 230,400,000 as 2.304×10^8. If we look instead at the number 0.00002304, we have the same value for a, but this time the decimal moved 5 places to the right ($n = -5$). Thus, 0.00002304 can be written as 2.304×10^{-5}. Using this notation makes it simple to compare very large or very small numbers. By comparing exponents, it is easy to see that 3.28×10^4 is smaller than 1.51×10^5, because 4 is less than 5.

Review Video: Scientific Notation
Visit mometrix.com/academy and enter code: 976454

Sets and Logic

Sets

Element of a Set

A set is a mathematical collection of items, and an element is an item that is included in the set. These items are typically sets of numbers, or sets of geometrical points, or even sets of sets.

Whether an item is an **element of a set** is a binary property. In other words, a particular item either is or is not an element of a given set. There are not different degrees of belonging to a set, and one element of a set cannot be more an element than another. Additionally, the elements do not have any particular order, and there is no count of how many times an element appears in a set. for example, in the set $\{0, 2, 1, 2, 4\}$, the numbers 0, 1, 2, and 4 are elements of the set. Two is not more of an element than the others because it is listed twice. Any number other than these, such as 3, is not an element of the set.

The mathematical symbol $\in$ means "is an element of." for instance, "$1 \in A$" means that "the number 1 is an element of set A". the symbol can be negated with a diagonal slash, so "$1 \notin A$" means "the number 1 is NOT an element of set A."

Empty Set

The empty set contains no elements. the symbol for the **empty set** is a circle with a line through it, $\emptyset$, or the empty set can be written in roster form as $\{\ \}$. Although it may seem trivial, the empty set is important for the same reason that zero is an important number—without the empty set, many set operations and definitions would be incomplete. for instance, the intersection of two non-overlapping sets is the empty set. the set of all prime numbers that are perfect squares is the empty set, because there are no such numbers. Other sets can be constructed using the empty set. for instance, a set *containing* the empty set, $\{\{\ \}\}$ or $\{\emptyset\}$, is different from the empty set itself, since it's not actually empty—it contains one element, the empty set.

The empty set is, by definition, a subset of every set, including itself. This is because every element that is an element of the empty set is also an element of any other set, since the empty set contains no elements that could make this statement false.

Subset, Proper Subset, and Superset

Set A is a **subset** of set B if set A is contained entirely within set B. More formally, set A is a subset of set B if every element of set A is also in set B. We can write this as $\forall x \in A\ x \in B$. the symbol for subset is $\subseteq$, so we can write "$A \subseteq B$" to mean "set A is a subset of set B," or "$A \nsubseteq B$" to mean "set A is NOT a subset of set B".

Any set is a subset of itself, since naturally any element in a set is in that set. a **proper subset** means a subset that it not equal to the other set. In other words, set A is a proper subset of set B if set A is a subset of set B but they are not the same, so $A \subseteq B$ but $B \nsubseteq A$. for example, $\{0, 1, 2\}$ is a proper subset of $\{0, 1, 2, 3\}$ because every element in the first set is included in the second set but the two sets are not identical. the symbol for proper subset is $\subset$, so we write "$A \subset B$" to mean "set A is a proper subset of set B," and "$A \not\subset B$" to mean "set A is not a proper subset of set B."

The converse of a subset is a **superset**. If A is a subset of B, then B is a superset of A. In the example above, $\{0, 1, 2, 3\}$ is a superset of $\{0, 1, 2\}$ because the first set contains every element of the second plus more.

UNION OF TWO OR MORE SETS

The **union** of two or more sets includes all the elements that are included in all of the sets. an element is in the union of sets A and B if it is in set A or in set B, or in both. the union is written with the symbol ∪, so "$A \cup B$" (read "A union B") means the union of sets A and B.

For example, given the sets $A = \{1, 2, 3, 4\}$ and $B = \{2, 4, 6, 8\}$, $A \cup B = \{1, 2, 3, 4, 6, 8\}$. 5 and 7 do not appear in $A \cup B$ because they are not elements of A or B. 1 and 3 are in $A \cup B$ because they are in set A, and 6 and 8 are in $A \cup B$ because they are in set B. 2 and 4 appear in both a and B, so they are in $A \cup B$, but they only appear once.

The union operation on sets is both commutative and associative. That is, $A \cup B = B \cup A$, and $(A \cup B) \cup C = A \cup (B \cup C)$.

INTERSECTION OF TWO OR MORE SETS

The intersection of two or more sets is a set including every element that appears in *all* of the sets. an element is in the intersection of sets A and B if and only if the element appears in both set A and set B. for instance, if set $A = \{0, 1, 2, 3\}$ and set $B = \{2, 3, 4, 5\}$, the intersection of sets A and B includes the elements 2 and 3, because these are the only elements that appear in both sets. the intersection is written with the symbol ∩, so "$A \cap B$" (read "A intersection B") means the intersection of sets A and B.

The intersection operation on sets is both commutative and associative. That is, $A \cap B = B \cap A$, and $(A \cap B) \cap C = A \cap (B \cap C)$. the union and intersection operations also jointly have distributive properties: $A \cap (B \cup C) = (A \cap B) \cup (A \cap C)$ and $A \cup (B \cap C) = (A \cup B) \cap (A \cup C)$.

COMPLEMENT OF A SET

The complement of a set is a set containing all the elements that are *not* in the original set. To determine this, we must also define the **universe of discourse**—the set of all possible elements we're considering, abbreviated U. for mathematical applications, the universe of discourse is commonly the set of all integers (abbreviated $\mathbb{Z}$), or the set of all real numbers (abbreviated $\mathbb{R}$). If U is the set of all integers, for example, then the complement of the set $A = \{1, 2, 3\}$ would include elements such as -3, 0, or 6, but it would not include elements such as $\sqrt{7}$ or $\frac{1}{4}$, because these are not in the universe of discourse.

The **complement of a set** is often written either by drawing a line over the name of the original set, or by adding an apostrophe or a superscripted C. the complement of set A, for instance, could be written as $\bar{A}$, as A', or as A^C.

For example, given set $A = \{2, 4, 6, 8\}$ with a universe of discourse of $U = \{1, 2, 3, 4, 5, 6, 7, 8, 9, 10\}$, the complement of a would be $\{1, 3, 5, 7, 9, 10\}$—all the elements of U that are not in A.

DIFFERENCE OF TWO SETS

The difference of two sets is a set containing all the elements that are in the first set but not in the second. the difference of sets A and B is also referred to as the **relative complement** of set A with respect to set B, and is written $A \setminus B$ or $A - B$. the difference is always a subset of the first set: $A \setminus B \subseteq A$. However, it is *not* necessarily the case that $A \setminus B \subseteq B$. In fact, because any element of $A \setminus$

B is by definition not an element of B, the only time that $A \setminus B$ can be a subset of B is if $A \setminus B$ has no elements, i.e. if $A \setminus B = \emptyset$, which is true if and only if $A \subseteq B$.

Unlike the union and intersection, the operation of the difference between sets is neither commutative nor associative. In general, $A \setminus B \neq B \setminus A$, and $A \setminus (B \setminus C) \neq (A \setminus B) \setminus C$.

For example, consider the sets $A = \{1, 2, 3\}$, $B = \{2, 4\}$, and $C = \{1, 2\}$. Then $A \setminus B = \{1, 3\}$ since 1 and 3 are in set A but not in set B. Similarly, $B \setminus A = \{4\}$, $B \setminus C = \{4\}$, $C \setminus B = \{1\}$, and $A \setminus C = \{3\}$. However, $C \setminus A = \emptyset$, i.e., set C is a subset of set A, so there are no elements that appear in C but not in A, which means the difference between C and A is the empty set.

Set Builder Notation

Set builder notation is a way of defining a set in terms of characteristics shared by its members. the criteria are enclosed in braces, and stated in terms of a variable. There are two parts to the definition, separated by either a colon or a vertical line. To the right is a restriction on the variable, defining its possible values. To the left is a formula involving the variable. All values of that formula (using any possible value of the variable) are elements of the set. the formula may be just the variable itself, if the elements equal the possible values.

For instance, consider the set of integers, $\{x : x < 5\}$, which defines a set containing all integers less than 5. Similarly, $\{2x : x < 5\}$ contains all *even* integers less than or equal to 8. We calculate the greatest possible value by taking the largest integer less than 5 and multiplying by 2: $2(4) = 8$. $\{2x + 1 : |x| < 10\}$ contains all odd integers between -17 and 19, inclusive. We calculate least and greatest values by taking the greatest and least integers that will satisfy the equation $|x| < 10$, and plug these values into the formula to the left of the colon: $2(9) + 1 = 19, 2(-9) + 1 = -17$.

The above examples verbally stated that they used sets of integers, but set builder notation can also directly state the domain of the variable in the notation. for instance, to specify all integers less than 5, we can write $\{x \in \mathbb{Z} : x < 5\}$ or $\{x : x \in \mathbb{Z} \wedge x < 5\}$.

Roster Form

Roster form refers to writing a set by explicitly listing all its elements. the elements are separated by commas, and the entire list of elements is enclosed in braces. Since the elements of a set are not ordered, the order in which they are written doesn't matter. for example, the **roster forms** $\{1, 2, 4\}$, $\{2, 4, 1\}$, and $\{2, 1, 4\}$ all describe the same set. Each element should be listed only once, since an element cannot exist more than once in a set. Thus $\{1, 2, 1, 4\}$ describes the same set as $\{1, 2, 4\}$, but does so in a redundant way.

Roster form is useful because it allows the reader to easily see the elements at a glance, but it becomes unwieldy for large sets. Sometimes an infinite set is written in roster form by using an ellipsis to indicate the continuation of a pattern. for example, the set of positive even integers could be written $\{2, 4, 6, 8, \ldots\}$. However, this convention does pose some problems, and formally infinite sets are usually better written in set builder form.

Symbols for Sets Commonly Used in Mathematics

Certain sets are used frequently enough in mathematics to have their own symbols. the standard symbols for these sets resemble upper-case letters of the Latin alphabet, but in a typeface with double lines. Among the most commonly used **sets** are:

- $\mathbb{R}$ – the set of all real numbers
- $\mathbb{Z}$ – the set of all integers

- $\mathbb{N}$ – the set of all natural numbers
- $\mathbb{Q}$ – the set of all rational numbers (numbers that can be written as the ratio of two integers, $\frac{p}{q}$, where $q \neq 0$)
- $\mathbb{C}$ – the set of all complex numbers (numbers of the form $a + bi$, where a and b are real numbers and $i = \sqrt{-1}$)

A superscripted plus or minus sign is used to restrict the set to positive or negative numbers. for instance, $\mathbb{R}^+$ would be the set of all positive real numbers, and $\mathbb{Z}^-$ would be the set of all negative integers.

Some of these sets are, of course, subsets of others. Specifically, $\mathbb{N} \subset \mathbb{Z} \subset \mathbb{Q} \subset \mathbb{R} \subset \mathbb{C}$.

Set Operations with Venn Diagrams

A Venn diagram is a useful visual tool for representing two or three sets and their common elements. Each set is drawn as a **circle**, with the different circles overlapping. Elements are placed in the circle corresponding to the appropriate set or sets—or placed outside all the circles if they belong to the universe of discourse but not to any of the sets.

For example, suppose our universe of discourse is the integers from 1 to 9, and we have the three sets $A = \{1, 2, 3, 4, 5, 6\}$, $B = \{4, 5, 6, 7\}$, and $C = \{3, 6, 9\}$. This could be illustrated with the following **Venn diagram**:

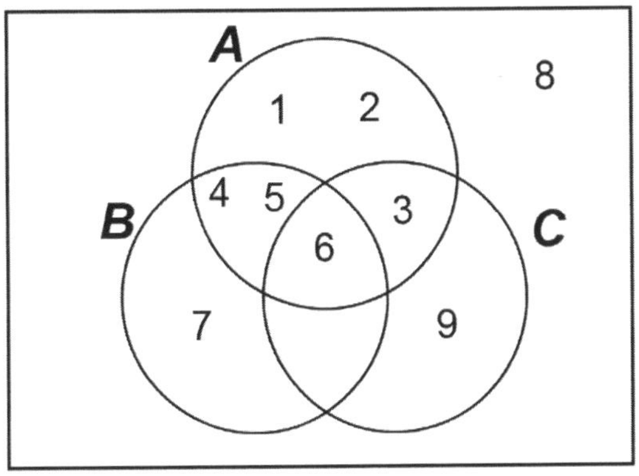

Note, for example, that 6 appears in the center of the diagram where all three circles overlap, because it is an element of all three sets. On the other hand, 8 is placed outside the three circles because it is not an element of any of the sets. Sometimes, instead of writing the elements themselves in the diagram, the total *number* of elements in each part of the Venn diagram is noted. This is especially useful for solving problems involving these numbers of elements.

Using Venn Diagrams to Solve Problems

Venn diagrams are useful for solving problems involving the numbers of elements in sets and in their intersections. By putting those numbers into a Venn diagram, it's simple to see how many must be in the "leftover" parts.

For example, suppose we're told that 200 voters were polled about two propositions, Proposition 1 and Proposition 2. Further,120 support Proposition 1, 85 support Proposition 2, and 50 support both propositions. To find how many of the voters support neither proposition, we can draw a Venn diagram with a circle representing the supporters of each proposition. We know 50 voters support both propositions, so we can write a 50 in the center of the diagram.

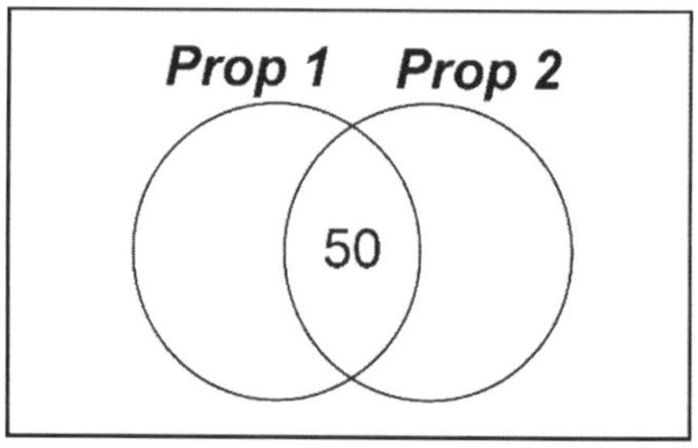

The Proposition 1 circle should contain 120 voters total, so subtracting the 50 voters in the overlap, the other section of the circle must contain $1200 - 50 = 70$. Similarly, the nonoverlapping part of the Proposition 2 circle should contain $85 - 50 = 35$.

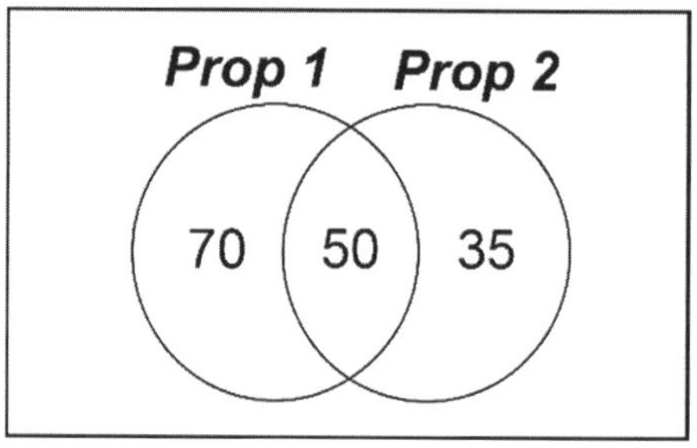

Adding all three sections, the total number of voters supporting either proposition is $70 + 50 + 35 = 155$, so there must be $200 - 155 = 45$ voters who support neither.

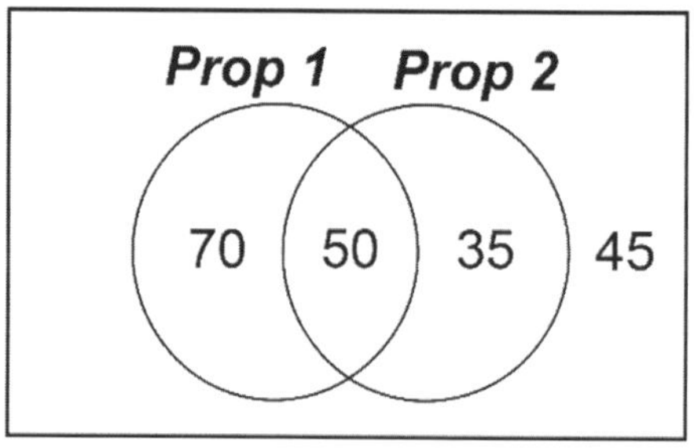

Properties of Infinite Sets

An infinite set has an infinite number of elements. a more technical definition is that a set is **infinite** if its elements can be put in one-to-one correspondence with the elements of one of its proper subsets. for instance, consider the set of all positive integers, $\mathbb{Z}^+$. If we remove the number 1, we can still match up every positive integer to an element of the remaining subset (by simply matching the number n to the number $n + 1$). $\mathbb{Z}^+$ is therefore an infinite set.

The union of an infinite set and any other set is always infinite. The intersection of two infinite sets may or may not be infinite. for instance, consider the set P of prime numbers, the set O of positive odd integers, and the set E of positive even integers—all infinite sets. $P \cap O$ is another infinite set, because there are infinitely many odd prime numbers. $P \cap E$ is finite, because there is only one even prime number. $E \cap O$ is the empty set. Likewise, the complement of an infinite set may be infinite, finite, or the empty set (if the set equals the universe of discourse).

Cardinality

Although all infinite sets have infinitely many members, they may still have different sizes. Two sets are defined to have the same size—or more technically the same **cardinality**—if each element of one set can be matched up to a unique element of the other, with none left over. for example, the set of all integers, $\mathbb{Z}$, and the set of all *even* integers have the same cardinality, even though the latter is a proper subset of the former: every number n in $\mathbb{Z}$ can be matched to a unique number $2n$ in the set of all *even* integers. Although it's more difficult to prove, the set of all rational numbers, $\mathbb{Q}$, also has the same cardinality as $\mathbb{Z}$. However, the set of all real numbers, $\mathbb{R}$, does *not* have the same cardinality—it is impossible to match each integer to a unique real number without any real numbers left over. the most famous proof of this fact was developed by Georg Cantor, and is called the *diagonal argument.*

Sets with the same cardinality as $\mathbb{Z}$ are said to be "countably infinite," or simply **countable**. Sets with a larger cardinality are said to be "uncountably infinite," or **uncountable**.

Logic

Premise and Argument

A premise is a statement that precedes a conclusion, in an argument. It is the proposition, or assumption, of an argument. An argument will have two or more premises.

Example:

If it is hot, then I will go swimming. (Premise)
It is hot. (Premise)
Therefore, I will go swimming. (Conclusion)

Simple and Compound Statements

A **statement** in propositional logic is any sentence or expression that has a truth value—that is, that may in principle be considered true or false. "Hello!", for example, is not a statement; there's no sense in which it could be considered true or false. On the other hand, "$2 = 3$" *is* a statement, albeit a clearly false one. a **compound statement** is a statement that contains one or more other statements, combined or modified in some way. a **simple statement**, or a **proposition**, is a statement that cannot be broken down further into smaller statements.

For example, consider the statement, "If it rains tomorrow, then the streets will be flooded and traffic will be slow." This is a compound statement, because two smaller statements are embedded within it: "it rains tomorrow" and "the streets will be flooded and traffic will be slow." the former cannot be broken down further, and is therefore a simple statement, but the latter is another compound statement, because it includes two simple statements: "the streets will be flooded" and "traffic will be slow."

Common operations used to combine and modify simple statements into compound statements include conjunction, disjunction, negation, and implication.

Conjunction

Conjunction is an operation that combines two or more statements into a compound statement that is true if and only if all of the component statements are true. When the statements are written out, conjunction is marked by the word "and." for example, the statement "Roses are red and violets are blue" is a compound statement that is a conjunction of the two simple statements "roses are red" and "violets are blue."

Conjunction is represented by the operator ∧. In the previous example, if proposition P is "roses are red" and proposition Q is "violets are blue," then the compound statement "roses are red and violets are blue" would be written as "$P \wedge Q$."

Disjunction

Disjunction is an operation that combines two or more statements into a compound statement that is true if and only if at least one of the component statements is true. When the statements are written out, disjunction is marked by the word "or." for example, the statement "I'll clean the closet today, or you'll clean it tomorrow" is a compound statement that is a disjunction of the simple statements "I'll clean the closet today" and "you'll clean the closet tomorrow."

Disjunction is represented by the operator ∨. In the previous example, if proposition P is "I'll clean the closet today" and proposition Q is "you'll clean the closet tomorrow," then the compound statement "I'll clean the closet today, or you'll clean it tomorrow" would be written as "$P \vee Q$."

Note that while in everyday language "or" implies exclusivity, as one or the other option but not both, in formal logic disjunction includes the possibility of both propositions being true. If I clean the closet today *and* you clean it tomorrow, then the sample statement "I'll clean the closet today, or you'll clean it tomorrow" is true.

Conditional and Biconditional Statements

A conditional statement, or **implication**, is a compound statement of the form "if P, then Q." for instance, the statement "if a snake has rattles, then it's venomous" is a conditional statement. It can also be written "P implies Q" ("that a snake has rattles implies that it's venomous") or "P only if Q" ("a snake has rattles only if it's venomous"). the conditional statement is true when both P and Q are true, and even when P is false, regardless of Q. In other words, the conditional statement is false only when P is true and Q is false. the conditional statement is written as "$P \rightarrow Q$." P is called the **premise** of the statement, and Q the **conclusion**.

A **biconditional statement** is a combination of two conditional statements: both "if P, then Q" and "if Q, then P." To state it more concisely, "P if and only if Q." an example is "A number is even if and only if it is divisible by 2." the biconditional statement is true when P and Q are either both true or both false; it is false if P is true and Q is false or vice versa. the biconditional statement is written "$P \leftrightarrow Q$."

Existential and Universal Quantifiers

A **quantifier** is a logical construct used in a compound statement to give information on the number of subjects for which a statement is true. the **existential quantifier** specifies that the statement is true for at least one subject. It is usually introduced as "there exists," such as "there exists a real number that is equal to its own square." the symbol ∃ is used to signify the existential quantifier. for example, the preceding statement could be written as "$\exists x \in \mathbb{R}\ x = x^2$." the **universal quantifier** specifies that the statement is true for *every* subject. It is usually said as "all" or "for all", such as "all real numbers are less than their own squares plus one." the symbol ∀ is used to signify the universal quantifier. for example, the preceding statement could be written as "$\forall x \in \mathbb{R}\ x < x^2 + 1$."

Sometimes it is useful to specify that there exists *exactly* one subject that meets a given criterion. In other words, there exists a *unique* such subject. This can be signified by adding an exclamation mark after the existential quantifier: "$\exists! \, x \in \mathbb{R} \, |x| = 0$" means "there exists a unique real number that has an absolute value of zero."

Truth Tables

A truth table shows the truth value of one or more compound statements for each possible combination of truth values of the propositions within it. the truth table contains one column for each **proposition**, and one column for each of the **compound statements** to be analyzed. It has one row for each combination of **truth values** of the propositions. Since each proposition has two possible truth values, the number of possible combinations for N propositions is 2^N, so the truth table will have 2^N rows.

The table below is a simple truth table for some common compound statements involving two propositions.

P	Q	$P \wedge Q$	$P \vee Q$	$\neg P$	$\neg Q$	$P \Rightarrow Q$	$Q \Rightarrow P$	$P \leftrightarrow Q$
T	T	T	T	F	F	T	T	T
T	F	F	T	F	T	F	T	F
F	T	F	T	T	F	T	F	F
F	F	F	F	T	T	T	T	T

Truth tables are useful for comparing two compound statements to see if they are equivalent. They are also useful for analyzing whether complicated compound statements are true or false. a table can have a column for each of the increasingly complex compound statements that combine to form the total statement.

Truth Table to Validate the Rule of Detachment

The Rule of Detachment states that given the premises, $P \to Q$ and P, the valid conclusion is Q.

In other words, for every case where $(P \to Q) \wedge P$ is true, Q will also be true. The truth table below illustrates this fact:

P	Q	$P \to Q$	$(P \to Q) \wedge P$
T	T	T	T
T	F	F	F
F	T	T	F
F	F	T	F

Notice the first cell under $(P \to Q) \wedge P$ is true, while the first cell under Q is also true. Thus, for every case where $(P \to Q) \wedge P$ was true, Q was also true.

Truth Table to Validate the Chain Rule

The Chain Rule states that given the premises, $P \to Q$ and $Q \to R$, the valid conclusion is $P \to R$.

In other words, for every case where $(P \to Q) \wedge (Q \to R)$ is true, $P \to R$ will also be true. The truth table below illustrates this fact:

P	Q	R	$P \to Q$	$Q \to R$	$(P \to Q) \wedge (Q \to R)$	$P \to R$
T	T	T	T	T	T	T
T	T	F	T	F	F	F
T	F	T	F	T	F	T
T	F	F	F	T	F	F
F	T	T	T	T	T	T
F	T	F	T	F	F	T
F	F	T	T	T	T	T
F	F	F	T	T	T	T

Notice that for every case where $(P \to Q) \wedge (Q \to R)$ was true, $P \to R$ was also true.

For example, consider the premises below:

If I hike a mountain, I will not eat a sandwich.
If I do not eat a sandwich, I will drink some water.
I will not drink some water.

Write a valid conclusive statement. Explain how you arrived at your answer. Be specific in your explanation.

Valid conclusive statement: I will not hike a mountain.

Application of the chain rule and rule of contraposition give the valid conclusion of $\neg P$. According to the chain rule, given $P \to \neg Q$ and $\neg Q \to R$, then $P \to R$. According to the rule of contraposition, $P \to R$ and $\neg R$ yields $\neg P$. On a truth table, for every place where $(P \to R) \wedge \neg R$ is true, $\neg P$ is also true. Thus, this is a valid conclusive statement.

Negation

In propositional logic, negation refers to the inversion of the truth value of a statement. the **negation** of a statement is true if the original statement is false, and false if the original statement is true. Negation can be signified by the word "not." for instance, the negation of the statement "Bob's cat is black" is "Bob's cat is not black." the symbol for negation is $\neg$. So, if the proposition *P* is "Bob's cat is black," then $\neg P$ would be "Bob's cat is not black." Two negations cancel each other out: $\neg\neg P = P$, or "not not *P* equals *P*."

It's important to be careful when combining negation with **quantifiers**. the negation of "there exists a cow that has a blue horn" is not "there exists a cow that does not have a blue horn." Rather, the negation is "there does not exist a cow that has a blue horn." the statements $\neg\exists x\ P(x)$ and $\exists x\ \neg P(x)$ are not equivalent. the same is true for the universal quantifier: $\neg\forall x\ P(x)$ and $\forall x\ \neg P(x)$ do not mean the same thing. There is, however, a connection between the negated quantifiers: $\neg\exists x\ P(x)$ is equivalent to $\forall x\ \neg P(x)$, and $\exists x\ \neg P(x)$ is equivalent to $\neg\forall x\ P(x)$.

De Morgan's Laws

De Morgan's Laws are a set of useful relations connecting negation, conjunction, and disjunction. They can be stated briefly as "the negation of a conjunction is the disjunction of the negations" and "the negation of a disjunction is the conjunction of the negations." This can be written as:

$$\neg(P \wedge Q) \leftrightarrow (\neg P) \vee (\neg Q) \text{ and } \neg(P \vee Q) \leftrightarrow (\neg P) \wedge (\neg Q)$$

For instance, if proposition P is "$x > 3$" and proposition Q is "$y > 3$", then De Morgan's Laws state that "it is not true that both x and y are greater than 3" is equivalent to "either x is not greater than 3, or y is not greater than 3."

The validity of **De Morgan's Laws** can be shown with truth tables. Note that the columns highlighted in the same color match:

P	Q	$\neg P$	$\neg Q$	$(\neg P) \wedge (\neg Q)$	$(\neg P) \vee (\neg Q)$	$P \wedge Q$	$P \vee Q$	$\neg(P \wedge Q)$	$\neg(P \vee Q)$
T	T	F	F	F	F	T	T	F	F
T	F	F	T	F	T	F	T	T	F
F	T	T	F	F	T	F	T	T	F
F	F	T	T	T	T	F	F	T	T

De Morgan's laws have an analogue in set theory, as well, replacing conjunction with intersection, disjunction with union, and negation with taking the complement:

$$\overline{A \cap B} = \bar{A} \cup \bar{B} \text{ and } \overline{A \cup B} = \bar{A} \cap \bar{B}$$

Converse, Inverse, and Contrapositive of a Conditional Statement

The converse of a conditional statement is a conditional statement with the premise and conclusion interchanged. the converse of $P \rightarrow Q$ is $Q \rightarrow P$. the **inverse** has the premise and conclusion both negated. the inverse of $P \rightarrow Q$ is $\neg P \rightarrow \neg Q$. the **contrapositive** has the premise and conclusion both negated *and* interchanged. the contrapositive of $P \rightarrow Q$ is $\neg Q \rightarrow \neg P$.

For example, given the **conditional statement**, "If there is a key in the lock, then someone is home," the **converse** is "if someone is home, then there is a key in the lock," the **inverse** is "if there is not a key in the lock, then no one is home," and the **contrapositive** is "if no one is home, then there is not a key in the lock."

Note that these statements are *not* logically equivalent. for instance, the statement "if $x = 4$, then $x > 2$" is true, but its converse "if $x > 2$, then $x = 4$" is not, because there are many numbers greater than 2, not just 4. a statement *is*, however, logically equivalent to its contrapositive—and the converse and inverse, while not equivalent to the original statement, are equivalent to each other. the following truth table summarizes the relationships:

P	Q	$P \rightarrow Q$	$Q \rightarrow P$ (converse)	$\neg P \rightarrow \neg Q$ (inverse)	$\neg Q \rightarrow \neg P$ (contrapositive)
T	T	T	T	T	T
T	F	F	T	T	F
F	T	T	F	F	T
F	F	T	T	T	T

Inductive Reasoning

Inductive reasoning is a method used to make a conjecture, based on patterns and observations. The conclusion of an inductive argument may be true or false.

Mathematical Example:

A cube has 6 faces, 8 vertices, and 12 edges. A square pyramid has 5 faces, 5 vertices, and 8 edges. A triangular prism has 5 faces, 6 vertices, and 9 edges. Thus, the sum of the numbers of faces and vertices, minus the number of edges, will always equal 2, for any solid.

Non-Mathematical Example:

Almost all summer days in Tucson are hot. It is a summer day in Tucson. Therefore, it will probably be hot.

Deductive Reasoning

Deductive reasoning is a method that proves a hypothesis or set of premises. The conclusion of a valid deductive argument will be true, given that the premises are true. Deductive reasoning utilizes logic to determine a conclusion.

Example:

If a ding is a dong, then a ping is a pong.
If a ping is a pong, then a ring is a ting.
A ding is a dong.
___
Therefore, a ring is a ting.

Rules of Logic

The rules of logic are related to deductive reasoning because one conclusion must be made, given a set of premises (or statements). A truth table may be used to determine the validity of an argument. In all cases, the determination of the conclusion is based on a top-down approach, whereby a set of premises yields a certain conclusion, albeit true or false, depending on the truth values of all premises.

Mathematical Induction Proof Utilizing Inductive Reasoning

A mathematical induction proof utilizes inductive reasoning in its assumption that if $P(k)$ is true, then $P(k+1)$ is also true. The induction hypothesis is $P(k)$. This step utilizes inductive reasoning because an observation is used to make the conjecture that $P(k+1)$ is also true.

Example:

For all natural numbers, n, the sum is equal to $(n+1)\left(\frac{n}{2}\right)$.
Show that $P(1)$ is true.
$1 = (1+1)\left(\frac{1}{2}\right)$.
Assume P(k) is true.
$1 + 2 + 3 + 4 + \cdots + k = (k+1)\left(\frac{k}{2}\right)$.

This previous step is the inductive hypothesis. This hypothesis may be used to write the conjecture that $P(k+1)$ is also true: $(1+2+3+4+\cdots+k)+(k+1)=[(k+1)+1]\left(\frac{k+1}{2}\right)$

$$(k+1)\left(\frac{k}{2}\right)+(k+1)=[(k+1)+1]\left(\frac{k}{2}+\frac{1}{2}\right)$$
$$(k+1)\left(\frac{k}{2}\right)+(k+1)=\left(\frac{k}{2}(k+1)+\frac{k}{2}\right)+\left(\frac{1}{2}(k+1)+\frac{1}{2}(1)\right)$$
$$(k+1)\left(\frac{k}{2}\right)+(k+1)=\frac{k}{2}(k+1)+\frac{k}{2}+\frac{k+1}{2}+\frac{1}{2}$$
$$(k+1)\left(\frac{k}{2}\right)+(k+1)=\frac{k}{2}(k+1)+\frac{2k+2}{2}$$
$$(k+1)\left(\frac{k}{2}\right)+(k+1)=\frac{k}{2}(k+1)+(k+1)$$

Formal Reasoning

Formal reasoning, in mathematics, involves justification using formal steps and processes to arrive at a conclusion. Formal reasoning is utilized when writing proofs and using logic. For example, when applying logic, validity of a conclusion is determined by truth tables. A set of premises will yield a given conclusion. This type of thinking is formal reasoning. Writing a geometric proof also employs formal reasoning.

Example:

If a quadrilateral has four congruent sides, it is a rhombus.
If a shape is a rhombus, then the diagonals are perpendicular.
A quadrilateral has four congruent sides.

Therefore, the diagonals are perpendicular.

Informal Reasoning

Informal reasoning, in mathematics, uses patterns and observations to make conjectures. The conjecture may be true or false. Several, or even many, examples may show a certain pattern, shedding light on a possible conclusion. However, informal reasoning does not provide a justifiable conclusion. A conjecture may certainly be deemed as likely or probable. However, informal reasoning will not reveal a certain conclusion.

Example:

Mathematical Idea – Given a sequence that starts with 1 and each term decreases by a factor of $\frac{1}{2}$, the limit of the sum of the sequence will be 2.

Informal Reasoning – The sum of 1 and $\frac{1}{2}$ is $1\frac{1}{2}$. The sum of 1, $\frac{1}{2}$, and $\frac{1}{4}$ is $1\frac{3}{4}$. The sum of 1, $\frac{1}{2}$, $\frac{1}{4}$, and $\frac{1}{8}$ is $1\frac{7}{8}$. Thus, it appears that as the sequence approaches infinity, the sum of the sequence approaches 2.

Problems

Use informal reasoning to justify the statement, "If n is a whole number, then n^2+n+1 is odd." Explain the reasoning steps used.

Using the sequence, 0, 1, 2, 3, 4, 5, 6, ... for n, evaluation of the expression, $n^2 + n + 1$, gives $0^2 + 0 + 1$, $1^2 + 1 + 1$, $2^2 + 2 + 1$, $3^2 + 3 + 1$, $4^2 + 4 + 1$, $5^2 + 5 + 1$, and $6^2 + 6 + 1$, or 1, 3, 7, 13, 21, 31, and 43, all of which are odd numbers. Thus, it appears that given any whole number, n, evaluation of the expression $n^2 + n + 1$ will yield an odd number.

Use formal reasoning to justify the statement, "If a divides b, a divides c, and a divides d, then a divides the sum of b, c, and d." Show the formal proof.

Direct Proof:

Assume a divides b, a divides c, and a divides d.

Given the definition of divides, a divides b indicates that there exists some integer, r, such that $b = a \times r$. Also, a divides c indicates that there exists some integer, s, such that $c = a \times s$. Finally, a divides d indicates that there exists some integer, t, such that $d = a \times t$. By substitution, the sum of b, c, and d may be written as $(a \times r) + (a \times s) + (a \times t)$. Factoring out an a gives $a(r + s + t)$. The factor $(r + s + t)$ is an integer, according to the closure property under addition. Thus, a divides the sum of b, c, and d.

Euler Circles

Euler circles (pronounced "oiler" and named after the eighteenth-century Swiss mathematician) are circles or other shapes that diagrammatically represent sets and their contents. the relative positions of the sets reflect their relationships: a subset is completely enclosed by the superset, and two circles overlap if and only if they have elements in common. Euler circles may be colored, with the colors blending where the circles overlap. a diagram consisting of multiple Euler circles is called an **Euler diagram**. Euler diagrams are similar to Venn diagrams but may be more complex, because while Venn diagrams are generally used with two or three sets, Euler diagrams generalize easily to larger numbers of sets. Furthermore, Euler diagrams allow the viewer to see at a glance the relationship between two sets.

For example, consider the sets $A = \{1,2,3\}$, $B = \{1,3,5,7,9\}$, $C = \{4,5,6,7,8\}$, $D = \{6,7,8\}$, and $E = \{6\}$. These sets could be represented in an Euler diagram as shown below:

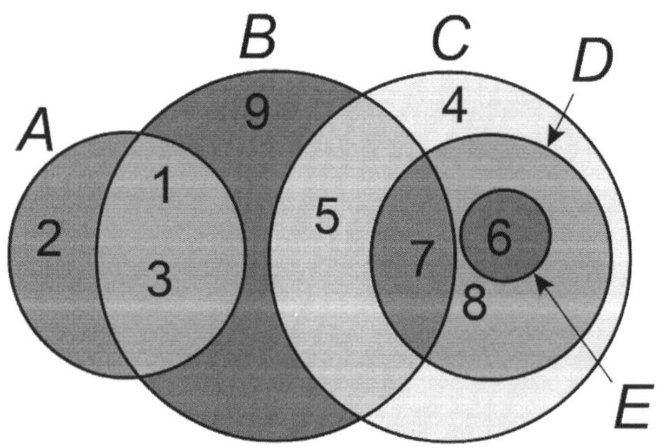

Metric System, Conversions, and Geometry

Measurement Conversion

When going from a larger unit to a smaller unit, multiply the number of the known amount by the **equivalent amount**. When going from a smaller unit to a larger unit, divide the number of the known amount by the equivalent amount.

Review Video: Metric System Conversions
Visit mometrix.com/academy and enter code: 163709

Also, you can set up conversion fractions. In these fractions, one fraction is the **conversion factor**. The other fraction has the unknown amount in the numerator. So, the known value is placed in the denominator. Sometimes the second fraction has the known value from the problem in the numerator, and the unknown in the denominator. Multiply the two fractions to get the converted measurement.

Conversion Units

Metric Conversions

1000 μg (microgram)	1 mg
1000 mg (milligram)	1 g
1000 g (gram)	1 kg
1000 kg (kilogram)	1 metric ton
1000 mL (milliliter)	1 L
1000 μm (micrometer)	1 mm
1000 mm (millimeter)	1 m
100 cm (centimeter)	1 m
1000 m (meter)	1 km

U.S. and Metric Equivalents

Unit	U.S. equivalent	Metric equivalent
Inch	1 inch	2.54 centimeters
Foot	12 inches	0.305 meters
Yard	3 feet	0.914 meters
Mile	5280 feet	1.609 kilometers

Capacity Measurements

Unit	U.S. equivalent	Metric equivalent
Ounce	8 drams	29.573 milliliters
Cup	8 ounces	0.237 liter
Pint	16 ounces	0.473 liter
Quart	2 pints	0.946 liter
Gallon	4 quarts	3.785 liters

Weight Measurements

Unit	U.S. equivalent	Metric equivalent
Ounce	16 drams	28.35 grams

Unit	U.S. equivalent	Metric equivalent
Pound	16 ounces	453.6 grams
Ton	2,000 pounds	907.2 kilograms

Fluid Measurements

Unit	U.S. equivalent	Metric equivalent
1 tsp	1.333 fluid drams	5 milliliters
3 tsp	4 fluid drams	15 or 16 milliliters
2 tbsp	1 fluid ounce	30 milliliters
1 glass	8 fluid ounces	240 milliliters

Measurement Conversion Practice Problems

Metric Examples

Convert 1.4 meters to centimeters.

$$1.4\text{ m} \times \frac{100\text{ cm}}{1\text{ m}} = 140\text{ cm}$$

Convert 218 centimeters to meters.

$$218\text{ cm} \times \frac{1\text{ m}}{100\text{ cm}} = 2.18\text{ m}$$

U.S. Examples

Convert 42 inches to feet.

$$42\text{ in} \times \frac{1\text{ ft}}{12\text{ in}} = 3.5\text{ ft}$$

Convert 15 feet to yards.

$$15\text{ ft} \times \frac{1\text{ yd}}{3\text{ ft}} = 5\text{ yd}$$

How many pounds are in 80 ounces?

$$80\text{ ounces} \times \frac{1\text{ pound}}{16\text{ ounces}} = 5\text{ pounds}$$

How many pints are in 9 gallons?

$$9\text{ gallons} \times \frac{4\text{ quarts}}{1\text{ gallon}} \times \frac{2\text{ pints}}{1\text{ quarts}} = 72\text{ pints}$$

Metric U.S. Conversion Examples

How many pounds are in 15 kilograms?

$$15\text{ kilograms} \times \frac{2.2\text{ pounds}}{1\text{ kilogram}} = 33\text{ pounds}$$

How many kilometers are in 2 miles?

$$2 \text{ miles } \times \frac{1.609 \text{ kilometers}}{1 \text{ mile}} = 3.218 \text{ kilometers}$$

How many centimeters are in 5 feet?

$$5 \text{ feet } \times \frac{12 \text{ inches}}{1 \text{ foot}} \times \frac{2.54 \text{ centimeters}}{1 \text{ inch}} = 152.4 \text{ centimeters}$$

How many gallons are in 15.14 liters?

$$15.14 \text{ liters } \times \frac{1 \text{ gallon}}{3.785 \text{ liters}} = 4 \text{ gallons}$$

How many liters are in 8 quarts?

$$8 \text{ quarts } \times \frac{1 \text{ gallon}}{4 \text{ quarts}} \times \frac{3.785 \text{ liters}}{1 \text{ gallon}} = 7.57 \text{ liters}$$

How many grams are in 13.2 pounds?

$$13.2 \text{ pounds } \times \frac{1 \text{ kilogram}}{2.2 \text{ pounds}} \times \frac{1000 \text{ grams}}{1 \text{ kilogram}} = 6000 \text{ grams}$$

Geometry

Lines and Planes

A **point** is a fixed location in space; has no size or dimensions; commonly represented by a dot.

A **line** is a set of points that extends infinitely in two opposite directions. It has length, but no width or depth. A line can be defined by any two distinct points that it contains. A line segment is a portion of a line that has definite endpoints. A ray is a portion of a line that extends from a single point on that line in one direction along the line. It has a definite beginning, but no ending.

A **plane** is a two-dimensional flat surface defined by three non-collinear points. A plane extends an infinite distance in all directions in those two dimensions. It contains an infinite number of points, parallel lines and segments, intersecting lines and segments, as well as parallel or intersecting rays. A plane will never contain a three-dimensional figure or skew lines, which are lines that don't intersect and are not parallel. Two given planes are either parallel or they intersect at a line. A plane may intersect a circular conic surface to form **conic sections**, such as a parabola, hyperbola, circle or ellipse.

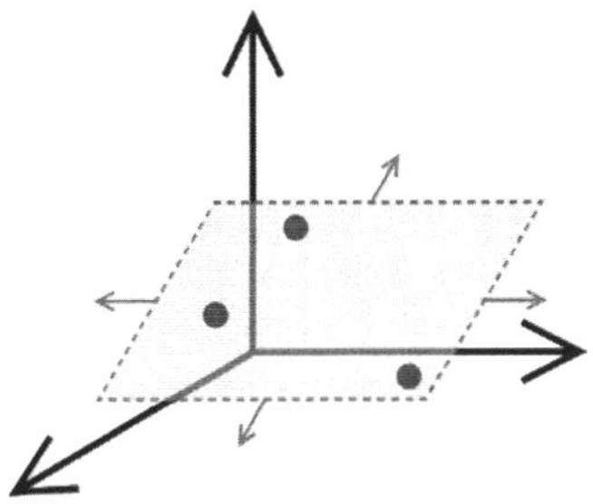

Review Video: Lines and Planes
Visit mometrix.com/academy and enter code: 554267

Perpendicular lines are lines that intersect at right angles. They are represented by the symbol ⊥. The shortest distance from a line to a point not on the line is a perpendicular segment from the point to the line.

Parallel lines are lines in the same plane that have no points in common and never meet. It is possible for lines to be in different planes, have no points in common, and never meet, but they are not parallel because they are in different planes.

A **bisector** is a line or line segment that divides another line segment into two equal lengths. A perpendicular bisector of a line segment is composed of points that are equidistant from the endpoints of the segment it is dividing.

Intersecting lines are lines that have exactly one point in common. Concurrent lines are multiple lines that intersect at a single point.

A **transversal** is a line that intersects at least two other lines, which may or may not be parallel to one another. A transversal that intersects parallel lines is a common occurrence in geometry.

ANGLES

An **angle** is formed when two lines or line segments meet at a common point. It may be a common starting point for a pair of segments or rays, or it may be the intersection of lines. Angles are represented by the symbol ∠.

The **vertex** is the point at which two segments or rays meet to form an angle. If the angle is formed by intersecting rays, lines, and/or line segments, the vertex is the point at which four angles are formed. The pairs of angles opposite one another are called vertical angles, and their measures are equal.

An **acute angle** is an angle with a degree measure less than 90°.

A **right angle** is an angle with a degree measure of exactly 90°.

An **obtuse angle** is an angle with a degree measure greater than 90° but less than 180°.

A **straight angle** is an angle with a degree measure of exactly 180°. This is also a semicircle.

A **reflex angle** is an angle with a degree measure greater than 180° but less than 360°.

A **full angle** is an angle with a degree measure of exactly 360°. This is also a circle.

Review Video: Angles
Visit mometrix.com/academy and enter code: 264624

Two angles whose sum is exactly 90° are said to be **complementary**. The two angles may or may not be adjacent. In a right triangle, the two acute angles are complementary.

Two angles whose sum is exactly 180° are said to be **supplementary**. The two angles may or may not be adjacent. Two intersecting lines always form two pairs of supplementary angles. Adjacent supplementary angles will always form a straight line.

Two angles that have the same vertex and share a side are said to be **adjacent**. Vertical angles are not adjacent because they share a vertex but no common side.

Review Video: Adjacent Angles
Visit mometrix.com/academy and enter code: 100375

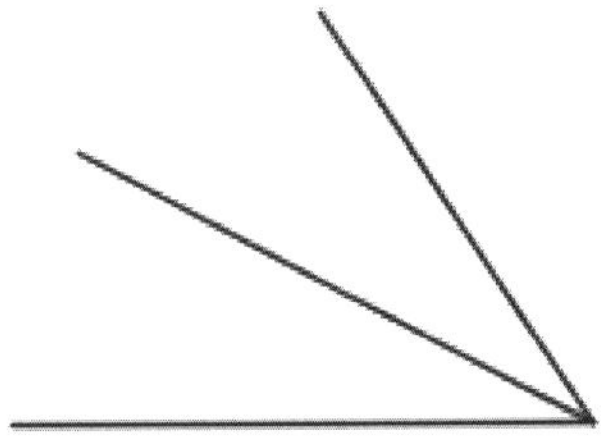

Adjacent — **Share vertex and side**

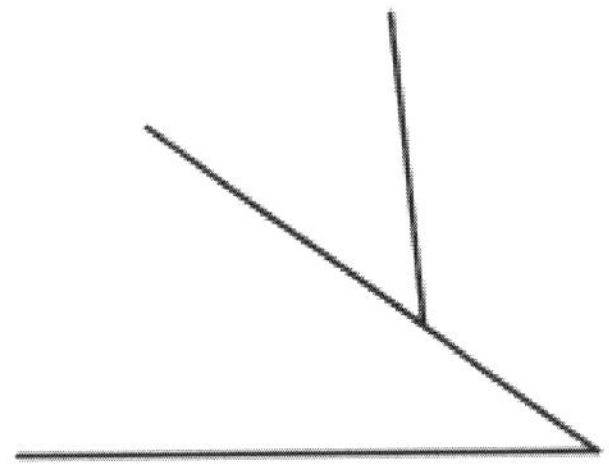

Not adjacent — **Share part of side, but not vertex**

When two parallel lines are cut by a transversal, the angles that are between the two parallel lines are **interior angles**. In the diagram below, angles 3, 4, 5, and 6 are interior angles.

When two parallel lines are cut by a transversal, the angles that are outside the parallel lines are **exterior angles**. In the diagram below, angles 1, 2, 7, and 8 are exterior angles.

When two parallel lines are cut by a transversal, the angles that are in the same position relative to the transversal and a parallel line are **corresponding angles**. The diagram below has four pairs of corresponding angles: angles 1 and 5; angles 2 and 6; angles 3 and 7; and angles 4 and 8. Corresponding angles formed by parallel lines are congruent.

When two parallel lines are cut by a transversal, the two interior angles that are on opposite sides of the transversal are called **alternate interior angles**. In the diagram below, there are two pairs of alternate interior angles: angles 3 and 6, and angles 4 and 5. Alternate interior angles formed by parallel lines are congruent.

When two parallel lines are cut by a transversal, the two exterior angles that are on opposite sides of the transversal are called **alternate exterior angles**.

In the diagram below, there are two pairs of alternate exterior angles: angles 1 and 8, and angles 2 and 7. Alternate exterior angles formed by parallel lines are congruent.

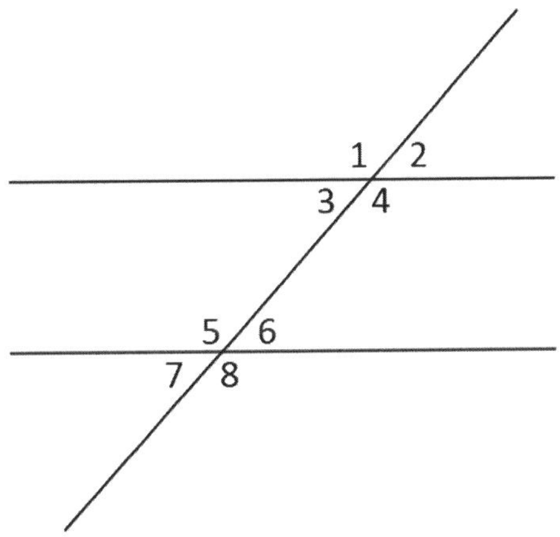

When two lines intersect, four angles are formed. The non-adjacent angles at this vertex are called vertical angles. Vertical angles are congruent. In the diagram, $\angle ABD \cong \angle CBE$ and $\angle ABC \cong \angle DBE$.

Review Video: Congruent Angles
Visit mometrix.com/academy and enter code: 642874

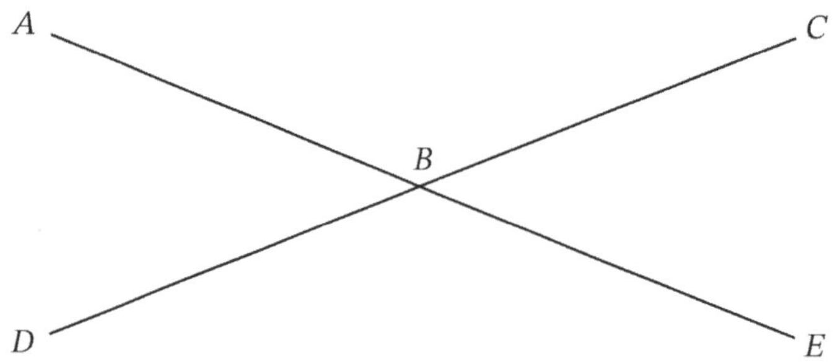

POLYGONS

Each straight line segment of a polygon is called a **side**.

The point at which two sides of a polygon intersect is called the **vertex**. In a polygon, the number of sides is always equal to the number of vertices.

A polygon with all sides congruent and all angles equal is called a **regular polygon**. Polygons must have three or more sides. Common polygons are:

$$\begin{aligned} \text{Triangle} &= 3 \text{ sides} \\ \text{Quadrilateral} &= 4 \text{ sides} \\ \text{Pentagon} &= 5 \text{ sides} \\ \text{Hexagon} &= 6 \text{ sides} \\ \text{Heptagon} &= 7 \text{ sides} \\ \text{Octagon} &= 8 \text{ sides} \\ \text{Nonagon} &= 9 \text{ sides} \\ \text{Decagon} &= 10 \text{ sides} \\ \text{Dodecagon} &= 12 \text{ sides} \end{aligned}$$

Generally, an n-gon is a polygon that has more than 12 angles and sides. The space of n is for the number of sides. Also, an 11-sided polygon is known as an 11-gon.

The sum of the interior angles of an n-sided polygon is $(n - 2) \times 180°$. For example, in a triangle $n = 3$. So the sum of the interior angles is $(3 - 2) \times 180° = 180°$. In a quadrilateral, $n = 4$, and the sum of the angles is $(4 - 2) \times 180° = 360°$.

A line segment from the center of a polygon that is perpendicular to a side of the polygon is called the **apothem**. A line segment from the center of a polygon to a vertex of the polygon is called a

radius. In a regular polygon, the apothem can be used to find the area of the polygon using the formula $A = \frac{1}{2}ap$, where a is the apothem, and p is the perimeter.

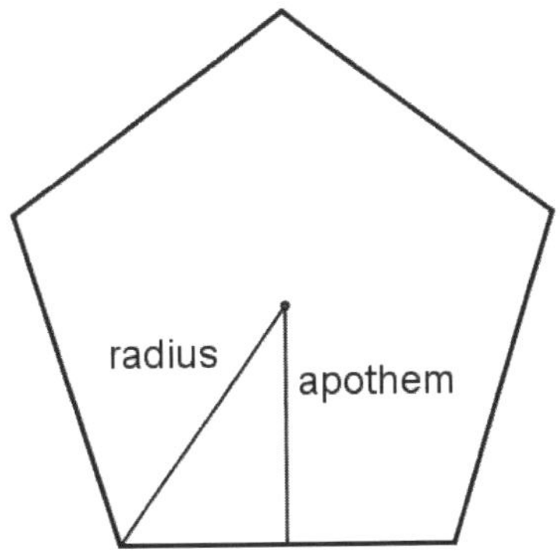

A **diagonal** is a line segment that joins two non-adjacent vertices of a polygon.

A **convex polygon** is a polygon whose diagonals all lie within the interior of the polygon. A **concave polygon** is a polygon with a least one diagonal that is outside the polygon. In the diagram below, quadrilateral $ABCD$ is concave because diagonal $\overline{AC}$ lies outside the polygon.

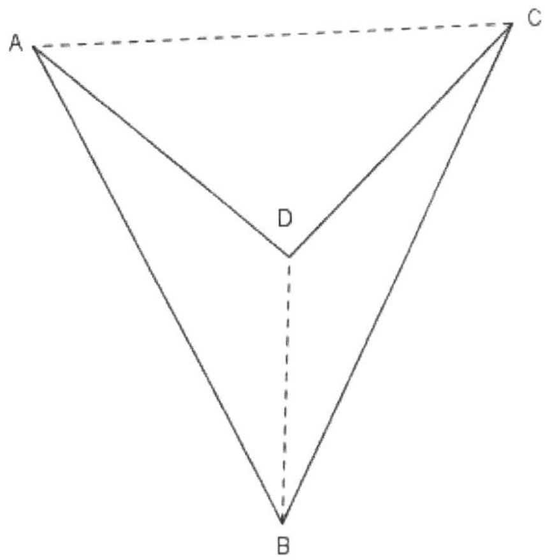

The number of diagonals that a polygon has can be found by using the formula: $\frac{n(n-3)}{2}$; where n is the number of sides in the polygon. This formula works for all polygons.

Congruent figures are geometric figures that have the same size and shape. All corresponding angles are equal, and all corresponding sides are equal. Congruence is indicated by the symbol $\cong$.

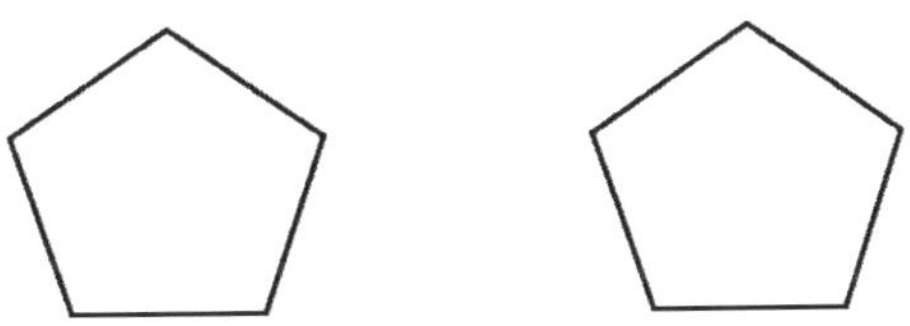

Congruent polygons

Similar figures are geometric figures that have the same shape, but may not have the same size. All corresponding angles are equal, and all corresponding sides are proportional. However, they do not have to be equal. Similarity is shown by the symbol $\sim$.

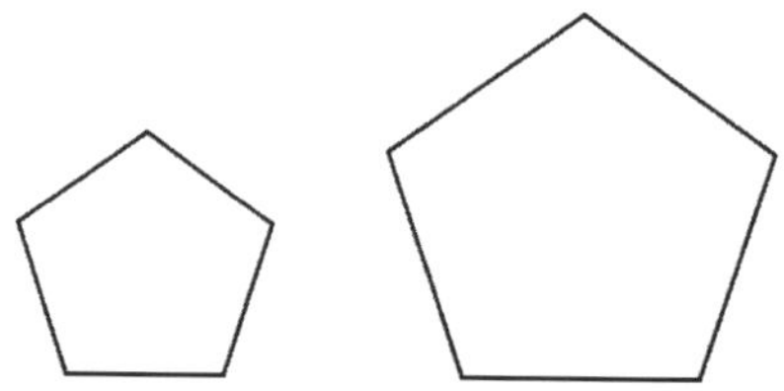

Similar polygons

Note that all congruent figures are also similar. However, not all similar figures are congruent.

Review Video: Intro to Polygons
Visit mometrix.com/academy and enter code: 271869

LINE OF SYMMETRY

Line of Symmetry: The line that divides a figure or object into equal parts. Each part is congruent to the other. An object may have no lines of symmetry, one line of symmetry, or multiple (i.e., more than one) lines of symmetry.

Lines of symmetry:

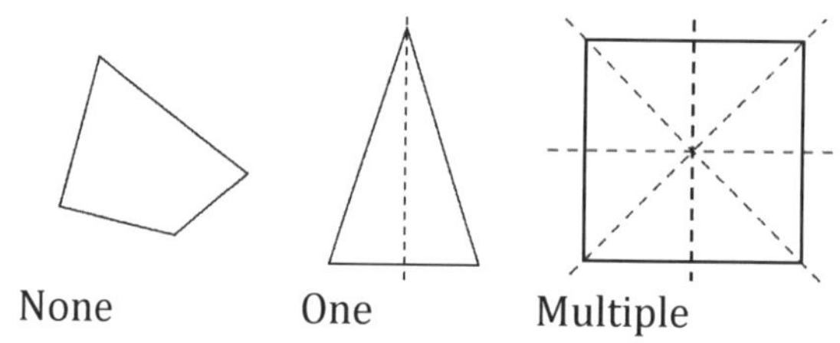

Review Video: Symmetry
Visit mometrix.com/academy and enter code: 528106

TRIANGLES

An **equilateral triangle** is a triangle with three congruent sides. An equilateral triangle will also have three congruent angles, each 60°. All equilateral triangles are also acute triangles.

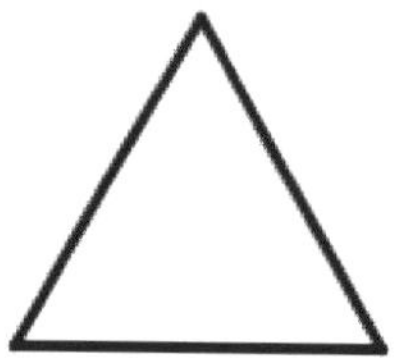

An **isosceles triangle** is a triangle with two congruent sides. An isosceles triangle will also have two congruent angles opposite the two congruent sides.

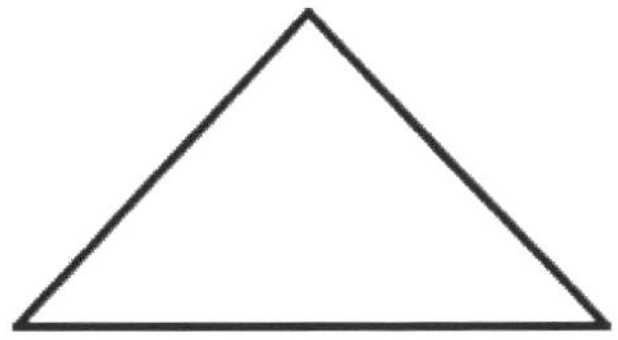

A **scalene triangle** is a triangle with no congruent sides. A scalene triangle will also have three angles of different measures. The angle with the largest measure is opposite the longest side, and the angle with the smallest measure is opposite the shortest side.

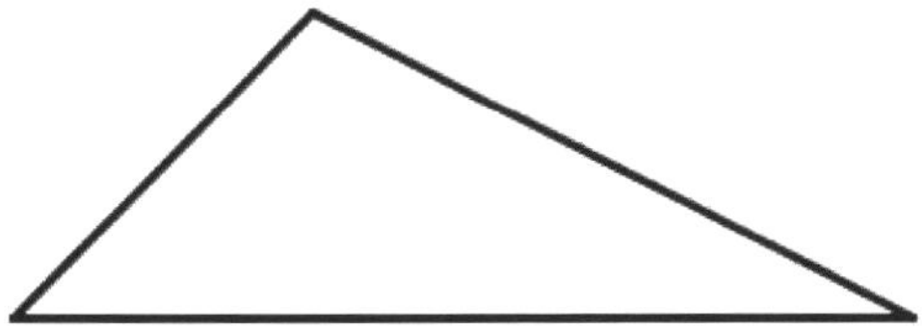

An **acute triangle** is a triangle whose three angles are all less than 90°. If two of the angles are equal, the acute triangle is also an isosceles triangle. If the three angles are all equal, the acute triangle is also an equilateral triangle.

A **right triangle** is a triangle with exactly one angle equal to 90°. All right triangles follow the Pythagorean theorem. A right triangle can never be acute or obtuse.

An **obtuse triangle** is a triangle with exactly one angle greater than 90°. The other two angles may or may not be equal. If the two remaining angles are equal, the obtuse triangle is also an isosceles triangle.

Review Video: Introduction to Types of Triangles
Visit mometrix.com/academy and enter code: 511711

TERMINOLOGY

ALTITUDE OF A TRIANGLE

A line segment drawn from one vertex perpendicular to the opposite side. In the diagram below, $\overline{BE}$, $\overline{AD}$, and $\overline{CF}$ are altitudes. The three altitudes in a triangle are always concurrent.

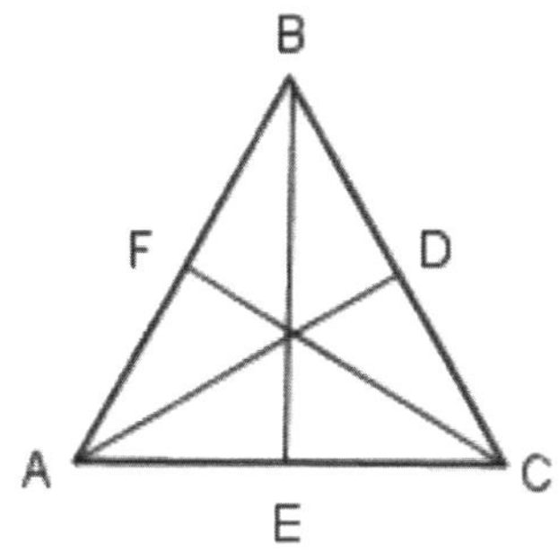

Height of a triangle

The length of the altitude, although the two terms are often used interchangeably.

Orthocenter of a triangle

The point of concurrency of the altitudes of a triangle. Note that in an obtuse triangle, the orthocenter will be outside the triangle, and in a right triangle, the orthocenter is the vertex of the right angle.

Median of a triangle

A line segment drawn from one vertex to the midpoint of the opposite side. This is not the same as the altitude, except the altitude to the base of an isosceles triangle and all three altitudes of an equilateral triangle.

Centroid of a triangle

The point of concurrency of the medians of a triangle. This is the same point as the orthocenter only in an equilateral triangle. Unlike the orthocenter, the centroid is always inside the triangle. The centroid can also be considered the exact center of the triangle. Any shape triangle can be perfectly balanced on a tip placed at the centroid. The centroid is also the point that is two-thirds the distance from the vertex to the opposite side.

General Rules

The *triangle inequality theorem* states that the sum of the measures of any two sides of a triangle is always greater than the measure of the third side. If the sum of the measures of two sides were equal to the third side, a triangle would be impossible because the two sides would lie flat across the third side and there would be no vertex. If the sum of the measures of two of the sides was less than the third side, a closed figure would be impossible because the two shortest sides would never meet.

The sum of the measures of the interior angles of a triangle is always 180°. Therefore, a triangle can never have more than one angle greater than or equal to 90°.

In any triangle, the angles opposite congruent sides are congruent, and the sides opposite congruent angles are congruent. The largest angle is always opposite the longest side, and the smallest angle is always opposite the shortest side.

The line segment that joins the midpoints of any two sides of a triangle is always parallel to the third side and exactly half the length of the third side.

Pythagorean Theorem

The side of a triangle opposite the right angle is called the **hypotenuse**. The other two sides are called the legs. The Pythagorean theorem states a relationship among the legs and hypotenuse of a right triangle: $a^2 + b^2 = c^2$, where a and b are the lengths of the legs of a right triangle, and c is the length of the hypotenuse. Note that this formula will only work with right triangles.

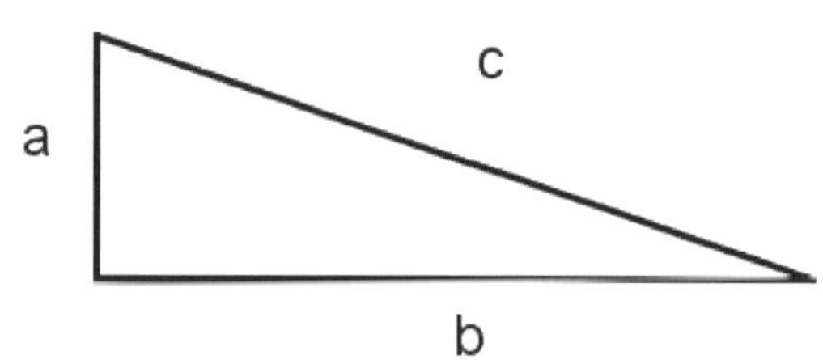

Review Video: Pythagorean Theorem
Visit mometrix.com/academy and enter code: 906576

Laws of Sines and Cosines

The **law of sines** states that $\frac{\sin A}{a} = \frac{\sin B}{b} = \frac{\sin C}{c}$, where A, B, and C are the angles of a triangle, and a, b, and c are the sides opposite their respective angles. This formula will work with all triangles, not just right triangles.

The **law of cosines** is given by the formula $c^2 = a^2 + b^2 - 2ab(\cos C)$, where a, b, and c are the sides of a triangle, and C is the angle opposite side c. This formula is similar to the *pythagorean theorem*, but unlike the pythagorean theorem, it can be used on any triangle.

Review Video: Cosine
Visit mometrix.com/academy and enter code: 361120

Similarity and Congruence Rules

Similar triangles are triangles whose corresponding angles are equal and whose corresponding sides are proportional. Represented by AAA. Similar triangles whose corresponding sides are congruent are also congruent triangles.

Triangles can be shown to be **congruent** in 5 ways:

- **SSS**: Three sides of one triangle are congruent to the three corresponding sides of the second triangle.
- **SAS**: Two sides and the included angle (the angle formed by those two sides) of one triangle are congruent to the corresponding two sides and included angle of the second triangle.
- **ASA**: Two angles and the included side (the side that joins the two angles) of one triangle are congruent to the corresponding two angles and included side of the second triangle.
- **AAS**: Two angles and a non-included side of one triangle are congruent to the corresponding two angles and non-included side of the second triangle.
- **HL**: The hypotenuse and leg of one right triangle are congruent to the corresponding hypotenuse and leg of the second right triangle.

Review Video: Similar Triangles
Visit mometrix.com/academy and enter code: 398538

Quadrilaterals

Quadrilateral: A closed two-dimensional geometric figure that has four straight sides. The sum of the interior angles of any quadrilateral is 360°.

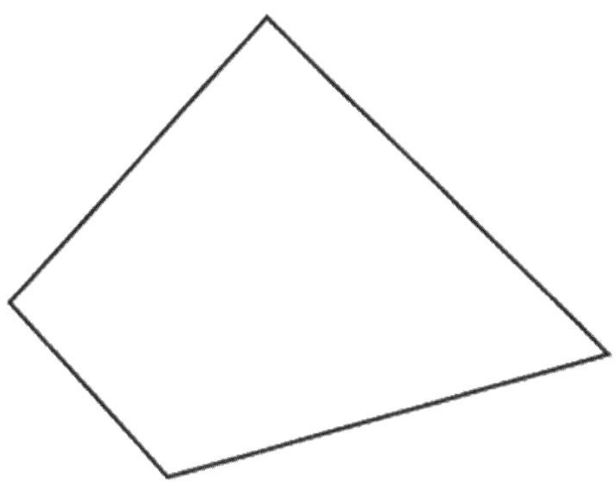

Kite: A quadrilateral with two pairs of adjacent sides that are congruent. A result of this is perpendicular diagonals. A kite can be concave or convex and has one line of symmetry.

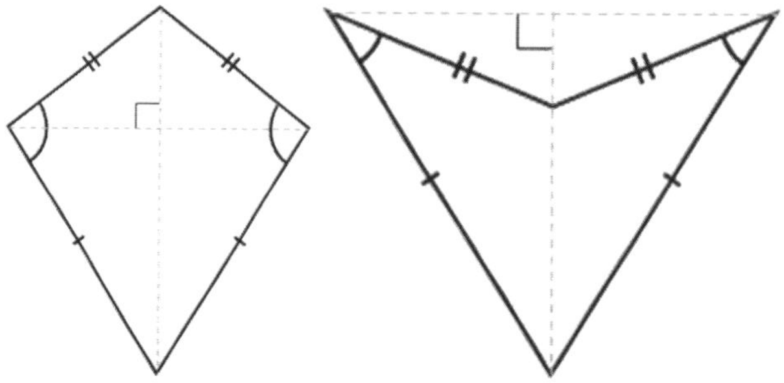

Trapezoid: A trapezoid is defined as a quadrilateral that has at least one pair of parallel sides. There are no rules for the second pair of sides. So there are no rules for the diagonals and no lines of symmetry for a trapezoid.

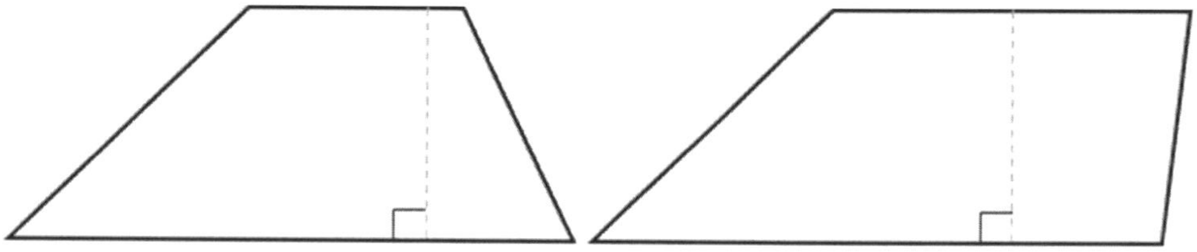

Parallelogram: A quadrilateral that has two pairs of opposite parallel sides. As such it is a special type of trapezoid. The sides that are parallel are also congruent. The opposite interior angles are always congruent, and the consecutive interior angles are supplementary. The diagonals of a parallelogram divide each other. Each diagonal divides the parallelogram into two congruent triangles. A parallelogram has no line of symmetry, but does have 180-degree rotational symmetry about the midpoint.

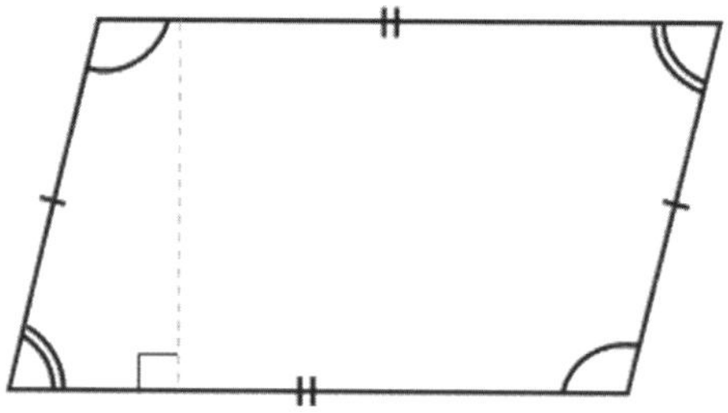

Review Video: Area and Perimeter of a Parallelogram
Visit mometrix.com/academy and enter code: 718313

Isosceles Trapezoid: A trapezoid with equal base angles. This gives rise to other properties including: the two nonparallel sides have the same length, the two non-base angles are also equal, and there is one line of symmetry through the midpoints of the parallel sides.

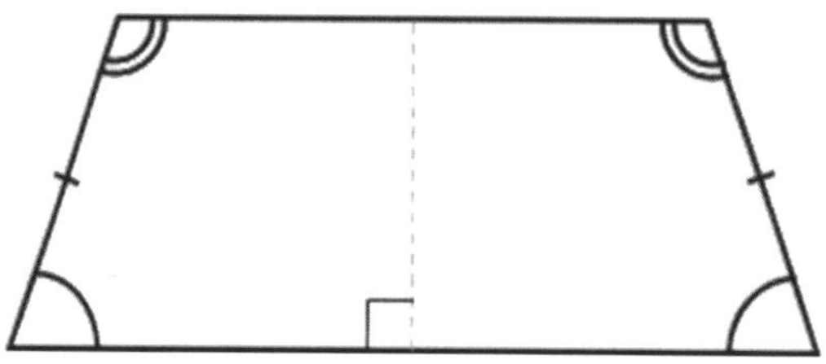

Rectangle: A quadrilateral with four right angles. All rectangles are parallelograms and trapezoids, but not all parallelograms or trapezoids are rectangles. The diagonals of a rectangle are congruent. Rectangles have 2 lines of symmetry (through each pair of opposing midpoints) and 180-degree rotational symmetry about the midpoint.

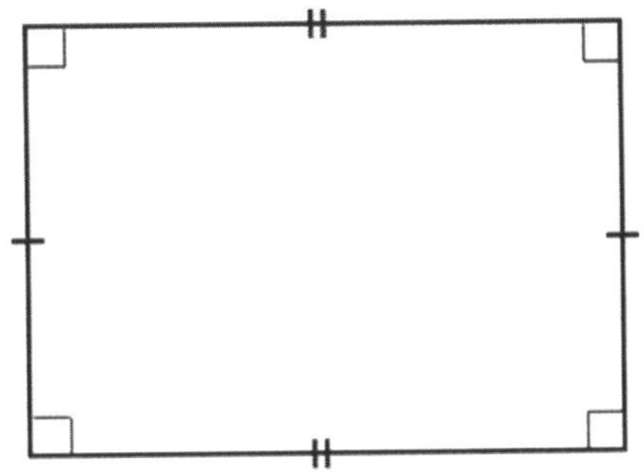

Rhombus: A quadrilateral with four congruent sides. All rhombuses are parallelograms and kites; thus, they inherit all the properties of both types of quadrilaterals. The diagonals of a rhombus are perpendicular to each other. Rhombi have 2 lines of symmetry (along each of the diagonals) and 180-degree rotational symmetry.

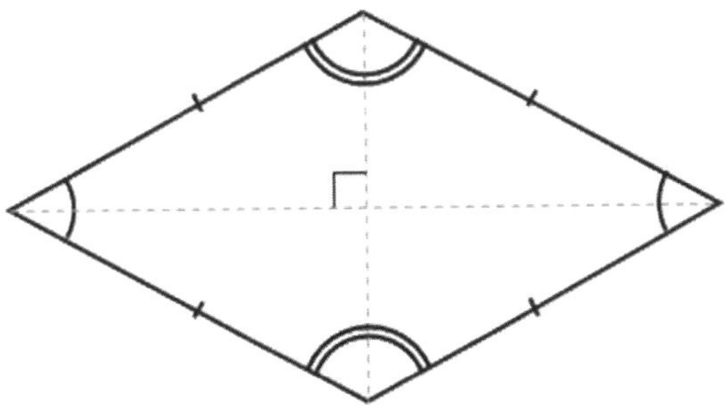

Review Video: Diagonals of Parallelograms, Rectangles, and Rhombi
Visit mometrix.com/academy and enter code: 320040

Square: A quadrilateral with four right angles and four congruent sides. Squares satisfy the criteria of all other types of quadrilaterals. The diagonals of a square are congruent and perpendicular to each other. Squares have 4 lines of symmetry (through each pair of opposing midpoints and along each of the diagonals) as well as 90-degree rotational symmetry about the midpoint.

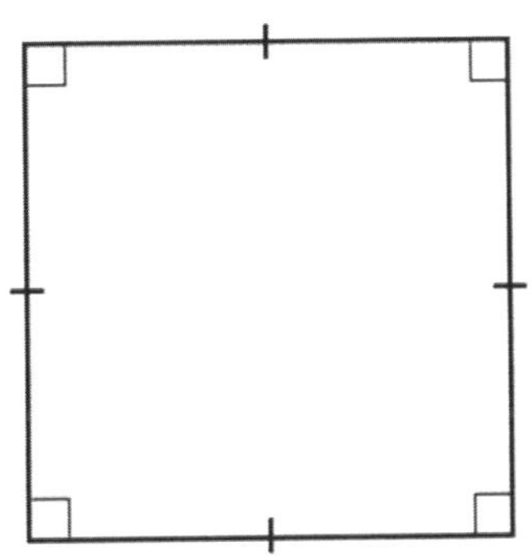

The hierarchy of quadrilaterals can be shown as follows:

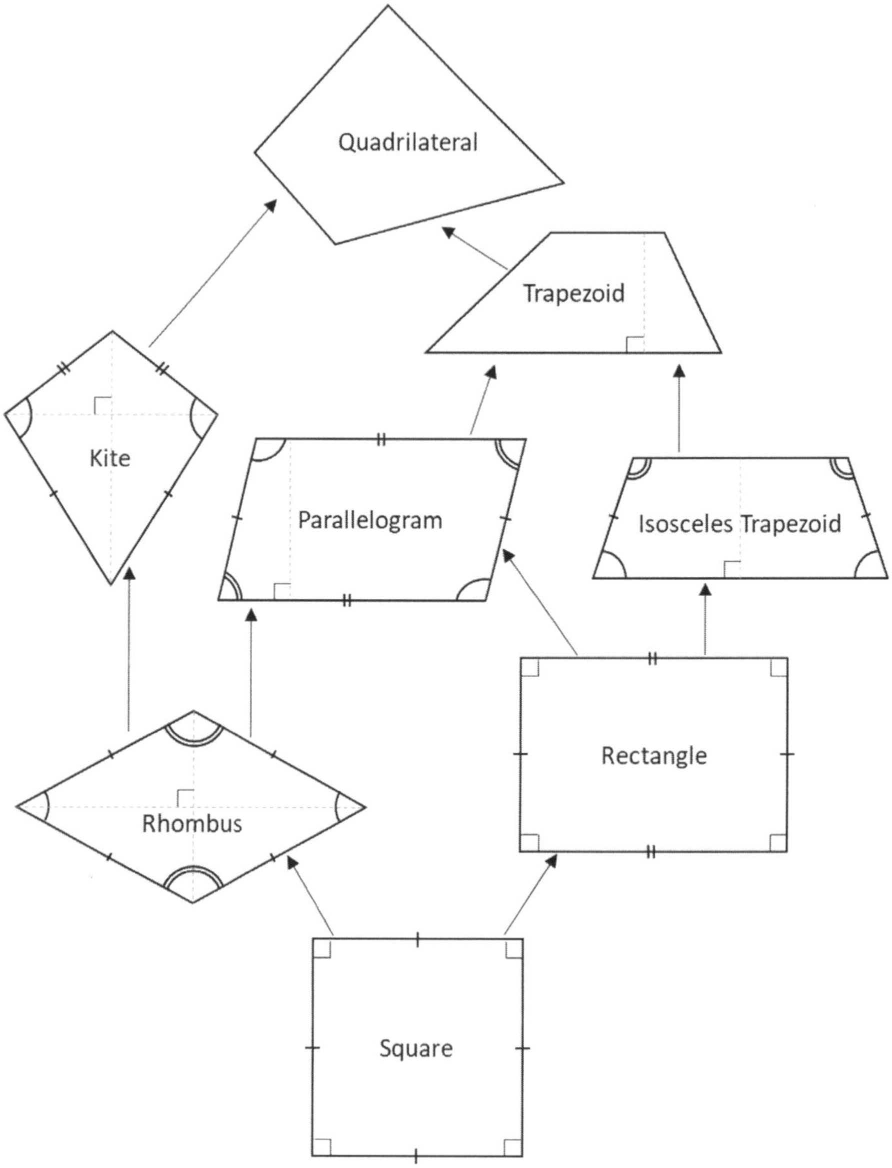

Area and Perimeter Formulas

Triangle

The *perimeter of any triangle* is found by summing the three side lengths; $P = a + b + c$. For an equilateral triangle, this is the same as $P = 3s$, where s is any side length, since all three sides are the same length.

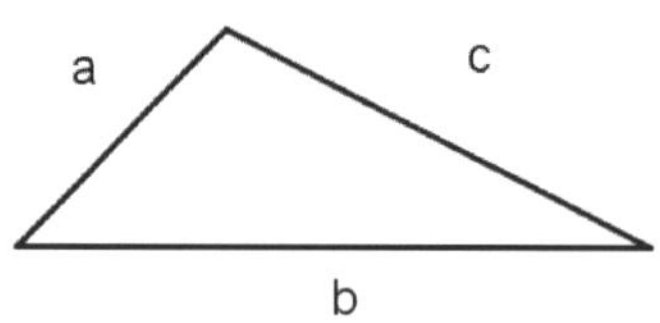

The area of any triangle can be found by taking half the product of one side length (base or b) and the perpendicular distance from that side to the opposite vertex (height or h). In equation form, $A = \frac{1}{2}bh$. For many triangles, it may be difficult to calculate h, so using one of the other formulas given here may be easier.

Review Video: Area and Perimeter of a Triangle
Visit mometrix.com/academy and enter code: 853779

Another formula that works for any triangle is $A = \sqrt{s(s-a)(s-b)(s-c)}$, where A is the area, s is the semiperimeter $s = \frac{a+b+c}{2}$, and a, b, and c are the lengths of the three sides.

The area of an equilateral triangle can be found by the formula $A = \frac{\sqrt{3}}{4}s^2$, where A is the area and s is the length of a side. You could use the $30° - 60° - 90°$ ratios to find the height of the triangle and then use the standard triangle area formula, but this is faster.

The area of an isosceles triangle can be found by the formula, $A = \frac{1}{2}b\sqrt{a^2 - \frac{b^2}{4}}$, where A is the area, b is the base (the unique side), and a is the length of one of the two congruent sides. If you do not remember this formula, you can use the Pythagorean Theorem to find the height so you can use the standard formula for the area of a triangle.

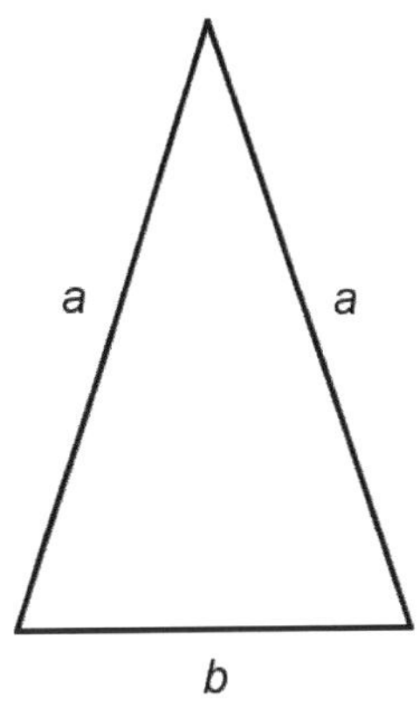

Square

The *area of a square* is found by using the formula $A = s^2$, where and s is the length of one side.

The *perimeter of a square* is found by using the formula $P = 4s$, where s is the length of one side. Because all four sides are equal in a square, it is faster to multiply the length of one side by 4 than to add the same number four times. You could use the formulas for rectangles and get the same answer.

Rectangle

The *area of a rectangle* is found by the formula $A = lw$, where A is the area of the rectangle, l is the length (usually considered to be the longer side) and w is the width (usually considered to be the shorter side). The numbers for l and w are interchangeable.

The *perimeter of a rectangle* is found by the formula $P = 2l + 2w$ or $P = 2(l + w)$, where l is the length, and w is the width. It may be easier to add the length and width first and then double the result, as in the second formula.

PARALLELOGRAM

The *area of a parallelogram* is found by the formula $A = bh$, where b is the length of the base, and h is the height. Note that the base and height correspond to the length and width in a rectangle, so this formula would apply to rectangles as well. Do not confuse the height of a parallelogram with the length of the second side. The two are only the same measure in the case of a rectangle.

The *perimeter of a parallelogram* is found by the formula $P = 2a + 2b$ or $P = 2(a + b)$, where a and b are the lengths of the two sides.

TRAPEZOID

The *area of a trapezoid* is found by the formula $A = \frac{1}{2}h(b_1 + b_2)$, where h is the height (segment joining and perpendicular to the parallel bases), and b_1 and b_2 are the two parallel sides (bases). Do not use one of the other two sides as the height unless that side is also perpendicular to the parallel bases.

The *perimeter of a trapezoid* is found by the formula $P = a + b_1 + c + b_2$, where a, b_1, c, and b_2 are the four sides of the trapezoid.

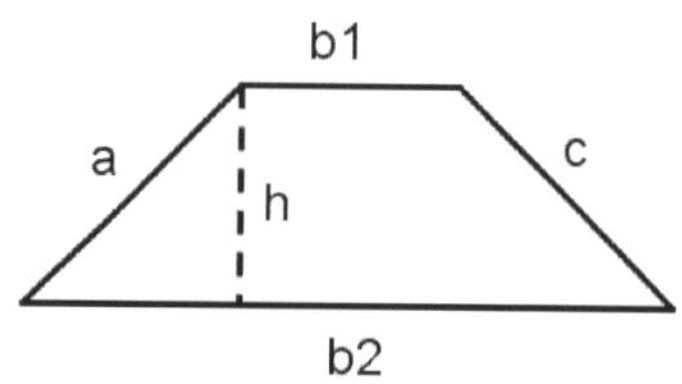

Review Video: Area and Perimeter of a Trapezoid
Visit mometrix.com/academy and enter code: 587523

ROTATION, CENTER OF ROTATION, AND ANGLE OF ROTATION

A *rotation* is a transformation that turns a figure around a point called the **center of rotation**, which can lie anywhere in the plane. If a line is drawn from a point on a figure to the center of rotation, and another line is drawn from the center to the rotated image of that point, the angle between the two lines is the **angle of rotation**. The vertex of the angle of rotation is the center of rotation.

Review Video: Rotation
Visit mometrix.com/academy and enter code: 602600

REFLECTION OVER A LINE AND REFLECTION IN A POINT

A reflection of a figure over a *line* (a "flip") creates a congruent image that is the same distance from the line as the original figure but on the opposite side. The **line of reflection** is the perpendicular bisector of any line segment drawn from a point on the original figure to its reflected image (unless the point and its reflected image happen to be the same point, which happens when a figure is reflected over one of its own sides).

A reflection of a figure in a *point* is the same as the rotation of the figure 180° about that point. The image of the figure is congruent to the original figure. The **point of reflection** is the midpoint of a line segment which connects a point in the figure to its image (unless the point and its reflected image happen to be the same point, which happens when a figure is reflected in one of its own points).

Review Video: Reflection
Visit mometrix.com/academy and enter code: 955068

EXAMPLE

Use the coordinate plane of the given image below to reflect the image across the y-axis.

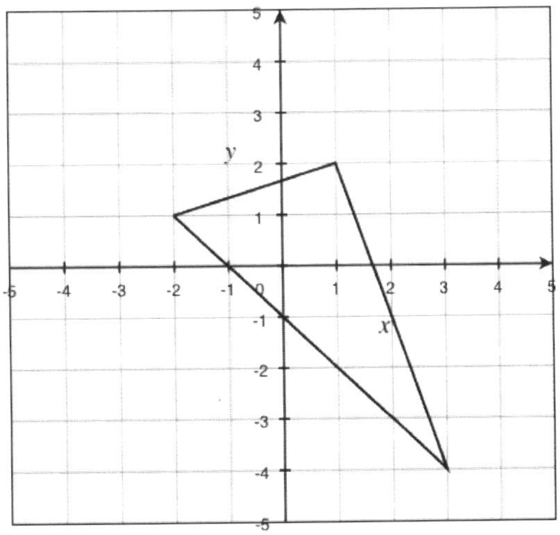

To reflect the image across the y-axis, replace each x-coordinate of the points that are the vertex of the triangle, x, with its negative, $-x$.

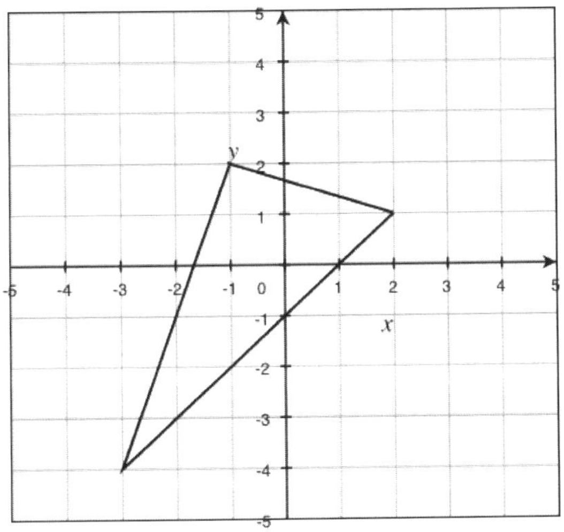

TRANSLATION

A *translation* is a transformation which slides a figure from one position in the plane to another position in the plane. The original figure and the translated figure have the same size, shape, and orientation.

Review Video: Translation
Visit mometrix.com/academy and enter code: 718628

Dilation

A **dilation** is a transformation which proportionally stretches or shrinks a figure by a **scale factor**. The dilated image is the same shape and orientation as the original image but a different size. A polygon and its dilated image are similar.

Example

Use the coordinate plane to create a dilation of the given image below, where the dilation is the enlargement of the original image.

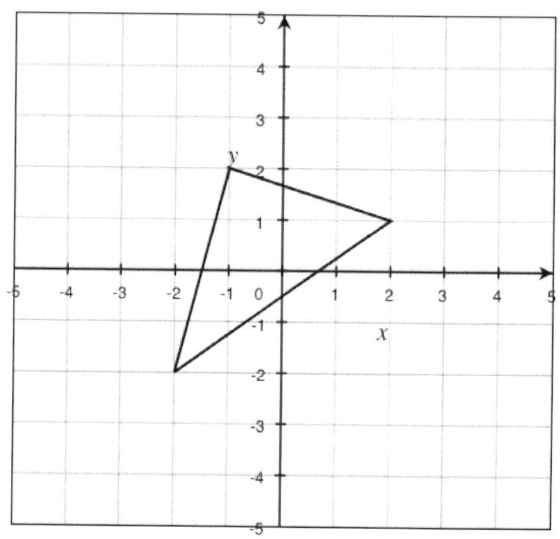

An enlargement can be found by multiplying each coordinate of the coordinate pairs located at the triangles vertices by a constant. If the figure is enlarged by a factor of 2, the new image would be:

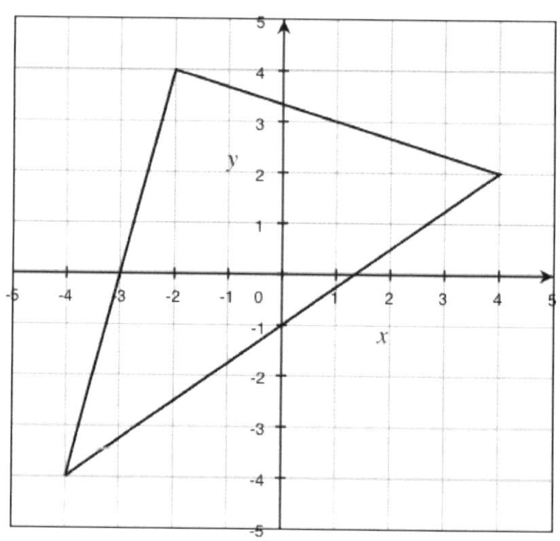

Review Video: Dilation
Visit mometrix.com/academy and enter code: 471630

CIRCLES

The center is the single point inside the circle that is equidistant from every point on the circle. The point O is in the diagram below. The radius is a line segment that joins the center of the circle and any one point on the circle. All radii of a circle are equal. The segments OX, OY, and OZ in the diagram below are radii.

The **diameter** is a line segment that passes through the center of the circle and has both endpoints inside the circle. The length of the diameter is twice the length of the radius. The segment XZ in the diagram below is a diameter. Concentric circles are circles that have the same center but not the same length of radii. A bulls-eye target is an example of concentric circles.

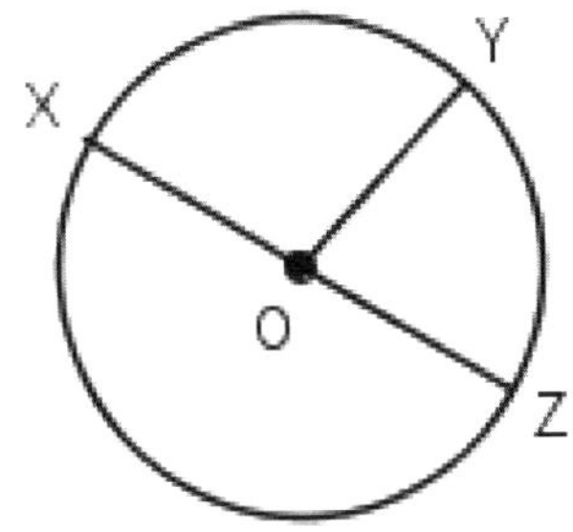

The **area of a circle** is found with the formula $A = \pi r^2$, where r is the length of the radius. If the diameter of the circle is given, divide it in half to get the radius before using the formula. (Note: In the following formulas, 3.14 is used for π.)

FIND THE RADIUS OF A CIRCLE GIVEN THE AREA

Example: The area of a circle is 30cm². Find the radius.

First, set up the equation to set apart the radius: $30 = \pi r^2$.
Then, divide both sides by π: $\frac{30}{\pi} = \frac{\pi r^2}{\pi}$
Now, take the square root of both sides: $\sqrt{9.55} \cong \sqrt{r^2}$ and you are left with: $3.09 \cong r$.

Note: You may have the area, and you are asked to find the diameter of the circle. So, follow the steps above to find the radius. Then, multiply the radius by 2 for the diameter.

The **circumference of a circle** is found by the formula $C = 2\pi r$, where r is the radius.

FIND THE RADIUS OF A CIRCLE GIVEN THE CIRCUMFERENCE

Example: The circumference is 20cm. Find the radius.

First, set up the equation to set apart the radius: $20 = 2\pi r$.
Then, divide both sides by 2: $\frac{20}{2} = \frac{2\pi r}{2}$.
Now, divide both sides by π: $\frac{10}{\pi} = \frac{\pi r}{\pi}$ and you are left with $3.18 \cong r$

Note: You may have the circumference, and you are asked to find the diameter of the circle. So, follow the steps above to find the radius. Then, multiply the radius by 2 for the diameter.

VOLUME AND SURFACE AREA FORMULAS

The **surface area** of a solid object is the area of all sides or exterior surfaces. For objects like prisms and pyramids, there is a difference between base surface area (B) and lateral surface area (LA). For a prism, the total surface area (SA) is $SA = LA + 2B$. For a pyramid or cone, the total surface area is $SA = LA + B$.

SPHERE

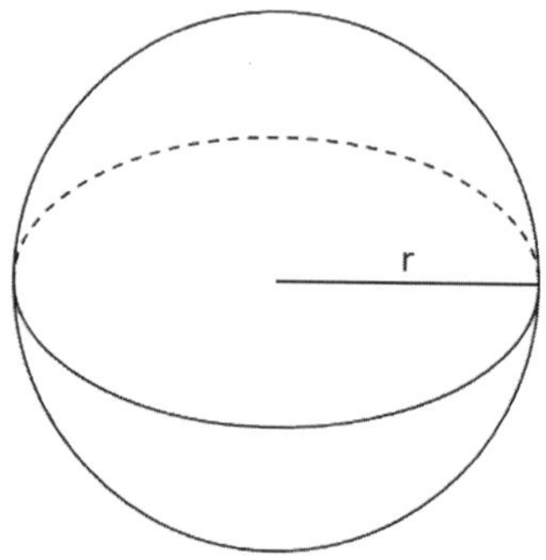

The **volume of a sphere** can be found with the formula $V = \frac{4}{3}\pi r^3$, where r is the radius. Sometimes, you may be asked to give the volume of a sphere in terms of π. For example, the volume of the sphere is 30π.

FIND THE RADIUS OF A SPHERE GIVEN THE VOLUME

Example: The volume of a sphere is 100 cm³. Find the radius.

First, set up the equation and simplify: $\frac{3}{4} \times \frac{4}{3}\pi r^3 = 100 \times \frac{3}{4}$ and you are left with: $\pi r^3 = 75$

Then, divide both sides by π: $\frac{\pi r^3}{\pi} = \frac{75}{\pi}$ and you are left with: $r^3 = \frac{75}{\pi} \cong 23.87$

Now, take the cubed root of both sides to solve for the radius: $\sqrt[3]{r^3} \cong \sqrt[3]{23.87}$. Thus, $r \cong 2.88$

The **surface area of a sphere** can be found with the formula $SA = 4\pi r^2$, where r is the radius.

FIND THE RADIUS OF A SPHERE GIVEN THE SURFACE AREA

Example: The surface area of a sphere is 100 cm². Find the radius.

First, set up the equation to set apart the radius: $SA = 4\pi r^2$.

Then, you move 4π to the other side of the equal sign and cancel out the 4π on the right side of the formula: $\frac{SA}{4\pi} = r^2$.

Next, you square both sides to set apart the radius: $\sqrt{\frac{SA}{4\pi}} = \sqrt{r^2}$ and you are left with $r = \sqrt{\frac{SA}{4\pi}}$

Now, solve the equation: $\sqrt{\frac{100}{4\pi}} \cong \sqrt{\frac{100}{12.57}} \cong 2.82$. Thus, the radius approximately equals 2.82 cm.

PRISM

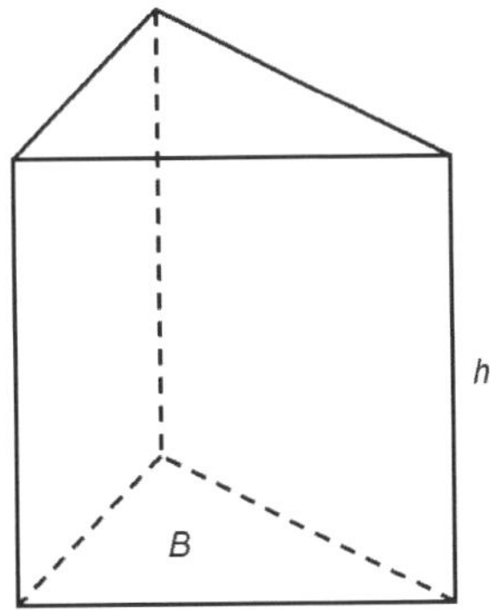

The **volume of any prism** is found with the formula $V = Bh$, where B is the area of the base, and h is the height. The perpendicular distance between the bases is the height.

FIND THE AREA OF THE BASE OR THE HEIGHT OF A PRISM GIVEN THE VOLUME

Example: The volume of the prism is 200 cm³. The area of the base is 10cm. Find the height.

First, set up the equation to set apart the height: $200 = 10h$.

Then, divide both sides by 10: $\frac{200}{10} = \frac{10h}{10}$.

Now, you are left with $20 = h$

The **surface area of any prism** is the sum of the areas of both bases and all sides. So, the formula for a sphere is $SA = 2B + Ph$, where B is the area of the base, P is the perimeter of the base, and h is the height of the prism.

FIND THE AREA OF THE BASE GIVEN THE SURFACE AREA

Example: The surface area of the prism is 100 cm². The perimeter of the base is 10cm, and the height is 2cm. Find the area of the base.

First, set up the equation to set apart the area of the base: $100 = 2B + 20$.

Then, subtract 20 from both sides: $100 - 20 = 2B + 20 - 20$.

Now, you are left with $80 = 2B$. So, divide both sides by 2 and you have $40 = B$.

FIND THE PERIMETER OF THE BASE OR THE HEIGHT OF A PRISM GIVEN THE SURFACE AREA

Example: The surface area of the prism is 280 cm². The area of the base is 15cm², and the perimeter of the base is 10cm. Find the height.

First, set up the equation to set apart the height: $280 = 2(15) + (10)h$ or $250 = 30 + (10)h$

Then, subtract 30 from both sides: $280 - 30 = 30 + (10)h - 30$ and you are left with: $250 = (10)h$.

Now, divide both sides by 10: $\frac{250}{10} = \frac{(10)h}{10} = 25$. Thus, the height of the prism is 25cm.

RECTANGULAR PRISM

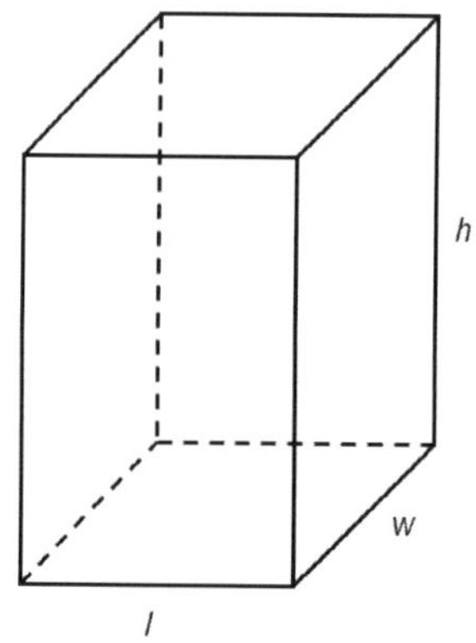

The **volume of a rectangular prism** can be found with the formula $V = lwh$, where V is the volume, l is the length, w is the width, and h is the height.

FIND THE LENGTH, WIDTH, OR HEIGHT OF A RECTANGULAR PRISM GIVEN THE VOLUME

Example: The volume of the rectangular prism is 200 cm^3. The width is 10cm, and the height is 10cm. Find the length.

First, set up the equation to set apart the length: $200 = l(10)(10)$ that becomes $200 = (100)l$.

Now, divide both sides by 100: $\frac{200}{100} = \frac{(100)l}{100}$ and you are left with $2 = l$.

The **surface area of a rectangular prism** can be calculated as $SA = 2lw + 2hl + 2wh$ or $SA = 2(lw + hl + wh)$.

FIND THE LENGTH, WIDTH, OR HEIGHT OF A RECTANGULAR PRISM GIVEN THE SURFACE AREA

Example: The surface area of the rectangular prism is 200 cm^2. The width is 15cm, and the height is 5cm. Find the length.

First, set up the equation to set apart the length: $200 = 2(15)l + 2(5)l + 2(15)(5)$ which simplifies to $200 = (40)l + 150$.

Then, subtract 150 from both sides: $200 - 150 = (40)l + 150 - 150$ and you get $50 = (40)l$.

Now, divide both sides by 40 to find l: $\frac{50}{40} = \frac{(40)l}{40}$ and you are left with $1.25 = l$.

CUBE

A cube is a special rectangular prism where all the sides have the same length, or $l = w = h$. The **volume of a cube** can be found with the formula $V = s^3$, where s is the length of a side.

FIND THE SIDE OF A CUBE GIVEN THE VOLUME

Example: The volume of a cube is 20 cm^3. Find the side.

First, set up the equation to set apart the side length: $20 = s^3$

Then, take the cube root of both sides: $\sqrt[3]{20} = \sqrt[3]{s^3}$ and you are left with $\sqrt[3]{20} = s$

Now, solve for the side length: $\sqrt[3]{20} \cong 2.71$. Thus, s approximately equals 2.71.

The **surface area of a cube** is calculated as $SA = 6s^2$, where SA is the total surface area and s is the length of a side.

FIND THE SIDE OF A CUBE GIVEN THE SURFACE AREA

Example: The surface area of a cube is 60 cm². Find the side.

First, set up the equation to set apart the side length: $60 = 6s^2$.

Then, divide both sides by 6: $\frac{60}{6} = \frac{6s^2}{6}$ and you are left with $10 = s^2$.

Now, take the square root of both sides to solve for s: $\sqrt{10} = \sqrt{s^2}$. Thus, $3.16 = s$

CYLINDER

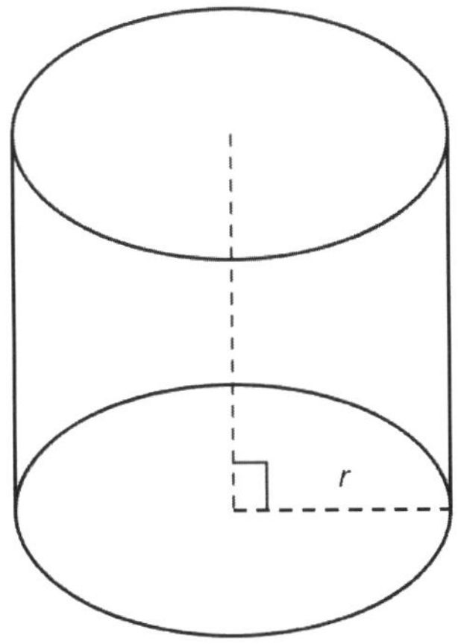

The **volume of a cylinder** can be found with the formula $V = \pi r^2 h$, where r is the radius, and h is the height.

FIND THE HEIGHT OF A CYLINDER GIVEN THE VOLUME

Example: The volume of a cylinder is 300 cm³ and the radius is 5 cm. Find the height.

First, set up the equation and substitute: $300 = \pi 5^2 h$.

Then, since $\pi 5^2 \cong 78.5$ you have $300 \cong 78.5h$.

Now, divide both sides by 78.5: $\frac{300}{78.5} \cong \frac{78.5h}{78.5}$ and you are left with: $3.82 \cong h$

FIND THE RADIUS OF A CYLINDER GIVEN THE VOLUME

Example: The volume of a cylinder is 200 cm³ and the radius is 15cm. Find the radius.

First, set up the equation to set apart the radius: $200 = \pi(15)r^2$.

Then, divide both sides of the equation by $\pi(15)$: $\frac{200}{\pi(15)} = \frac{\pi(15)r^2}{\pi(15)}$ and you are left with: $4.25 \cong r^2$.

Now, take the square root of both sides: $\sqrt{4.25} \cong \sqrt{r^2}$ and you have $2.06 \cong r$.

The **surface area of a cylinder** can be found with the formula $SA = 2\pi r^2 + 2\pi rh$.

The first term (i.e., $2\pi r^2$) is the base area multiplied by two. The second term (i.e., $2\pi rh$) is the perimeter of the base multiplied by the height.

FIND THE HEIGHT OF A CYLINDER GIVEN THE SURFACE AREA

Example: The surface area of a cylinder is 150 cm² and the radius is 2 cm. Find the height.

First, set up the equation and substitute: $150 = 2\pi 2^2 + 2\pi(2)h$ or $150 \cong 25.12 + 12.56h$.

Then, subtract 25.12 from both sides of the equation: $150 - 25.12 = 25.12 + 12.56h - 25.12$ and you have $124.85 = 12.56h$.

Now, divide both sides by 12.56: $\frac{124.85}{12.56} = \frac{12.56h}{12.56}$ and you are left with $9.94 = h$.

FIND THE RADIUS OF A CYLINDER GIVEN THE SURFACE AREA

Example: The surface area of a cylinder is 327 cm², and the height is 12cm. Find the radius.

First, set up the equation and substitute: $327 = 2\pi r^2 + 2\pi 12(r)$ or $327 \cong 6.28r^2 + 75.36r$.

Then, rearrange to the quadratic form: $6.28r^2 + 75.36r - 327 \cong 0$.

Next, fill in the quadratic formula with the coefficients: $r \cong \frac{-75.36 \pm \sqrt{(75.36)^2 - 4(6.28)(-327)}}{2(6.28)}$.

Now, simplify the result to find the radius approximately equals positive 3.39.

PYRAMID

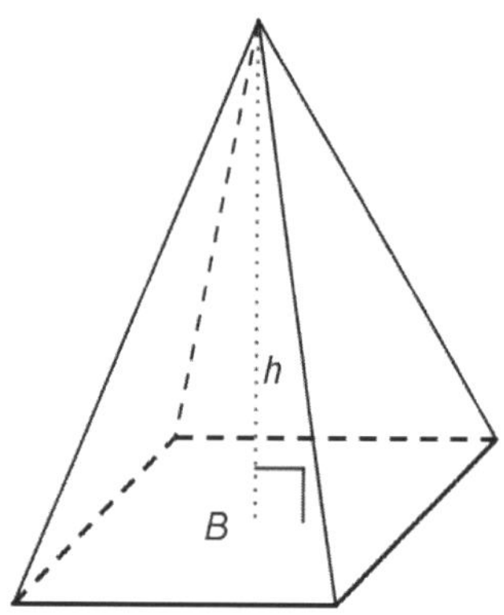

The **volume of a pyramid** is found with the formula $V = \frac{1}{3}Bh$, where B is the area of the base, and h is the height. The perpendicular distance from the vertex to the base is the height. This formula is the same as $\frac{1}{3}$ times the volume of a prism. Like a prism, the base of a pyramid can be any shape.

FIND THE AREA OF THE BASE OR THE HEIGHT OF A PYRAMID GIVEN THE VOLUME

Example: The volume of the pyramid is 100 cm³. The area of the base is 5cm². Find the height.

First, set up the equation to set apart the height: $100 = \frac{1}{3}5h$.

Then, multiply both sides by 3: $100 \times 3 = \frac{1}{3}5h \times 3$ and you have $300 = 5h$.

Now, divide both sides by 5: $\frac{300}{5} = \frac{5h}{5}$ and you have found that the height is 60.

A right pyramid means that the base is a regular polygon. Also, the vertex is directly over the center of that polygon. If the pyramid is a right pyramid, the **surface area** can be calculated as $SA = B + \frac{1}{2}Ph_s$, where P is the perimeter of the base, and h_s is the slant height. The distance from the vertex to the midpoint of one side of the base is the slant height.

If the pyramid is irregular, the area of each triangle side must be calculated one at a time. Then, take the sum of the areas and the base to have the surface area.

FIND THE AREA OF THE BASE, THE PERIMETER OF THE BASE, OR THE HEIGHT GIVEN THE SURFACE AREA

Example: The surface area of the pyramid is 100 cm^2. The area of the base is 40cm^2, and the height is 12cm.

First, set up the equation to set apart the perimeter of the base: $100 = 40 + \frac{1}{2}12P$.

Then, multiply the height by $\frac{1}{2}$: $100 = 40 + 6P$.

Next, subtract 40 from both sides of the equation: $100 - 40 = 40 + 6P - 40$ and you have $60 = 6P$

Now, divide both sides by 6: $\frac{60}{6} = \frac{6P}{6}$ and you are left with P=10cm.

CONE

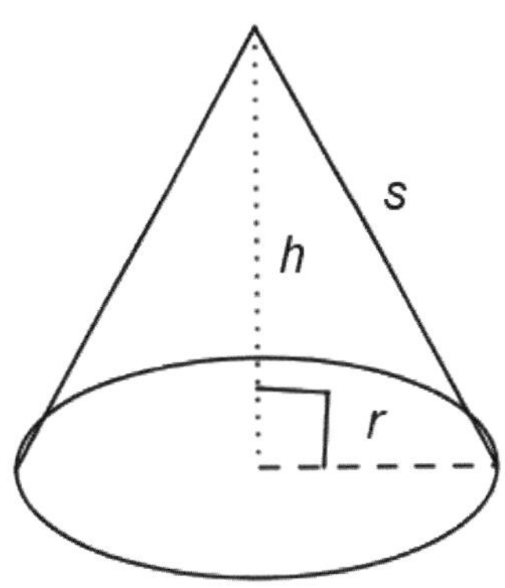

The **volume of a cone** is found with the formula $V = \frac{1}{3}\pi r^2 h$, where r is the radius, h is the height, and s is the slant height. This formula is the same as $\frac{1}{3}$ times the volume of a cylinder.

FIND THE RADIUS OR HEIGHT OF A CONE GIVEN THE VOLUME

Example: The volume of the cone is 47.12 cm^3. The height is 5cm. Find the radius.

First, set up the equation to set apart the radius: $47.12 = \frac{1}{3}\pi 5r^2$.

Then, multiply both sides by 3: $47.12 \times 3 = \frac{1}{3}\pi 5r^2 \times 3$ and you have $141.36 = \pi 5r^2$.

Next, divide both sides by 5π: $\frac{141.36}{5\pi} = \frac{\pi 5r^2}{5\pi}$ and you have $9 \cong r^2$.

Now, take the square root of both sides: $\sqrt{9} \cong \sqrt{r^2}$ and you have $3 \cong r$

The **surface area of a cone** can be found with the formula $SA = \pi r^2 + \pi rs$, where s is the slant height. The slant height can be found with the Pythagorean Theorem to be $\sqrt{r^2 + h^2}$. So, the surface area formula for a cone can also be written as $SA = \pi r^2 + \pi r\sqrt{r^2 + h^2}$.

FIND THE RADIUS OF A CONE GIVEN THE SURFACE AREA

Example: The surface area of the cone is 43.97 cm². The slant height is 5cm. Find the radius.

First, set up the equation to set apart the radius: $43.97 = \pi r^2 + 5\pi r$.

Then, divide both sides by π: $\frac{43.97}{\pi} = \frac{\pi r^2 + 5\pi r}{\pi}$ and you have: $14 \cong r^2 + 5r$.

Next, subtract 14 from both sides, and you have: $0 \cong r^2 + 5r - 14$

Now, use the quadratic formula: $r \cong \frac{-5 \pm \sqrt{5^2 - 4(1)(-14)}}{2(1)}$ and find $r \cong +2$.

FIND THE SLANT HEIGHT OF A CONE GIVEN THE SURFACE AREA

Example: The surface area of the cone is 37.68 cm². The radius is 2cm. Find the slant height.

First, set up the equation to set apart the slant height: $37.68 = \pi 2^2 + \pi 2s$.

Then, calculate both sides: $37.68 \cong 12.56 + 6.28s$

Next, divide all three terms by 6.28: $\frac{37.68}{6.28} \cong \frac{12.56}{6.28} + \frac{6.28s}{6.28}$ and you have $6 \cong 2 + s$.

Now, subtract 2 from both sides: $6 - 2 \cong 2 + s - 2$ and you are left with $4 \cong s$

Review Video: Volume and Surface Area of a Right Circular Cone
Visit mometrix.com/academy and enter code: 573574

Algebra, Graphs, and Functions

Proportions and Ratios

Proportions

A proportion is a relationship between two quantities that dictates how one changes when the other changes. A **direct proportion** describes a relationship in which a quantity increases by a set amount for every increase in the other quantity, or decreases by that same amount for every decrease in the other quantity. Example: Assuming a constant driving speed, the time required for a car trip increases as the distance of the trip increases. The distance to be traveled and the time required to travel are directly proportional.

An **inverse proportion** is a relationship in which an increase in one quantity is accompanied by a decrease in the other, or vice versa. Example: the time required for a car trip decreases as the speed increases, and increases as the speed decreases, so the time required is inversely proportional to the speed of the car.

Review Video: Proportions
Visit mometrix.com/academy and enter code: 505355

Ratios

A **ratio** is a comparison of two quantities in a particular order. Example: If there are 14 computers in a lab, and the class has 20 students, there is a student to computer ratio of 20 to 14, commonly written as 20:14. Ratios are normally reduced to their smallest whole number representation, so 20:14 would be reduced to 10:7 by dividing both sides by 2.

Review Video: Ratios
Visit mometrix.com/academy and enter code: 996914

Real World Problems with Proportions and Ratios

Example 1

A thermos has a leak and loses 100 mg of hot chocolate every two hours. How much hot chocolate will the thermos lose in five hours?

Using proportional reasoning, since five hours is two and a half times as long as two hours, the thermos will lose two and a half times as much hot chocolate, $2.5 \times 100 \text{ mg} = 250 \text{ mg}$, in five hours. To compute the answer, first write the amount of hot chocolate per 2 hours as a ratio: $\frac{100 \text{ mg}}{2 \text{ hours}}$. Next setup a proportion to relate the time increments of 2 hours and 5 hours: $\frac{100 \text{ mg}}{2 \text{ hours}} = \frac{x \text{ mg}}{5 \text{ hours}}$ where x is the amount of hot chocolate the thermos loses in five hours. Make sure to keep the same units in either the numerator or denominator. In this case the numerator units must be mg for both ratios and the denominator units must be hours for both ratios.

Use cross multiplication and division to solve for x:

$$\frac{100 \text{ mg}}{2 \text{ hours}} = \frac{x \text{ mg}}{5 \text{ hours}}$$

$$\begin{aligned} 100(5) &= 2(x) \\ 500 &= 2x \\ 500 \div 2 &= 2x \div 2 \\ 250 &= x \end{aligned}$$

Therefore, the thermos loses 250 mg every five hours.

Example 2

At a school, for every 20 female students there are 15 male students. This same student ratio happens to exist at another school. If there are 100 female students at the second school, how many male students are there?

One way to find the number of male students is to set up and solve a proportion.

$$\frac{\text{number of female students}}{\text{number of male students}} = \frac{20}{15} = \frac{100}{\text{number of male students}}$$

Represent the unknown number of male students as the variable x.

$$\frac{20}{15} = \frac{100}{x}$$

Cross multiply. $20 \times x = 15 \times 100$, so $20x = 1500$.

Divide each side of the equation by 20 to get $x = 75$

Example 3

In a hospital emergency room, there are 4 nurses for every 12 patients. What is the ratio of nurses to patients? If the nurse-to-patient ratio remains constant, how many nurses must be present to care for 24 patients?

The ratio of nurses to patients can be written as 4 to 12, 4:12, or $\frac{4}{12}$. Because four and twelve have a common factor of four, the ratio should be reduced to 1:3, which means that there is one nurse present for every three patients. If this ratio remains constant, there must be eight nurses present to care for 24 patients.

Example 4

In a bank, the banker-to-customer ratio is 1:2. If seven bankers are on duty, how many customers are currently in the bank?

Use proportional reasoning or set up a proportion to solve. Because there are twice as many customers as bankers, there must be fourteen customers when seven bankers are on duty. Setting up and solving a proportion gives the same result:

$$\frac{\text{number of bankers}}{\text{number of customers}} = \frac{1}{2} = \frac{7}{\text{number of customers}}$$

Represent the unknown number of customers as the variable x.

$$\frac{1}{2} = \frac{7}{x}$$

To solve for x, cross multiply: $1 \times x = 7 \times 2$, so $x = 14$.

Constant of Proportionality

When two quantities have a proportional relationship, there exists a **constant of proportionality** between the quantities. The product of this constant and one of the quantities is equal to the other quantity. For example, if one lemon costs \$0.25, two lemons cost \$0.50, and three lemons cost \$0.75, there is a proportional relationship between the total cost of lemons and the number of lemons purchased. The constant of proportionality is the **unit price**, namely \$0.25/lemon. Notice that the total price of lemons, t, can be found by multiplying the unit price of lemons, p, and the number of lemons, n: $t = pn$.

Work/Unit Rate

Unit rate expresses a quantity of one thing in terms of one unit of another. For example, if you travel 30 miles every two hours, a unit rate expresses this comparison in terms of one hour: in one hour you travel 15 miles, so your unit rate is 15 miles per hour. Other examples are how much one ounce of food costs (price per ounce) or figuring out how much one egg costs out of the dozen (price per 1 egg, instead of price per 12 eggs). The denominator of a unit rate is always 1. Unit rates are used to compare different situations to solve problems. For example, to make sure you get the best deal when deciding which kind of soda to buy, you can find the unit rate of each. If Soda #1 costs \$1.50 for a 1-liter bottle, and soda #2 costs \$2.75 for a 2-liter bottle, it would be a better deal to buy Soda #2, because its unit rate is only \$1.375 per 1-liter, which is cheaper than Soda #1. Unit rates can also help determine the length of time a given event will take. For example, if you can paint 2 rooms in 4.5 hours, you can determine how long it will take you to paint 5 rooms by solving for the unit rate per room and then multiplying that by 5.

Review Video: Rates and Unit Rates
Visit mometrix.com/academy and enter code: 185363

Example 1

Janice made \$40 during the first 5 hours she spent babysitting. She will continue to earn money at this rate until she finishes babysitting in 3 more hours. Find how much money Janice earned babysitting and how much she earns per hour.

Janice will earn \$64 babysitting in her 8 total hours (adding the first 5 hours to the remaining 3 gives the 8 hour total). This can be found by setting up a proportion comparing money earned to babysitting hours. Since she earns \$40 for 5 hours and since the rate is constant, she will earn a proportional amount in 8 hours: $\frac{40}{5} = \frac{x}{8}$. Cross multiplying will yield $5x = 320$, and division by 5 shows that $x = 64$.

Janice earns \$8 per hour. This can be found by taking her total amount earned, \$64, and dividing it by the total number of hours worked, 8. Since $\frac{64}{8} = 8$, Janice makes \$8 in one hour. This can also be found by finding the unit rate, money earned per hour: $\frac{64}{8} = \frac{x}{1}$. Since cross multiplying yields $8x = 64$, and division by 8 shows that $x = 8$, Janice earns \$8 per hour.

EXAMPLE 2

The McDonalds are taking a family road trip, driving 300 miles to their cabin. It took them 2 hours to drive the first 120 miles. They will drive at the same speed all the way to their cabin. Find the speed at which the McDonalds are driving and how much longer it will take them to get to their cabin.

The McDonalds are driving 60 miles per hour. This can be found by setting up a proportion to find the unit rate, the number of miles they drive per one hour: $\frac{120}{2} = \frac{x}{1}$. Cross multiplying yields $2x = 120$ and division by 2 shows that $x = 60$.

Since the McDonalds will drive this same speed for the remaining miles, it will take them another 3 hours to get to their cabin. This can be found by first finding how many miles the McDonalds have left to drive, which is $300 - 120 = 180$. The McDonalds are driving at 60 miles per hour, so a proportion can be set up to determine how many hours it will take them to drive 180 miles: $\frac{180}{x} = \frac{60}{1}$. Cross multiplying yields $60x = 180$, and division by 60 shows that $x = 3$. This can also be found by using the formula $D = r \times t$ (or Distance = rate × time), where $180 = 60 \times t$, and division by 60 shows that $t = 3$.

EXAMPLE 3

It takes Andy 10 minutes to read 6 pages of his book. He has already read 150 pages in his book that is 210 pages long. Find how long it takes Andy to read 1 page and also find how long it will take him to finish his book if he continues to read at the same speed.

It takes Andy 1 minute and 40 seconds to read one page in his book. This can be found by finding the unit rate per one page, by dividing the total time it takes him to read 6 pages by 6. Since it takes him 10 minutes to read 6 pages, $\frac{10}{6} = 1\frac{2}{3}$ minutes, which is 1 minute and 40 seconds.

It will take Andy another 100 minutes, or 1 hour and 40 minutes to finish his book. This can be found by first figuring out how many pages Andy has left to read, which is $210 - 150 = 60$. Since it is now known that it takes him $1\frac{2}{3}$ minutes to read each page, then that rate must be multiplied by however many pages he has left to read (60) to find the time he'll need: $60 \times 1\frac{2}{3} = 100$, so it will take him 100 minutes, or 1 hour and 40 minutes, to read the rest of his book.

Functions

Function and Relation

When expressing functional relationships, the **variables** x and y are typically used. These values are often written as the **coordinates** (x, y). The x-value is the independent variable and the y-value is the dependent variable. A **relation** is a set of data in which there is not a unique y-value for each x-value in the dataset. This means that there can be two of the same x-values assigned to different y-values. A relation is simply a relationship between the x and y-values in each coordinate but does not apply to the relationship between the values of x and y in the data set. A **function** is a relation where one quantity depends on the other. For example, the amount of money that you make depends on the number of hours that you work. In a function, each x-value in the data set has one unique y-value because the y-value depends on the x-value.

Determining a Function

You can determine whether an equation is a **function** by substituting different values into the equation for x. These values are called input values. All possible input values are referred to as the **domain**. The result of substituting these values into the equation is called the output, or **range**. You can display and organize these numbers in a data table. A **data table** contains the values for x and y, which you can also list as coordinates. In order for a function to exist, the table cannot contain any repeating x-values that correspond with different y-values. If each x-coordinate maps to one and only one y-coordinate, the table contains a function. However, there can be repeating y-values that correspond with different x-values. An example of this is when the function contains an exponent. For example, if $x^2 = y$, then both $x = 2$ and $x = -2$ will correspond to $y = 4$, since $2^2 = 4$, and $(-2)^2 = 4$.

Review Video: Definition of a Function
Visit mometrix.com/academy and enter code: 784611

Equation Using Independent and Dependent Variables

To write an equation, you must first assign **variables** to the unknown values in the problem and then translate the words and phrases into expressions containing numbers and symbols. For example, if Ray earns \$10 an hour, this can be represented by the expression $10x$, where x is equal to the number of hours that Ray works. The value of x represents the number of hours because it is the **independent variable**, or the amount that you can choose and can manipulate. To find out how much money he earns in y hours, you would write the equation $10x = y$. The variable y is the **dependent variable** because it depends on x and cannot be manipulated. Once you have the equation for the function, you can choose any number of hours to find the corresponding amount that he earns. For example, if you want to know how much he would earn working 36 hours, you would substitute 36 in for x and multiply to find that he would earn \$360.

Review Video: Dependent and Independent Variables and Inverting Functions
Visit mometrix.com/academy and enter code: 704764

Writing a Function Rule Using a Table

If given a set of data, place the corresponding x- and y-values into a table and analyze the relationship between them. Consider what you can do to each x-value to obtain the corresponding y-value. Try adding or subtracting different numbers to and from x and then try multiplying or dividing different numbers to and from x. If none of these **operations** give you the y-value, try combining the operations. Once you find a rule that works for one pair, make sure to try it with each additional set of ordered pairs in the table. If the same operation or combination of operations satisfies each set of coordinates, then the table contains a function. The rule is then used to write the equation of the function in "$y = f(x)$" form.

EQUATIONS AND GRAPHING

When algebraic functions and equations are shown graphically, they are usually shown on a ***Cartesian coordinate plane***. The Cartesian coordinate plane consists of two number lines placed perpendicular to each other, and intersecting at the zero point, also known as the origin. The horizontal number line is known as the x-axis, with positive values to the right of the origin, and negative values to the left of the origin. The vertical number line is known as the y-axis, with positive values above the origin, and negative values below the origin. Any point on the plane can be identified by an ordered pair in the form (x, y), called coordinates. The x-value of the coordinate is called the abscissa, and the y-value of the coordinate is called the ordinate. The two number lines divide the plane into **four quadrants**: I, II, III, and IV.

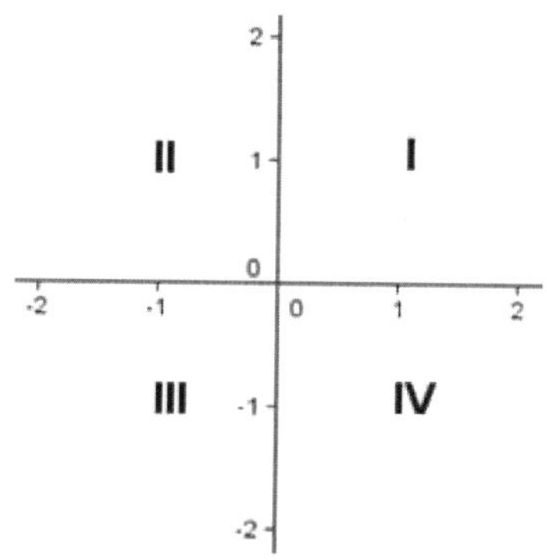

Before learning the different forms in which equations can be written, it is important to understand some terminology. A ratio of the change in the vertical distance to the change in horizontal distance is called the **slope** and is often given the variable m. On a graph with two points, (x_1, y_1) and (x_2, y_2), the slope is represented by the formula:

$$m = \frac{y_2 - y_1}{x_2 - x_1};\ x_1 \neq x_2$$

If the value of the slope is positive, the line slopes upward from left to right. If the value of the slope is negative, the line slopes downward from left to right. If the y-coordinates are the same for both points, the slope is 0 and the line is a **horizontal line**. If the x-coordinates are the same for both points, there is no slope and the line is a ***vertical line***. Two or more lines that have equal slopes are **parallel lines**. **Perpendicular lines** have slopes that are negative reciprocals of each other, such as $\frac{a}{b}$ and $\frac{-b}{a}$.

Review Video: How to Graph a Function
Visit mometrix.com/academy and enter code: 492785

MONOMIALS AND POLYNOMIALS

A **monomial** is a single constant, variable, or product of constants and variables, such as 7, x, $2x$, or x^3y. There will never be addition or subtraction symbols in a monomial. Like monomials have like variables, but they may have different coefficients. **Polynomials** are algebraic expressions which use addition and subtraction to combine two or more monomials. Two terms make a binomial;

three terms make a trinomial; etc.. The **degree of a monomial** is the sum of the exponents of the variables. The **degree of a polynomial** is the highest degree of any individual term.

LINEAR EQUATIONS

Linear equations can be written many ways. Below is a list of the many forms linear equations can take.

- **Standard Form**: $Ax + By = C$; the slope is $\frac{-A}{B}$ and the y-intercept is $\frac{C}{B}$
- **Slope Intercept Form**: $y = mx + b$, where m is the slope and b is the y-intercept
- **Point-Slope Form**: $y - y_1 = m(x - x_1)$, where m is the slope and (x_1, y_1) is a point on the line
- **Two-Point Form**: $\frac{y-y_1}{x-x_1} = \frac{y_2-y_1}{x_2-x_1}$, where (x_1, y_1) and (x_2, y_2) are two points on the given line
- **Intercept Form**: $\frac{x}{x_1} + \frac{y}{y_1} = 1$, where $(x_1, 0)$ is the point at which a line intersects the x-axis, and $(0, y_1)$ is the point at which the same line intersects the y-axis

Review Video: Slope-Intercept and Point-Slope Forms
Visit mometrix.com/academy and enter code: 113216

A linear equation in the form $ax + b = 0$, where $a \neq 0$ is referred to as **one variable linear equations**. A solution to such an equation is called a **root**. In the case where we have the equation $5x + 10 = 0$, if we solve for x we get a solution of $x = -2$. In other words, the root of the equation is -2. This is found by first subtracting 10 from both sides, which gives $5x = -10$. Next, simply divide both sides by the coefficient of the variable, in this case 5, to get $x = -2$. This can be checked by plugging -2 back into the original equation $(5)(-2) + 10 = -10 + 10 = 0$.

The **solution set** is the set of all solutions of an equation. In our example, the solution set would simply be -2. If there were more solutions (there usually are in multivariable equations) then they would also be included in the solution set. When an equation has no true solutions, this is referred to as an **empty set**. Equations with identical solution sets are ***equivalent equations***. An **identity** is a term whose value or determinant is equal to 1.

Review Video: Linear Equations Basics
Visit mometrix.com/academy and enter code: 793005

MANIPULATION OF FUNCTIONS

Horizontal and vertical shift occur when values are added to or subtracted from the x or y values, respectively.

If a constant is added to the y portion of each point, the graph shifts up. If a constant is subtracted from the y portion of each point, the graph shifts down. This is represented by the expression $f(x) \pm k$, where k is a constant.

If a constant is added to the x portion of each point, the graph shifts left. If a constant is subtracted from the x portion of each point, the graph shifts right. This is represented by the expression $f(x \pm k)$, where k is a constant.

Stretch, compression, and reflection occur when different parts of a function are multiplied by different groups of constants. If the function as a whole is multiplied by a real number constant greater than 1, $(k \times f(x))$, the graph is stretched vertically. If k in the previous equation is greater than zero but less than 1, the graph is compressed vertically. If k is less than zero, the graph is reflected about the x-axis, in addition to being either stretched or compressed vertically if k is less than or greater than -1, respectively. If instead, just the x-term is multiplied by a constant greater than 1 ($f(k \times x)$), the graph is compressed horizontally. If k in the previous equation is greater than zero but less than 1, the graph is stretched horizontally. If k is less than zero, the graph is reflected about the y-axis, in addition to being either stretched or compressed horizontally if k is greater than or less than -1, respectively.

Classification of Functions

There are many different ways to classify functions based on their structure or behavior. Listed here are a few common classifications.

Constant functions are given by the equation $y = b$ or $f(x) = b$, where b is a real number. There is no independent variable present in the equation, so the function has a constant value for all x. The graph of a constant function is a horizontal line of slope 0 that is positioned b units from the x-axis. If b is positive, the line is above the x-axis; if b is negative, the line is below the x-axis.

Identity functions are identified by the equation $y = x$ or $f(x) = x$, where every value of y is equal to its corresponding value of x. The only zero is the point $(0, 0)$. The graph is a diagonal line with slope 1.

In **linear functions**, the value of the function changes in direct proportion to x. The rate of change,represented by the slope on its graph, is constant throughout. The standard form of a linear equation is $ax + by = c$, where a, b, and c are real numbers. As a function, this equation is commonly written as $y = mx + b$ or $f(x) = mx + b$. This is known as the slope-intercept form, because the coefficients give the slope of the graphed function (m) and its y-intercept (b). Solve the equation $mx + b = 0$ for x to get $x = -\frac{b}{m}$, which is the only zero of the function. The domain and range are both the set of all real numbers.

> **Review Video: Linear Functions**
> Visit mometrix.com/academy and enter code: 200735

A **polynomial function** is a function with multiple terms and multiple powers of x, such as:

$$f(x) = a_n x^n + a_{n-1} x^{n-1} + a_{n-2} x^{n-2} + \cdots + a_1 x + a_0$$

where n is a non-negative integer that is the highest exponent in the polynomial, and $a_n \neq 0$. The domain of a polynomial function is the set of all real numbers. If the greatest exponent in the polynomial is even, the polynomial is said to be of even degree and the range is the set of real numbers that satisfy the function. If the greatest exponent in the polynomial is odd, the polynomial is said to be odd and the range, like the domain, is the set of all real numbers.

> **Review Video: Simplifying Rational Polynomial Functions**
> Visit mometrix.com/academy and enter code: 351038

A **quadratic function** is a polynomial function that follows the equation pattern $y = ax^2 + bx + c$, or $f(x) = ax^2 + bx + c$, where a, b, and c are real numbers and $a \neq 0$. The domain of a quadratic function is the set of all real numbers. The range is also real numbers, but only those in the subset of the domain that satisfy the equation. The root(s) of any quadratic function can be found by plugging the values of a, b, and c into the **quadratic formula**:

$$x = \frac{-b \pm \sqrt{b^2 - 4ac}}{2a}$$

If the expression $b^2 - 4ac$, the discriminant, is negative, you will instead find complex roots.

A quadratic function has a parabola for its graph. In the equation $f(x) = ax^2 + bx + c$, if a is positive, the parabola will open upward. If a is negative, the parabola will open downward. The axis of symmetry is a vertical line that passes through the vertex. To determine whether or not the parabola will intersect the x-axis, check the number of real roots. An equation with two real roots will cross the x-axis twice. An equation with one real root will have its vertex on the x-axis. An equation with no real roots will not contact the x-axis.

Review Video: Using the Quadratic Formula
Visit mometrix.com/academy and enter code: 163102

Review Video: Changing Constants in Graphs of Functions: Quadratic Equations
Visit mometrix.com/academy and enter code: 476276

An **absolute value function** is in the format $f(x) = |ax + b|$. Like other functions, the domain is the set of all real numbers. However, because absolute value indicates positive numbers, the range is limited to positive real numbers. To find the zero of an absolute value function, set the portion inside the absolute value sign equal to zero and solve for x. An absolute value function is also known as a piecewise function because it must be solved in pieces—one for if the value inside the absolute value sign is positive, and one for if the value is negative. The function can be expressed as

$$f(x) = \begin{cases} ax + b \text{ if } ax + b \geq 0 \\ -(ax + b) \text{ if } ax + b < 0 \end{cases}$$

This will allow for an accurate statement of the range.

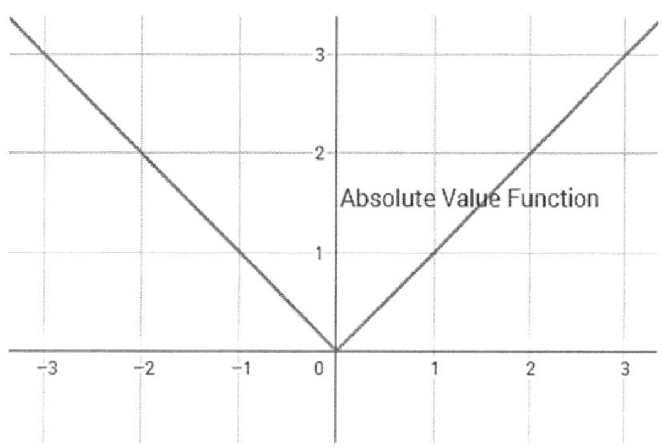

In a **one-to-one function**, each value of x has exactly one value for y (this is the definition of a function) *and* each value of y has exactly one value for x. While the vertical line test will determine if a graph is that of a function, the horizontal line test will determine if a function is a one-to-one function. If a horizontal line drawn at any value of y intersects the graph in more than one place, the graph is not that of a one-to-one function. Do not make the mistake of using the horizontal line test exclusively in determining if a graph is that of a one-to-one function. A one-to-one function must pass both the vertical line test and the horizontal line test. One-to-one functions are also **invertible functions**.

A **monotone function** is a function whose graph either constantly increases or constantly decreases. Examples include the functions $f(x) = x$, $f(x) = -x$, or $f(x) = x^3$.

An **even function** has a graph that is symmetric with respect to the y-axis and satisfies the equation $f(x) = f(-x)$. Examples include the functions $f(x) = x^2$ and $f(x) = ax^n$, where a is any real number and n is a positive even integer.

An **odd function** has a graph that is symmetric with respect to the origin and satisfies the equation $f(x) = -f(-x)$. Examples include the functions $f(x) = x^3$ and $f(x) = ax^n$, where a is any real number and n is a positive odd integer.

Review Video: Even and Odd Functions
Visit mometrix.com/academy and enter code: 278985

Algebraic functions are those that exclusively use polynomials and roots. These would include polynomial functions, rational functions, square root functions, and all combinations of these functions, such as polynomials as the radicand. These combinations may be joined by addition, subtraction, multiplication, or division, but may not include variables as exponents.

Review Video: Common Functions
Visit mometrix.com/academy and enter code: 629798

Transcendental functions are all functions that are non-algebraic. Any function that includes logarithms, trigonometric functions, variables as exponents, or any combination that includes any of these is not algebraic in nature, even if the function includes polynomials or roots.

Related Concepts

According to the **fundamental theorem of algebra**, every non-constant, single variable polynomial has exactly as many roots as the polynomial's highest exponent. For example, if x^4 is the largest exponent of a term, the polynomial will have exactly 4 roots. However, some of these roots may have multiplicity or be non-real numbers. For instance, in the function $f(x) = x^4 - 4x + 3$, the only real roots are 1 and -1. The root 1 has multiplicity of 2 and there is one non-real root $(-1 - \sqrt{2}i)$.

The **remainder theorem** is useful for determining the remainder when a polynomial is divided by a binomial. The Remainder Theorem states that if a polynomial function $f(x)$ is divided by a binomial $x - a$, where a is a real number, the remainder of the division will be the value of $f(a)$. If $f(a) = 0$, then a is a root of the polynomial.

The **factor theorem** is related to the Remainder Theorem and states that if $f(a) = 0$ then $(x - a)$ is a factor of the function.

According to the **rational root theorem,** any rational root of a polynomial function $f(x) = a_n x^n + a_{n-1}x^{n-1} + \cdots + a_1 x + a_0$ with integer coefficients will, when reduced to its lowest terms, be a positive or negative fraction such that the numerator is a factor of a_0 and the denominator is a factor of a_n. For instance, if the polynomial function $f(x) = x^3 + 3x^2 - 4$ has any rational roots, the numerators of those roots can only be factors of 4 (1, 2, 4), and the denominators can only be factors of 1 (1). The function in this example has roots of 1 $\left(\text{or } \frac{1}{1}\right)$ and -2 $\left(\text{or } -\frac{2}{1}\right)$.

Variables that vary directly are those that either both increase at the same rate or both decrease at the same rate. For example, in the functions $y = kx$ or $y = kx^n$, where k and n are positive, the value of y increases as the value of x increases and decreases as the value of x decreases.

Variables that vary inversely are those where one increases while the other decreases. For example, in the functions $y = \frac{k}{x}$ or $y = \frac{k}{x^n}$ where k and n are positive, the value of y increases as the value of x decreases and decreases as the value of x increases.

In both cases, k is the constant of variation.

Applying the Basic Operations to Functions

For each of the basic operations, we will use these functions as examples: $f(x) = x^2$ and $g(x) = x$.

To find the sum of two functions f and g, assuming the domains are compatible, simply add the two functions together: $(f + g)(x) = f(x) + g(x) = x^2 + x$

To find the difference of two functions f and g, assuming the domains are compatible, simply subtract the second function from the first: $(f - g)(x) = f(x) - g(x) = x^2 - x$.

To find the product of two functions f and g, assuming the domains are compatible, multiply the two functions together: $(f \times g)(x) = f(x) \times g(x) = x^2 \times x = x^3$.

To find the quotient of two functions f and g, assuming the domains are compatible, divide the first function by the second: $\frac{f}{g}(x) = \frac{f(x)}{g(x)} = \frac{x^2}{x} = x\,; x \neq 0$.

The example given in each case is fairly simple, but on a given problem, if you are looking only for the value of the sum, difference, product or quotient of two functions at a particular x-value, it may be simpler to solve the functions individually and then perform the given operation using those values.

The composite of two functions f and g, written as $(f \circ g)(x)$ simply means that the output of the second function is used as the input of the first. This can also be written as $f(g(x))$. In general, this can be solved by substituting $g(x)$ for all instances of x in $f(x)$ and simplifying. Using the example functions $f(x) = x^2 - x + 2$ and $g(x) = x + 1$, we can find that $(f \circ g)(x)$ or $f(g(x))$ is equal to $f(x + 1) = (x + 1)^2 - (x + 1) + 2$, which simplifies to $x^2 + x + 2$.

It is important to note that $(f \circ g)(x)$ is not necessarily the same as $(g \circ f)(x)$. The process is not commutative like addition or multiplication expressions. If $(f \circ g)(x)$ does equal $(g \circ f)(x)$, the two functions are inverses of each other.

Solve Equations in One Variable

Manipulating Equations

Sometimes you will have variables missing in equations. So, you need to find the missing variable. To do this, you need to remember one important thing: *whatever you do to one side of an equation, you need to do to the other side.* If you subtract 100 from one side of an equation, you need to subtract 100 from the other side of the equation. This will allow you to change the form of the equation to find missing values.

EXAMPLE

Ray earns $10 an hour at his job. Write an equation for his earnings as a function of time spent working. Determine how long Ray has to work in order to earn $360.

The number of dollars that Ray earns is dependent on the number of hours he works, so earnings will be represented by the dependent variable y and hours worked will be represented by the independent variable x. He earns 10 dollars per hour worked, so his earning can be calculated as

$$y = 10x$$

To calculate the number of hours Ray must work to earn $360, plug in 360 for y and solve for x:

$$360 = 10x$$

$$x = \frac{360}{10} = 36$$

So, Ray must work 36 hours in order to earn $360.

SOLVING ONE VARIABLE LINEAR EQUATIONS

Another way to write an equation is $ax + b = 0$ where $a \neq 0$. This is known as a **one-variable linear equation**. A solution to an equation is called a **root**. Consider the following equation:

$$5x + 10 = 0$$

If we solve for x, the solution is $x = -2$. In other words, the root of the equation is -2.

The first step is to subtract 10 from both sides. This gives $5x = -10$.

Next, divide both sides by the **coefficient** of the variable. For this example, that is 5. So, you should have $x = -2$. You can make sure that you have the correct answer by substituting -2 back into the original equation. So, the equation now looks like this: $(5)(-2) + 10 = -10 + 10 = 0$.

EXAMPLE 1

Given $\frac{45\%}{12\%} = \frac{15\%}{x}$, solve for x.

First, cross multiply; then, solve for x: $\frac{45\%}{12\%} = \frac{15\%}{x}$

$$\frac{0.45}{0.12} = \frac{0.15}{x}$$
$$0.45(x) = 0.12(0.15)$$
$$0.45x = 0.0180$$
$$0.45x \div 0.45 = 0.0180 \div 0.45$$
$$x = 0.04 = 4\%$$

Alternatively, notice that $\frac{45\% \div 3}{12\% \div 3} = \frac{15\%}{4\%}$. So, $x = 4\%$.

EXAMPLE 2

How do you solve for x in the proportion $\frac{0.50}{2} = \frac{1.50}{x}$?

First, cross multiply; then, solve for x.

$$\frac{0.50}{2} = \frac{1.50}{x}$$
$$0.50(x) = 2(1.50)$$
$$0.50x = 3$$
$$0.50x \div 0.50 = 3 \div 0.50$$
$$x = 6$$

Or, notice that $\frac{0.50 \times 3}{2 \times 3} = \frac{1.50}{6}$, so $x = 6$.

EXAMPLE 3

Given $\frac{40}{8} = \frac{x}{24}$, find x.

One way to solve for x is to first cross multiply.

$$\frac{40}{8} = \frac{x}{24}$$
$$40(24) = 8(x)$$
$$960 = 8x$$
$$120 = x$$

Or, notice that:

$$\frac{40 \times 3}{8 \times 3} = \frac{120}{24}, \text{so } x = 120$$

CALCULATIONS USING POINTS

Sometimes you need to perform calculations using only points on a graph as input data. Using points, you can determine what the **midpoint** and **distance** are. If you know the equation for a line you can calculate the distance between the line and the point.

To find the **midpoint** of two points (x_1, y_1) and (x_2, y_2), average the x-coordinates to get the x-coordinate of the midpoint, and average the y-coordinates to get the y-coordinate of the midpoint. The formula is Midpoint $= \left(\frac{x_1+x_2}{2}, \frac{y_1+y_2}{2}\right)$.

The **distance** between two points is the same as the length of the hypotenuse of a right triangle with the two given points as endpoints, and the two sides of the right triangle parallel to the x-axis and y-axis, respectively. The length of the segment parallel to the x-axis is the difference between the x-coordinates of the two points. The length of the segment parallel to the y-axis is the difference between the y-coordinates of the two points. Use the Pythagorean theorem $a^2 + b^2 = c^2$ or $c = \sqrt{a^2 + b^2}$ to find the distance. The formula is distance $= \sqrt{(x_2 - x_1)^2 + (y_2 - y_1)^2}$.

When a line is in the format $Ax + By + C = 0$, where A, B, and C are coefficients, you can use a point (x_1, y_1) not on the line and apply the formula $d = \frac{|Ax_1+By_1+C|}{\sqrt{A^2+B^2}}$ to find the distance between the line and the point (x_1, y_1).

Review Video: Calculations Using Points on a Graph
Visit mometrix.com/academy and enter code: 883228

EXAMPLE

Find the distance and midpoint between points (2, 4) and (8,6).

Midpoint

$$\text{Midpoint} = \left(\frac{x_1 + x_2}{2}, \frac{y_1 + y_2}{2}\right)$$
$$\text{Midpoint} = \left(\frac{2 + 8}{2}, \frac{4 + 6}{2}\right)$$
$$\text{Midpoint} = \left(\frac{10}{2}, \frac{10}{2}\right)$$
$$\text{Midpoint} = (5,5)$$

Distance

$$\text{Distance} = \sqrt{(x_2 - x_1)^2 + (y_2 - y_1)^2}$$
$$\text{Distance} = \sqrt{(8 - 2)^2 + (6 - 4)^2}$$
$$\text{Distance} = \sqrt{(6)^2 + (2)^2}$$
$$\text{Distance} = \sqrt{36 + 4}$$
$$\text{Distance} = \sqrt{40} \text{ or } 2\sqrt{10}$$

POLYNOMIAL ALGEBRA

To multiply two binomials, follow the **FOIL** method. FOIL stands for:

First: Multiply the first term of each binomial

Outer: Multiply the outer terms of each binomial

Inner: Multiply the inner terms of each binomial

Last: Multiply the last term of each binomial

Using FOIL $(Ax + By)(Cx + Dy) = ACx^2 + ADxy + BCxy + BDy^2$.

EXAMPLE

Use the FOIL method on binomials $(x + 2)$ and $(x - 3)$.

First: $(x + 2)(x - 3) = (x)(x) = x^2$

Outer: $(x + 2)\ (x - 3) = (x)(-3) = -3x$

Inner: $(x + 2)\ (x - 3) = (2)(x) = 2x$

Last: $(x + 2)(x - 3) = (2)(-3) = -6$

Combine like Terms:

$$(x^2) + (-3x + 2x) + (-6) = x^2 - x - 6$$

Review Video: Polynomials
Visit mometrix.com/academy and enter code: 305005

Dividing Polynomials

To divide polynomials, begin by arranging the terms of each polynomial in order of one variable. You may arrange in ascending or descending order, but make sure to be consistent with both polynomials. To get the first term of the quotient, divide the first term of the dividend by the first term of the divisor. Multiply the first term of the quotient by the entire divisor and subtract that product from the dividend. Repeat for the second and successive terms until you either get a remainder of zero or a remainder whose degree is less than the degree of the divisor. If the quotient has a remainder, write the answer as a mixed expression in the form:

$$\text{quotient} + \frac{\text{remainder}}{\text{divisor}}$$

The remainder would then be a rational expression. **Rational expressions** are fractions with polynomials in both the numerator and the denominator; the value of the polynomial in the denominator cannot be equal to zero. To add or subtract rational expressions, first find the common denominator, then rewrite each fraction as an equivalent fraction with the common denominator. Finally, add or subtract the numerators to get the numerator of the answer, and keep the common denominator as the denominator of the answer. When multiplying rational expressions factor each polynomial and cancel like factors (a factor which appears in both the numerator and the denominator). Then, multiply all remaining factors in the numerator to get the numerator of the product, and multiply the remaining factors in the denominator to get the denominator of the product. Remember – cancel entire factors, not individual terms. To divide rational expressions, take the reciprocal of the divisor (the rational expression you are dividing by) and multiply by the dividend.

Below are patterns of some special products to remember:

- Perfect trinomial squares:
  $$x^2 + 2xy + y^2 = (x + y)^2 \text{ and } x^2 - 2xy + y^2 = (x - y)^2$$
- Difference between two squares:
  $$x^2 - y^2 = (x + y)(x - y)$$
- Sum of two cubes:
  $$x^3 + y^3 = (x + y)(x^2 - xy + y^2)$$
  Note: the second factor is *not* the same as a perfect trinomial square, so do not try to factor it further.
- Difference between two cubes:
  $$x^3 - y^3 = (x - y)(x^2 + xy + y^2)$$
  Again, the second factor is *not* the same as a perfect trinomial square.
- Perfect cubes:
  $$x^3 + 3x^2y + 3xy^2 + y^3 = (x + y)^3 \text{ and } x^3 - 3x^2y + 3xy^2 - y^3 = (x - y)^3$$

In order to **factor a polynomial**, first check for a common monomial factor. When the greatest common monomial factor has been factored out, look for patterns of special products: differences of two squares, the sum or difference of two cubes for binomial factors, or perfect trinomial squares for trinomial factors. If the factor is a trinomial but not a perfect trinomial square, look for a factorable form, such as:

$$x^2 + (a + b)x + ab = (x + a)(x + b)$$

or

$$(ac)x^2 + (ad + bc)x + bd = (ax + b)(cx + d)$$

For factors with four terms, look for groups to factor. Once you have found the factors, write the original polynomial as the product of all the factors. Make sure all of the polynomial factors are prime. Monomial factors may be prime or composite. Check your work by multiplying the factors to make sure you get the original polynomial.

Solving Quadratic Equations

To solve a quadratic equation by factoring, begin by rewriting the equation in standard form, if necessary. Factor the side with the variable then set each of the factors equal to zero and solve the resulting linear equations. Check your answers by substituting the roots you found into the original equation. If, when writing the equation in standard form, you have $x^2 + c = 0$ or $x^2 - c = 0$, set $x^2 = -c$ or $x^2 = c$ and take the square root of c. If $c = 0$, the only real root is zero. If c is positive, there are two real roots—the positive and negative square root values. If c is negative, there are no real roots because you cannot take the square root of a negative number.

Review Video: Factoring Quadratic Equations
Visit mometrix.com/academy and enter code: 336566

To solve a quadratic equation by **completing the square**, rewrite the equation so that all terms containing the variable are on the left side of the equal sign, and all the constants are on the right side of the equal sign. Make sure the coefficient of the squared term is 1. If there is a coefficient with the squared term, divide each term on both sides of the equal side by that number. Next, work with the coefficient of the single-variable term. Square half of this coefficient and add that value to both sides. Now you can factor the left side (the side containing the variable) as the square of a binomial. $x^2 + 2ax + a^2 = C \Rightarrow (x + a)^2 = C$, where x is the variable, and a and C are constants. Take the square root of both sides and solve for the variable. Substitute the value of the variable in the original problem to check your work.

Quadratic Function

A **quadratic function** is a function in the form $y = ax^2 + bx + c; a \neq 0$. While a linear function forms a line, a quadratic function forms a **parabola**, which is a u-shaped figure that either opens upward or downward. A parabola that opens upward is said to be a **positive quadratic function** and a parabola that opens downward is said to be a **negative quadratic function**. The shape of a parabola can differ, depending on the values of *a, b,* and *c*. All parabolas contain a **vertex**, which is the highest possible point, the **maximum**, or the lowest possible point, the **minimum**. This is the point where the graph begins moving in the opposite direction. A quadratic function can have zero, one, or two solutions, and therefore, zero, one, or two x-intercepts. Recall that the x-intercepts are referred to as the zeros, or roots, of a function. A quadratic function will have only one y-intercept.

Understanding the basic components of a quadratic function can give you an idea of the shape of its graph.

Review Video: Solutions of a Quadratic Equation on a Graph
Visit mometrix.com/academy and enter code: 328231

Example graph of a positive quadratic function:

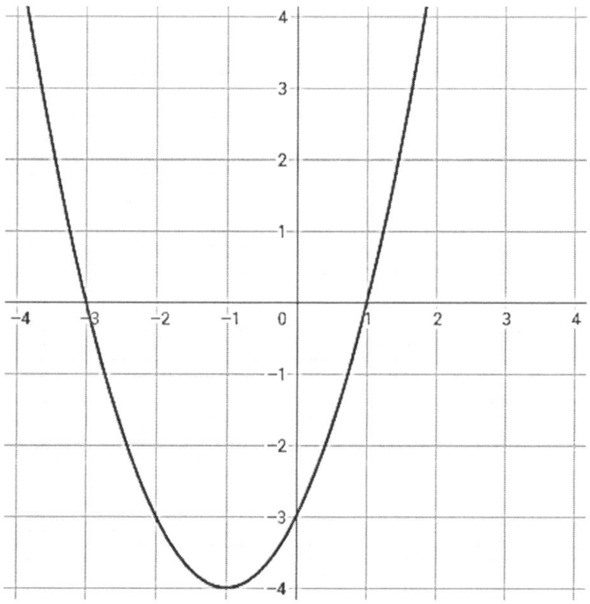

SIMPLIFYING POLYNOMIAL EXPRESSIONS

A polynomial is a group of monomials added or subtracted together. Simplifying polynomials requires combining like terms. The like terms in a polynomial expression are those that have the same variable raised to the same power. It is often helpful to connect the like terms with arrows or lines in order to separate them from the other monomials. Once you have determined the like terms, you can rearrange the polynomial by placing them together. Remember to include the sign that is in front of each term. Once the like terms are placed together, you can apply each operation and simplify. When adding and subtracting polynomials, only add and subtract the **coefficient**, or the number part; the variable and exponent stay the same.

Review Video: Adding and Subtracting Polynomials
Visit mometrix.com/academy and enter code: 124088

FINDING ROOTS

The **roots** of a quadratic equation are the solutions when $ax^2 + bx + c = 0$. As an example, to find the roots of $y = x^2 + 6x - 16$, first replace y with 0. If $0 = x^2 + 6x - 16$, then to find the values of x, you can factor the equation if possible. When factoring a quadratic equation where $a = 1$, find the factors of c that add up to b. That is the factors of -16 that add up to 6. The factors of -16 include, -4 and 4, -8 and 2 and -2 and 8. The factors that add up to equal 6 are -2 and 8. Write these factors as the product of two binomials, $0 = (x - 2)(x + 8)$. You can verify that these are the correct factors by using FOIL to multiply them together. Finally, since these binomials multiply together to equal zero, set them each equal to zero and solve for x. This results in $x - 2 = 0$, which simplifies to $x = 2$ and $x + 8 = 0$, which simplifies to $x = -8$. Therefore, the roots of the equation are 2 and −8. These values are important because they tell you where the graph of the equation crosses the x-axis. The points of intersection are $(2, 0)$ and $(-8, 0)$.

Example

List the steps used in solving $y = 2x^2 + 8x + 4$.

First, substitute 0 in for y in the quadratic equation: $0 = 2x^2 + 8x + 4$

Next, try to factor the quadratic equation. If $a \neq 1$, list the factors of ac, or 8:

$$(1, 8), (-1, -8), (2, 4), (-2, -4)$$

Look for the factors of ac that add up to b, or 8. Since none do, the equation cannot be factored with whole numbers. Substitute the values of a, b, and c into the quadratic formula, then use the order of operations to simplify:

$$x = \frac{-8 \pm \sqrt{8^2 - 4(2)(4)}}{2(2)}$$
$$x = \frac{-8 \pm \sqrt{64 - 32}}{4}$$
$$x = \frac{-8}{4} \pm \frac{\sqrt{32}}{4}$$
$$x = -2 \pm \sqrt{\frac{32}{16}}$$
$$x = -2 \pm \sqrt{2}$$

$$x = -2 + \sqrt{2} \quad x = -2 - \sqrt{2}$$

Check both solutions with the original equation to make sure they are valid.
Evaluate the square roots and round to two decimal places.

$$x = -3.41 \text{ and } x = -0.59$$

Using Given Roots to Find Quadratic Equation

Find a quadratic equation whose real roots are $x = 2$ and $x = -1$.

One way to find the roots of a quadratic equation is to factor the equation and use the **zero product property**, setting each factor of the equation equal to zero to find the corresponding root. We can use this technique in reverse to find an equation given its roots. Each root corresponds to a linear equation which in turn corresponds to a factor of the quadratic equation.

For example, the root $x = 2$ corresponds to the equation $x - 2 = 0$, and the root $x = -1$ corresponds to the equation $x + 1 = 0$. These two equations correspond to the factors $(x - 2)$ and $(x + 1)$, from which we can derive the equation $(x - 2)(x + 1) = 0$, or $x^2 - x - 2 = 0$.

Any integer multiple of this entire equation will also yield the same roots, as the integer will simply cancel out when the equation is factored.

For example, $2x^2 - 2x - 4 = 0$ factors as $2(x - 2)(x + 1) = 0$

Linear Systems and Inequalities

Systems of Equations

Systems of equations are sets of simultaneous equations that all use the same variables. A solution to a system of equations must be true for each equation in the system. **Consistent systems** are those with at least one solution. **Inconsistent systems** are systems of equations that have no solution.

Solving by Substitution

To solve a system of linear equations by **substitution**, start with the easier equation and solve for one of the variables. Express this variable in terms of the other variable. Substitute this expression in the other equation and solve for the other variable. The solution should be expressed in the form (x, y). Substitute the values into both of the original equations to check your answer. Consider the following system of equations:

$$x + 6y = 15$$
$$3x - 12y = 18$$

Solving the first equation for x: $x = 15 - 6y$

Substitute this value in place of x in the second equation, and solve for y:

$$\begin{aligned} 3(15 - 6y) - 12y &= 18 \\ 45 - 18y - 12y &= 18 \\ 30y &= 27 \\ y &= \frac{27}{30} = \frac{9}{10} = 0.9 \end{aligned}$$

Plug this value for y back into the first equation to solve for x:

$$x = 15 - 6(0.9) = 15 - 5.4 = 9.6$$

Check both equations if you have time:

$$\begin{aligned} 9.6 + 6(0.9) &= 15 \\ 9.6 + 5.4 &= 15 \\ 15 &= 15 \end{aligned} \qquad \begin{aligned} 3(9.6) - 12(0.9) &= 18 \\ 28.8 - 10.8 &= 18 \\ 18 &= 18 \end{aligned}$$

Therefore, the solution is (9.6,0.9).

Review Video: The Substitution Method
Visit mometrix.com/academy and enter code: 565151

Solving by Elimination

To solve a system of equations using **elimination**, begin by rewriting both equations in standard form $Ax + By = C$. Check to see if the coefficients of one pair of like variables add to zero. If not, multiply one or both of the equations by a non-zero number to make one set of like variables add to zero. Add the two equations to solve for one of the variables. Substitute this value into one of the original equations to solve for the other variable.

For example, solve the following system using elimination:

$$\begin{aligned} -4x - 3y &= 10 \\ 2x - 9y &= 16 \end{aligned}$$

If we multiply the first equation by -3, we can eliminate the y terms and solve for x:

$$\begin{array}{r} 12x + 9y = -30 \\ +\ 2x - 9y = \quad 16 \\ \hline 14x \qquad = -14 \end{array}$$

$$x = \frac{-14}{14} = -1$$

Plug the value for x back into either of the original equations and solve for y:

$$\begin{aligned} -4(-1) - 3y &= 10 \\ 4 - 3y &= 10 \\ y &= \frac{10 - 4}{-3} = -2 \end{aligned}$$

Check both equations if you have time:

$$\begin{aligned} -4x - 3y &= 10 \\ -4(-1) - 3(-2) &= 10 \\ 4 + 6 &= 10 \\ 10 &= 10 \end{aligned} \qquad \begin{aligned} 2x - 9y &= 16 \\ 2(-1) - 9(-2) &= 16 \\ -2 + 18 &= 16 \\ 16 &= 16 \end{aligned}$$

Therefore, the solution is $(-1, -2)$.

Review Video: Substitution and Elimination for Solving Linear Systems
Visit mometrix.com/academy and enter code: 958611

SOLVING GRAPHICALLY

To solve a system of linear equations **graphically**, plot both equations on the same graph. The solution of the equations is the point where both lines cross. If the lines do not cross (are parallel), then there is **no solution**. For example, consider the following system of equations:

$$y = 2x + 7$$
$$y = -x + 1$$

Since these equations are given in slope-intercept form, they are easy to graph; the y intercepts of the lines are $(0, 7)$ and $(0, 1)$. The respective slopes are 2 and -1, thus the graphs look like this:

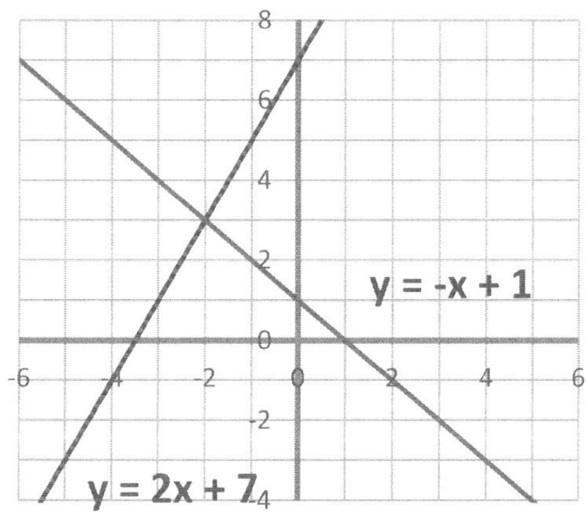

The two lines intersect at the point $(-2, 3)$, thus this is the solution to the system of equations.

Solving a system graphically is generally only practical if both coordinates of the solution are integers; otherwise the intersection will lie between gridlines on the graph and the coordinates will be difficult or impossible to determine exactly. It also helps if, as in this example, the equations are in slope-intercept form or some other form that makes them easy to graph. Otherwise, another method of solution (by substitution or elimination) is likely to be more useful.

Inequalities

GRAPHING INEQUALITIES

Graph the inequality $10 > -2x + 4$.

In order to graph the inequality $10 > -2x + 4$, you must first solve for x. The opposite of addition is subtraction, so subtract 4 from both sides. This results in $6 > -2x$. Next, the opposite of multiplication is division, so divide both sides by -2. Don't forget to flip the inequality symbol since you are dividing by a negative number. This results in $-3 < x$. You can rewrite this as $x > -3$. To graph an inequality, you create a number line and put a circle around the value that is being compared to x. If you are graphing a greater than or less than inequality, as the one shown, the circle remains open. This represents all of the values excluding -3. If the inequality happens to be a greater than or equal to or less than or equal to, you draw a closed circle around the value. This would represent all of the values including the number. Finally, take a look at the values that the solution represents and shade the number line in the appropriate direction. You are graphing all of the values greater than -3 so shade all of the numbers to the right of -3.

Other Important Concepts

Commonly in algebra and other upper-level fields of math you find yourself working with mathematical expressions that do not equal each other. The statement comparing such expressions with symbols such as < (less than) or > (greater than) is called an *inequality*. An example of an inequality is $7x > 5$. To solve for x, simply divide both sides by 7 and the solution is shown to be $x > \frac{5}{7}$. Graphs of the solution set of inequalities are represented on a number line. Open circles are used to show that an expression approaches a number but is never quite equal to that number.

Review Video: Solving Multi-Step Inequalities
Visit mometrix.com/academy and enter code: 347842

Conditional inequalities are those with certain values for the variable that will make the condition true and other values for the variable where the condition will be false. **Absolute inequalities** can have any real number as the value for the variable to make the condition true, while there is no real number value for the variable that will make the condition false. Solving inequalities is done by following the same rules as for solving equations with the exception that when multiplying or dividing by a negative number the direction of the inequality sign must be flipped or reversed. **double inequalities** are situations where two inequality statements apply to the same variable expression. An example of this is $-c < ax + b < c$.

Review Video: Conditional and Absolute Inequalities
Visit mometrix.com/academy and enter code: 980164

Determining Solutions to Inequalities

Determine whether $(-2, 4)$ is a solution of the inequality $y \geq -2x + 3$.

To determine whether a coordinate is a **solution of an inequality**, you can either use the inequality or its graph. Using $(-2, 4)$ as (x, y), substitute the values into the inequality to see if it makes a true statement. This results in $4 \geq -2(-2) + 3$. Using the integer rules, simplify the right side of the inequality by multiplying and then adding. The result is $4 \geq 7$, which is a false statement. Therefore, the coordinate is not a solution of the inequality. You can also use the **graph** of an inequality to see if a coordinate is a part of the solution. The graph of an inequality is shaded over the section of the coordinate grid that is included in the solution. The graph of $y \geq -2x + 3$ includes the solid line $y = -2x + 3$ and is shaded to the right of the line, representing all of the points greater than and including the points on the line. This excludes the point $(-2, 4)$, so it is not a solution of the inequality.

Exponents, Logarithms, and Financial Literacy

Exponential Functions and Logarithmic Functions

Exponential functions are equations that have the format $y = b^x$, where base $b > 0$ and $b \neq 1$. The exponential function can also be written $f(x) = b^x$.

Logarithmic functions are equations that have the format $y = \log_b x$ or $f(x) = \log_b x$, where b is the base and x is the antilogarithm or antilog. The base may be any number except one; however, the most common bases for logarithms are base 10 and base e. The log base e is known the natural logarithm, or *ln*, expressed by the function $f(x) = \ln x$.

Exponential functions and logarithmic functions are related in that one is the inverse of the other. If $f(x) = b^x$, then $f^{-1}(x) = \log_b x$. This can perhaps be expressed more clearly by the two equations: $y = b^x$ and $x = \log_b y$. The graphs of exponential function $f(x) = 2^x$ and logarithminc function $f(x) = \log_2 x$ are depicted below:

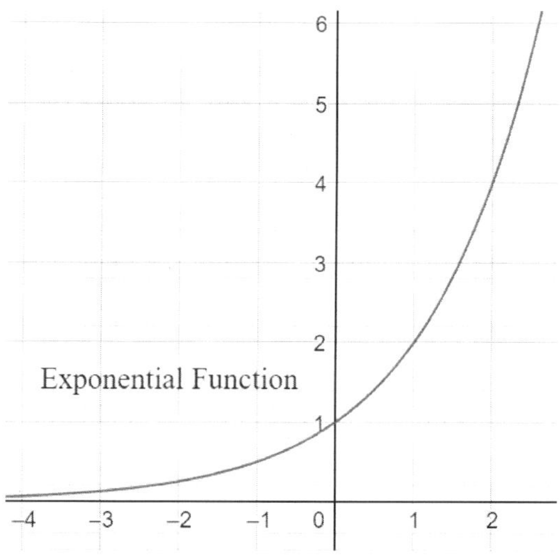

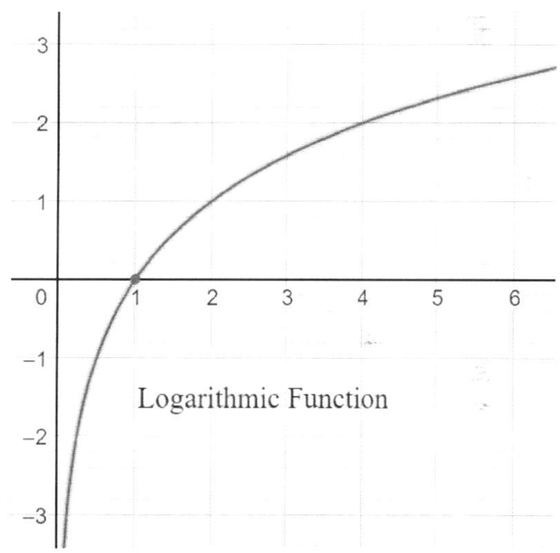

The **properties logarithms** are analogous to the laws of exponents:

- The logarithm of a number that is equal to the base is equal to 1: $\log_b b = 1$.
  Examples: $\log_3 3 = 1 \mid \log_{1000} 1000 = 1$
- The logarithm of any number with a base of 1 is undefined: $\log_1 M = undefined$.
- The logarithm of the number 1 with any base is equal to 0: $\log_b 1 = 0$.
  Examples: $\log_2 1 = 0 \mid \log_{10} 1 = 0$
- Add logarithms of equal base by multiplying the antilogs: $\log_b M + \log_b N = \log_b MN$
  Example: $\log_2 4 + \log_2 8 = \log_2 4 \times 8 = \log_2 32 = 5$
- Subtract logarithms of equal base by dividing the antilogs: $\log_b M - \log_b N = \log_b \left(\frac{M}{N}\right)$
  Example: $\log_4 6 - \log_4 2 = \log_4 \left(\frac{6}{2}\right) = \log_4 3$

- For an antilog is raised to an exponent, the value in the exponent can be moved to the coefficient of the logarithm: $\log_b M^p = p \log_b M$.
  Example: $\log_5 7^2 = 2\log_5 7$ | $\log_{99} 99^3 = 3\log_{99} 99 = 3(1) = 3$
- Convert the base of a logarithm to any other base (except a base of 1) with a ratio of logarithms: $\log_b M = \frac{\log_k M}{\log_k b}$
  Example: $\log_5 4 = \frac{\log_{10} 4}{\log_{10} 5}$

Note: Any logarithm that does not have an assigned value of b is assumed to be base 10:

$$\log x = \log_{10} x$$

EXAMPLE

Simplify $\frac{1+\log_{16} x}{\log_{16} 10-\log_{16} 5}$ using the properties of logarithms.

$$\begin{aligned}\frac{1+\log_{16} x}{\log_{16} 10-\log_{16} 5} &= \frac{1+\log_{16} x}{\log_{16}(10/5)} \\ &= \frac{\log_{16} 16+\log_{16} x}{\log_{16} 2} \\ &= \frac{\log_{16} 16x}{\log_{16} 2} \\ &= \log_2 16x \\ &= \log_2 16+\log_2 x \\ &= \log_2 2^4+\log_2 x \\ &= 4\log_2 2+\log_2 x \\ &= 4+\log_2 x\end{aligned}$$

Financial Literacy

Simple and Compound Interest Rates

The appropriate amount of interest to be paid on a loan that uses **simple interest rates** can be determined by multiplying the principal (the total amount borrowed) by the simple interest rate for the period of the loan. For example, if an individual has a \$10,000 loan with a 6% simple interest rate that must be paid off in one payment at the end of the year, the interest on the loan would be \$600. A **compound interest rate**, on the other hand, bases the amount of interest for the loan on the sum of the principal of the loan and the total amount of interest accrued each time the loan is compounded. For example, if an individual has a \$10,000 loan with 6% interest compounded semiannually, the interest the first time it compounds would be $\$600(\$10{,}000 \times 6\%)$. The interest the second time it compounds would be $\$600(\$10{,}000 \times 6\%)$, so the annual interest payment would be $\$1{,}236(\$600 + \$636)$

Price/Earnings Ratio

The **price/earnings ratio**, or p/e ratio, is a measure of the company's profits versus the current market price. The p/e ratio is calculated by finding the ratio of the current market price of the stock to the **earnings per share**, or EPS:

$$p/e = \frac{\begin{pmatrix}\text{current market}\\ \text{price per share}\end{pmatrix}}{\text{EPS}}$$

The EPS is a reflection on the profitability of the company, and the EPS for a period can be found as:

$$\text{EPS} = \frac{(\text{net income})}{(\text{outstanding shares})}$$

In general, a higher p/e ratio indicates that higher future earnings growth is expected, as compared to a similar company in a similar industry with a lower p/e ratio.

Dividend Yield Ratio

The **dividend yield ratio** measures the dividend earned by investors. It only measures the income from dividends, or the portion of a company's earnings distributed per share to shareholders, and not the income from any increase in share price. It also doesn't take into account any broker commission fees to purchase the stock. The dividend yield ratio is:

$$\text{dividend yield ratio} = \frac{(\text{dividend per share})}{(\text{market price per share})}$$

ROI

The **return on investment**, or ROI, is a percentage of return based on the capital invested, and measures the rate of return so that different investments with different capital investments and returns can be compared. To calculate the ROI, evaluate the formula:

$$\text{ROI} = \frac{\begin{pmatrix}\text{return from}\\ \text{investment}\end{pmatrix} - \begin{pmatrix}\text{capital}\\ \text{investment}\end{pmatrix}}{\begin{pmatrix}\text{capital}\\ \text{investment}\end{pmatrix}}$$

For example, if the capital investment of a stock is \$100, and the yield of the investment after a year is \$105, then:

$$\text{ROI} = \frac{105 - 100}{100} = 0.05 = 5\%$$

INSTALLMENT LOAN

The total installment cost of an installment loan is the cost of the amount paid in payments plus the down payment:

$$\begin{pmatrix}\text{total}\\\text{installment cost}\end{pmatrix} = \begin{pmatrix}\text{payment}\\\text{amount}\end{pmatrix} \times \begin{pmatrix}\text{number of}\\\text{payments}\end{pmatrix} + \begin{pmatrix}\text{down}\\\text{payment}\end{pmatrix}$$

The finance charge is the difference between the total installment amount and the cash price of the item:

$$\begin{pmatrix}\text{finance}\\\text{charge}\end{pmatrix} = \begin{pmatrix}\text{total}\\\text{installment cost}\end{pmatrix} - \begin{pmatrix}\text{cash}\\\text{price}\end{pmatrix}$$

The amount financed is the difference between the cash price and the down payment:

$$\begin{pmatrix}\text{amount}\\\text{financed}\end{pmatrix} = \begin{pmatrix}\text{cash}\\\text{price}\end{pmatrix} - \begin{pmatrix}\text{down}\\\text{payment}\end{pmatrix}$$

Example: Find the total installment cost, finance charge, and amount financed for an installment loan to pay for a dining set. Cash price of dining set: \$1,200.00, number of installments: 18, cash down: 20% of cash price. Each installment is \$75.00.

The amount financed is the cash price less the down payment. The down payment is 20% of the cash price, or: \$1,200.00 × 0.20 = \$240.00, so:

$$\begin{pmatrix}\text{amount}\\\text{financed}\end{pmatrix} = \$1{,}200.0 - \$240.00 = \$960.00$$

$$\begin{pmatrix}\text{total}\\\text{installment cost}\end{pmatrix} = \$75.00 \times 18 + \$240.00 = \$1{,}590.00$$

The finance charge is the difference between paying the cash price and paying the total installment cost: \$1,590.00 − \$1,200.00 = \$390.00

CALCULATING THE APPROXIMATE ANNUAL PERCENTAGE RATE (APR) FOR A LOAN PAID IN MONTHLY PAYMENTS

To calculate the approximate APR for a loan, first determine the finance and next determine the amount financed. Using these two quantities, and the total number of payments, calculate the approximate APR as follows:

$$\text{Approximate APR} = \frac{24 \times \begin{pmatrix}\text{finance}\\\text{charge}\end{pmatrix}}{\begin{pmatrix}\text{amount}\\\text{financed}\end{pmatrix} \times \left(1 + \begin{pmatrix}\text{number of}\\\text{payments}\end{pmatrix}\right)}$$

Example: Find the total installment cost, finance charge, amount financed, and approximate APR for an installment loan to pay for a used car. The cash price is \$4,800.00. The down payment is 15% of the cash price. The loan is paid in 36 installments, at \$135.00 each.

The down payment is 15% of the cash price: $4,800.00 × 0.15 = $720.00.

$$\binom{\text{amount}}{\text{financed}} = \$4{,}800.00 - \$720.00 = \$4080.00 \qquad \binom{\text{total}}{\text{installment cost}} = \$135.00 \times 36 + \$720.00 = \$5{,}580.00$$

Finance charge is: total installment cost − cash price = $5,580.00 − $4,800.00 = $780.00. Therefore, the approximate APR is:

$$\frac{24 \times \binom{\text{finance}}{\text{charge}}}{\binom{\text{amount}}{\text{financed}} \times \left(1 + \binom{\text{number of}}{\text{payments}}\right)} = \frac{24 \times 780}{4080(1 + 36)} = 0.124 = 12.4\%$$

Annuity

An **annuity** is a series of equal payments occurring at equal periods of time. With an **ordinary annuity** the cash flow occurs is at the end of a period. When unspecified, the term "annuity" refers to ordinary annuity. The term **annuity due** applies when the cash flow is at the beginning of the period, such as a rent payment.

Present Value

The **present value** of an annuity is the current value of a stream of money paid or received in equal amounts over future periods. The present value of an annuity can be calculated using the following formula:

$$PV = PMT \frac{[1 - (1 + i)^{-n}]}{i}$$

where:
PV = present value
PMT = payment (annuity amount)
i = interest rate
n = number of periods

Amortization

Amortization is the gradual reduction of the book value of an asset and represents the usage and obsolescence of the asset. Amortization is a way to spread the assets costs over its useful life. In addition, since amortization is an expense, it reduces a firm's taxable income. Amortization is similar to depreciation, but amortization typically refers to intangible assets, such as goodwill, patents, or copyrights, while depreciation refers to tangible assets.

Future Value

The **future value** is the equivalent amount of present cash flows at some time in the future. The future value of a present amount is found using the following formula:

$$FV = PV\,(1 + i)^n$$

where:
FV = future value
PV = present value
i = interest rate
n = number of periods

For example, if you invest \$1000 today at an annual interest rate of 4%, calculate the future value of your investment in 20 years.

First, define your known variables:

$$PV = \$1000$$
$$i = 4\% = 0.04$$
$$n = 20$$

Next, choose the appropriate formula: $FV = PV\,(1 + i)^n$

Finally, calculate the result: $FV = 1000\,(1 + 0.04)^{20} = 2191$

The future value of the investment is \$2,191.

APR

The **annual percentage rate**, or APR, is the annual interest rate plus the added costs of a loan or investment. Examples of extra costs added to the interest rate include application fees, processing fees, and closing costs. When borrowing money, the APR represents the cost of the loan. When using APR in calculations, remember it represents an annual rate. In order to use the future value, present value, and annuity formulas, the period must match the compounding of the interest rate.

Effective Annual Rate

The **effective annual rate**, or EAR, expresses a loan or investment's interest rate when compounding occurs more frequently than once per year. The following formula is used to calculate the effective annual rate:

$$EAR = \left(1 + \frac{i}{n}\right)^n - 1$$

where:
EAR = effective annual rate
i = annual interest rate
n = number of compounding periods

Probability and Statistics

Probability

Probability is a branch of statistics that deals with the likelihood of something taking place. One classic example is a coin toss. There are only two possible results: heads or tails. The likelihood, or probability, that the coin will land as heads is 1 out of 2 ($\frac{1}{2}$, 0.5, 50%). Tails has the same probability. Another common example is a 6-sided die roll. There are six possible results from rolling a single die, each with an equal chance of happening, so the probability of any given number coming up is 1 out of 6. The following terms are frequently used in probability:

- **Event** – a situation that produces results of some sort (a coin toss)
- **Compound event** – event that involves two or more independent events (rolling a pair of dice; taking the sum)
- **Outcome** – a possible result in an experiment or event (heads, tails)
- **Desired outcome** (or success)—an outcome that meets a particular set of criteria (a roll of 1 or 2 if we are looking for numbers less than 3)
- **Independent events**—two or more events whose outcomes do not affect one another (two coins tossed at the same time)
- **Dependent events**—two or more events whose outcomes affect one another (two cards drawn consecutively from the same deck)
- **Certain outcome**—probability of outcome is 100% or 1
- **Impossible outcome**—probability of outcome is 0% or 0
- **Mutually exclusive outcomes** – two or more outcomes with criteria that cannot be satisfied in a single event (a coin coming up heads and tails on the same toss)

Review Video: Intro to Probability
Visit mometrix.com/academy and enter code: 212374

Calculating Probability

Theoretical probability can usually be determined without actually performing the event. The likelihood of an outcome occurring, or the probability of an outcome occurring, is given by the formula:

$$P(A) = \frac{\text{Number of acceptable outcomes}}{\text{Number of possible outcomes}}$$

Where $P(A)$ is the probability of an outcome A occurring, and each outcome is just as likely to occur as any other outcome. If each outcome has the same probability of occurring as every other possible outcome, the outcomes are said to be equally likely to occur. The total number of acceptable outcomes must be less than or equal to the total number of possible outcomes. If the two are equal, then the outcome is certain to occur and the probability is 1. If the number of acceptable outcomes is zero, then the outcome is impossible and the probability is 0.

Review Video: Empirical Probability
Visit mometrix.com/academy and enter code: 513468

Permutations and Combinations

When trying to calculate the probability of an event using the $\frac{\text{desired outcomes}}{\text{total outcomes}}$ formula, you may frequently find that there are too many outcomes to individually count them. Permutation and combination formulas offer a shortcut to counting outcomes. A **permutation** is an arrangement of a specific number of a set of objects in a specific order. The number of permutations of *r* items given a set of *n* items can be calculated as:

$$_nP_r = \frac{n!}{(n-r)!}$$

Combinations are similar to permutations, except there are no restrictions regarding the order of the elements. While ABC is considered a different permutation than BCA, ABC and BCA are considered the same combination. The number of combinations of *r* items given a set of *n* items can be calculated as:

$$_nC_r = \frac{n!}{r!\,(n-r)!} \text{ or } _nC_r = \frac{_nP_r}{r!}$$

Example:

Suppose you want to calculate how many different 5-card hands can be drawn from a deck of 52 cards. This is a combination since the order of the cards in a hand does not matter. There are 52 cards available, and 5 to be selected. Thus, the number of different hands is

$$_{52}C_5 = \frac{52!}{5! \times 47!} = 2{,}598{,}960$$

Complement of an Event

Sometimes it may be easier to calculate the possibility of something not happening, or the **complement of an event**. Represented by the symbol $\bar{A}$, the complement of *A* is the probability that event *A* does not happen. When you know the probability of event *A* occurring, you can use the formula:

$$P(\bar{A}) = 1 - P(A)$$

Where $P(\bar{A})$ is the probability of event *A* not occurring, and $P(A)$ is the probability of event *A* occurring.

Addition Rule

The **addition rule** for probability is used for finding the probability of a compound event. Use the formula:

$$P(A \text{ or } B) = P(A) + P(B) - P(A \text{ and } B)$$

Where $P(A \text{ and } B)$ is the probability of both events occurring to find the probability of a compound event. The probability of both events occurring at the same time must be subtracted to eliminate any overlap in the first two probabilities. For mutually exclusive events, $P(A \text{ and } B) = 0$, so the addition rule simplifies to:

$$P(A \text{ or } B) = P(A) + P(B)$$

Conditional Probability

Conditional probability is the probability of an event occurring once another event has already occurred. Given event *A* and dependent event *B*, the probability of event *B* occurring when event *A* has already occurred is represented by the notation $P(A|B)$. To find the probability of event *B* occurring, take into account the fact that event A has already occurred and adjust the total number of possible outcomes. For example, suppose you have ten balls numbered 1–10 and you want ball number 7 to be pulled in two pulls. On the first pull, the probability of getting the 7 is $\frac{1}{10}$ because there is one ball with a 7 on it and 10 balls to choose from. Assuming the first pull did not yield a 7, the probability of pulling a 7 on the second pull is now $\frac{1}{9}$ because there are only 9 balls remaining.

Multiplication Rule

The **multiplication rule** can be used to find the probability of two independent events occurring using the formula:

$$P(A \text{ and } B) = P(A) \times P(B)$$

Where $P(A \text{ and } B)$ is the probability of two independent events occurring, $P(A)$ is the probability of the first event occurring, and $P(B)$ is the probability of the second event occurring.

The multiplication rule can also be used to find the probability of two dependent events occurring using the formula:

$$P(A \text{ and } B) = P(A) \times P(B|A)$$

Where $P(A \text{ and } B)$ is the probability of two dependent events occurring and $P(B|A)$ is the probability of the second event occurring after the first event has already occurred. This is the general form of the multiplication rule, since $P(B|A) = P(B)$ when events A and B are independent.

Use a **combination of the multiplication** rule and the rule of complements to find the probability that at least one outcome of the element will occur. This is given by the general formula $P(\text{at least one event occurring}) = 1 - P(\text{no outcomes occurring})$. For example, to find the probability that at least one even number will show when a pair of dice is rolled, find the probability that two odd numbers will be rolled (no even numbers) and subtract from one. You can always use a tree diagram or make a chart to list the possible outcomes when the sample space is small, such as in the dice-rolling example, but in most cases it will be much faster to use the multiplication and complement formulas.

Review Video: Multiplication Rule
Visit mometrix.com/academy and enter code: 782598

Expected Value

Expected value is a method of determining the expected outcome in a random situation. It is a sum of the weighted probabilities of the possible outcomes. Multiply the probability of an event occurring by the weight assigned to that probability (such as the amount of money won or lost). A practical application of the expected value is to determine whether a game of chance is really fair. If the sum of the weighted probabilities is equal to zero, the game is generally considered fair because the player has a fair chance to at least to break even. If the expected value is less than zero, then players are expected to lose more than they win. For example, a lottery drawing might allow the player to choose any three-digit number, 000–999. The probability of choosing the winning number is 1:1000. If it costs \$1 to play, and a winning number receives \$500, the expected value is:

$$\left(-\$1 \times \frac{999}{1{,}000}\right) + \left(\$500 \times \frac{1}{1{,}000}\right) = -0.499 \text{ or } -\$0.50$$

You can expect to lose on average 50 cents for every dollar you spend.

Empirical Probability

Most of the time, when we talk about probability, we mean theoretical probability. **Empirical probability**, or experimental probability or relative frequency, is the number of times an outcome occurs in a particular experiment or a certain number of observed events. While theoretical probability is based on what *should* happen, experimental probability is based on what *has* happened. Experimental probability is calculated in the same way as theoretical probability, except that actual outcomes are used instead of possible outcomes.

Theoretical and experimental probability do not always line up with one another. Theoretical probability says that out of 20 coin-tosses, 10 should be heads. However, if we were actually to toss 20 coins, we might record just 5 heads. This doesn't mean that our theoretical probability is incorrect; it just means that this particular experiment had results that were different from what was predicted. A practical application of empirical probability is the insurance industry. There are no set functions that define lifespan, health, or safety. Insurance companies look at factors from hundreds of thousands of individuals to find patterns that they then use to set the formulas for insurance premiums.

Objective Probability

Objective probability is based on mathematical formulas and documented evidence. Examples of objective probability include raffles or lottery drawings where there is a pre-determined number of possible outcomes and a predetermined number of outcomes that correspond to an event. Other cases of objective probability include probabilities of rolling dice, flipping coins, or drawing cards. Most gambling games are based on objective probability.

Subjective Probability

Subjective probability is based on personal or professional feelings and judgments. Often, there is a lot of guesswork following extensive research. Areas where subjective probability is applicable include sales trends and business expenses. Attractions set admission prices based on subjective probabilities of attendance based on varying admission rates in an effort to maximize their profit.

Sample Space

The total set of all possible results of a test or experiment is called a **sample space**, or sometimes a universal sample space. The sample space, represented by one of the variables S, Ω, or U (for universal sample space) has individual elements called outcomes. Other terms for outcome that may be used interchangeably include elementary outcome, simple event, or sample point. The number of outcomes in a given sample space could be infinite or finite, and some tests may yield multiple unique sample sets. For example, tests conducted by drawing playing cards from a standard deck would have one sample space of the card values, another sample space of the card suits, and a third sample space of suit-denomination combinations. For most tests, the sample spaces considered will be finite.

An **event**, represented by the variable E, is a portion of a sample space. It may be one outcome or a group of outcomes from the same sample space. If an event occurs, then the test or experiment will generate an outcome that satisfies the requirement of that event. For example, given a standard deck of 52 playing cards as the sample space, and defining the event as the collection of face cards, then the event will occur if the card drawn is a J, Q, or K. If any other card is drawn, the event is said to have not occurred.

For every sample space, each possible outcome has a specific likelihood, or probability, that it will occur. The probability measure, also called the **distribution**, is a function that assigns a real number probability, from zero to one, to each outcome. For a probability measure to be accurate, every outcome must have a real number probability measure that is greater than or equal to zero and less than or equal to one. Also, the probability measure of the sample space must equal one, and the probability measure of the union of multiple outcomes must equal the sum of the individual probability measures.

Probabilities of events are expressed as real numbers from zero to one. They give a numerical value to the chance that a particular event will occur. The probability of an event occurring is the sum of the probabilities of the individual elements of that event. For example, in a standard deck of 52 playing cards as the sample space and the collection of face cards as the event, the probability of drawing a specific face card is $\frac{1}{52} = 0.019$, but the probability of drawing any one of the twelve face cards is $12(0.019) = 0.228$. Note that rounding of numbers can generate different results. If you multiplied 12 by the fraction $\frac{1}{52}$ before converting to a decimal, you would get the answer $\frac{12}{52} = 0.231$.

Tree Diagram

For a simple sample space, possible outcomes may be determined by using a **tree diagram** or an organized chart. In either case, you can easily draw or list out the possible outcomes. For example, to determine all the possible ways three objects can be ordered, you can draw a tree diagram:

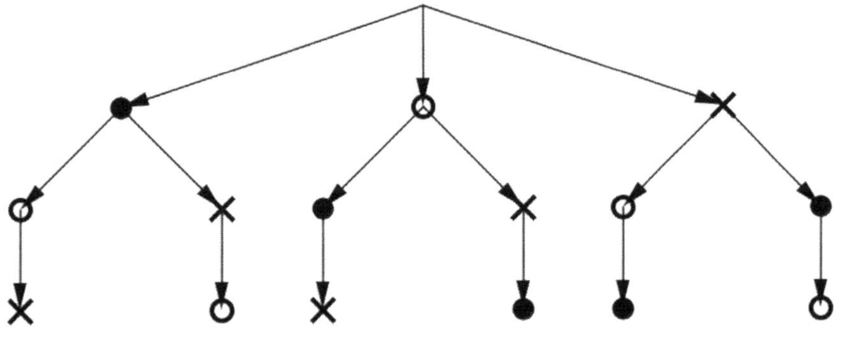

You can also make a chart to list all the possibilities:

First object	Second object	Third object
•	x	o
•	o	x
o	•	x
o	x	•
x	•	o
x	o	•

Either way, you can easily see there are six possible ways the three objects can be ordered.

Odds

In probability, the **odds in favor of an event** are the number of times the event will occur compared to the number of times the event will not occur. To calculate the odds in favor of an event, use the formula:

$$\frac{P(A)}{1 - P(A)}$$

Where $P(A)$ is the probability that the event will occur. Many times, odds in favor is given as a ratio in the form $\frac{a}{b}$ or $a:b$, where a is the probability of the event occurring and b is the complement of the event, the probability of the event not occurring. If the odds in favor are given as 2:5, that means that you can expect the event to occur two times for every 5 times that it does not occur. In other words, the probability that the event will occur is $\frac{2}{2+5} = \frac{2}{7}$.

In probability, the **odds against an event** are the number of times the event will not occur compared to the number of times the event will occur. To calculate the odds against an event, use the formula:

$$\frac{1 - P(A)}{P(A)}$$

This is the reciprocal of the odds in favor of an event.

Statistics

Statistics is the branch of mathematics that deals with collecting, recording, interpreting, illustrating, and analyzing large amounts of **data**. The following terms are often used in the discussion of data and **statistics**:

- **Data** – the collective name for pieces of *information* (singular is datum).
- **Quantitative data** – measurements (such as length, mass, and speed) that provide information about *quantities* in numbers
- **Qualitative data** – information (such as colors, scents, tastes, and shapes) that *cannot be measured* using numbers
- **Discrete data** – information that can be expressed only by a *specific value*, such as whole or half numbers. For example, since people can be counted only in whole numbers, a population count would be discrete data.
- **Continuous data** – information (such as time and temperature) that can be expressed by *any value within a given range*
- **Primary data** – information that has been *collected* directly from a survey, investigation, or experiment, such as a questionnaire or the recording of daily temperatures. Primary data that has not yet been organized or analyzed is called raw data.
- **Secondary data** – information that has been collected, sorted, and *processed* by the researcher
- **Ordinal data** – information that *can be placed in numerical order*, such as age or weight
- **Nominal data** – information that *cannot be placed in numerical order*, such as names or places.

Statistical Concepts

Population

In statistics, the **population** is the entire collection of people, plants, etc., that data can be collected from. For example, a study to determine how well students in the area schools perform on a standardized test would have a population of all the students enrolled in those schools, although a study may include just a small sample of students from each school. A **parameter** is a numerical value that gives information about the population, such as the mean, median, mode, or standard deviation. Remember that the symbol for the mean of a population is μ and the symbol for the standard deviation of a population is σ.

Sample

A **sample** is a portion of the entire population. Whereas a parameter helped describe the population, a **statistic** is a numerical value that gives information about the sample, such as mean, median, mode, or standard deviation. Keep in mind that the symbols for mean and standard deviation are different when they are referring to a sample rather than the entire population. For a sample, the symbol for mean is $\bar{x}$ and the symbol for standard deviation is s. The mean and standard deviation of a sample may or may not be identical to that of the entire population due to a sample only being a subset of the population. However, if the sample is random and large enough, statistically significant values can be attained. Samples are generally used when the population is too large to justify including every element or when acquiring data for the entire population is impossible.

Inferential Statistics

Inferential statistics is the branch of statistics that uses samples to make predictions about an entire population. This type of statistics is often seen in political polls, where a sample of the population is questioned about a particular topic or politician to gain an understanding about the attitudes of the entire population of the country. Often, exit polls are conducted on election days using this method. Inferential statistics can have a large margin of error if you do not have a valid sample.

Sampling Distribution

Statistical values calculated from various samples of the same size make up the **sampling distribution**. For example, if several samples of identical size are randomly selected from a large population and then the mean of each sample is calculated, the distribution of values of the means would be a sampling distribution.

The **sampling distribution of the mean** is the distribution of the sample mean, $\bar{x}$, derived from random samples of a given size. It has three important characteristics. First, the mean of the sampling distribution of the mean is equal to the mean of the population that was sampled. Second, assuming the standard deviation is non-zero, the standard deviation of the sampling distribution of the mean equals the standard deviation of the sampled population divided by the square root of the sample size. This is sometimes called the standard error. Finally, as the sample size gets larger, the sampling distribution of the mean gets closer to a normal distribution via the Central Limit Theorem.

Random Samples

For most studies, a **random sample** is necessary to produce valid results. Random samples should not have any particular influence to cause sampled subjects to behave one way or another. The goal is for the random sample to be a **representative sample**, or a sample whose characteristics give an accurate picture of the characteristics of the entire population. To accomplish this, you must make sure you have a proper **sample size**, or an appropriate number of elements in the sample.

Measures of Central Tendency

The **measure of central tendency** is a statistical value that gives a general tendency for the center of a group of data. There are several different ways of describing the measure of central tendency. Each one has a unique way it is calculated, and each one gives a slightly different perspective on the data set. Whenever you give a measure of central tendency, always make sure the units are the same. If the data has different units, such as hours, minutes, and seconds, convert all the data to the same unit, and use the same unit in the measure of central tendency. If no units are given in the data, do not give units for the measure of central tendency.

Mean

The **statistical mean** of a group of data is the same as the arithmetic average of that group. To find the mean of a set of data, first convert each value to the same units, if necessary. Then find the sum of all the values, and count the total number of data values, making sure you take into consideration each individual value. If a value appears more than once, count it more than once. Divide the sum of the values by the total number of values and apply the units, if any. Note that the mean does not have to be one of the data values in the set, and may not divide evenly.

$$\text{mean} = \frac{\text{sum of the data values}}{\text{quantity of data values}}$$

For instance, the mean of the data set $\{88, 72, 61, 90, 97, 68, 88, 79, 86, 93, 97, 71, 80, 84, 89\}$ would be the sum of the fifteen numbers divided by 15:

$$\frac{88 + 72 + 61 + 90 + 97 + 68 + 88 + 79 + 86 + 93 + 97 + 71 + 80 + 84 + 89}{15} = \frac{1242}{15}$$
$$= 82.8$$

While the mean is relatively easy to calculate and averages are understood by most people, the mean can be very misleading if it is used as the sole measure of central tendency. If the data set has outliers (data values that are unusually high or unusually low compared to the rest of the data values), the mean can be very distorted, especially if the data set has a small number of values. If unusually high values are countered with unusually low values, the mean is not affected as much. For example, if five of twenty students in a class get a 100 on a test, but the other 15 students have an average of 60 on the same test, the class average would appear as 70. Whenever the mean is skewed by outliers, it is always a good idea to include the median as an alternate measure of central tendency.

Median

The **statistical median** is the value in the middle of the set of data. To find the median, list all data values in order from smallest to largest or from largest to smallest. Any value that is repeated in the set must be listed the number of times it appears. If there are an odd number of data values, the median is the value in the middle of the list. If there is an even number of data values, the median is the arithmetic mean of the two middle values.

The median of the data set $\{88, 72, 61, 90, 97, 68, 88, 79, 86, 93, 97, 71, 80, 84, 89\}$ is 86, as that is the middle value of the ordered set $\{61, 68, 71, 72, 79, 80, 84, \mathbf{86}, 88, 88, 89, 90, 93, 97, 97\}$.

MODE

The **statistical mode** is the data value that occurs the most number of times in the data set. It is possible to have exactly one mode, more than one mode, or no mode. To find the mode of a set of data, arrange the data like you do to find the median (all values in order, listing all multiples of data values). Count the number of times each value appears in the data set. If all values appear an equal number of times, there is no mode. If one value appears more than any other value, that value is the mode. If two or more values appear the same number of times, but there are other values that appear fewer times and no values that appear more times, all of those values are the modes.

The big disadvantage of using the median as a measure of central tendency is that is relies solely on a value's relative size as compared to the other values in the set. When the individual values in a set of data are evenly dispersed, the median can be an accurate tool. However, if there is a group of rather large values or a group of rather small values that are not offset by a different group of values, the information that can be inferred from the median may not be accurate because the distribution of values is skewed.

The main disadvantage of the mode is that the values of the other data in the set have no bearing on the mode. The mode may be the largest value, the smallest value, or a value anywhere in between in the set. The mode only tells which value or values, if any, occurred the most number of times. It does not give any suggestions about the remaining values in the set.

The data set $\{88, 72, 61, 90, 97, 68, 88, 79, 86, 93, 97, 71, 80, 84, 89\}$ has two modes: 88 and 97, since they each occurred twice and all others only once.

Review Video: Mean, Median, and Mode
Visit mometrix.com/academy and enter code: 286207

MEASURES OF DISPERSION

The **measure of dispersion** is a single value that helps to "interpret" the measure of central tendency by providing more information about how the data values in the set are distributed about the measure of central tendency. The measure of dispersion helps to eliminate or reduce the disadvantages of using the mean, median, or mode as a single measure of central tendency, and give a more accurate picture of the dataset as a whole. To have a measure of dispersion, you must know or calculate the range, standard deviation, or variance of the data set.

RANGE

The **range** of a set of data is the difference between the greatest and lowest values of the data in the set. To calculate the range, you must first make sure the units for all data values are the same, and then identify the greatest and lowest values. Use the formula:

$$\text{range} = \text{highest value} - \text{lowest value}$$

Write the answer with the same units as the data values you used to do the calculations.

The range of the data set $\{88, 72, 61, 90, 97, 68, 88, 79, 86, 93, 97, 71, 80, 84, 89\}$ is $97 - 61 = 38$.

Review Video: Statistical Range
Visit mometrix.com/academy and enter code: 778541

Standard Deviation

Standard deviation is a measure of dispersion that compares all the data values in the set to the mean of the set. To find the standard deviation of a sample, use the formula:

$$\sigma = \sqrt{\frac{\sum_{i=1}^{n}(x_i - \bar{x})^2}{n-1}}$$

where σ is the standard deviation of a sample, x represents the individual values in the data set, $\bar{x}$ is the mean of the data values in the set, and n is the number of data values in the set. The higher the value of the standard deviation is, the greater the variance of the data values from the mean. The units associated with the standard deviation are the same as the units of the data values.

The standard deviation of the data set $\{88, 72, 61, 90, 97, 68, 88, 79, 86, 93, 97, 71, 80, 84, 89\}$ is:

$$\begin{aligned}
\sigma &= \sqrt{\frac{\sum_{i=1}^{15}(x_i - \bar{x})^2}{15-1}} \\
&= \sqrt{\frac{(88-82.87)^2 + (72-82.87)^2 + \cdots + (84-82.87)^2 + (89-82.87)^2}{14}} \\
&= \sqrt{\frac{(5.13)^2 + (-10.87)^2 + \cdots + (1.13)^2 + (6.13)^2}{14}} \\
&= \sqrt{\frac{26.3169 + 118.1569 + \cdots + 1.2769 + 37.5769}{14}} \\
&= \sqrt{\frac{1635.7335}{14}} \\
&\cong 10.81
\end{aligned}$$

Variance

The **variance** of a sample is the square of the standard deviation of that sample, σ^2. While the mean of a set of data gives the average of the set and gives information about where a specific data value lies in relation to the average, the variance of the sample gives information about the degree to which the data values are spread out and tell you how close an individual value is to the average compared to the other values. The units associated with variance are the same as the units of the data values squared.

The variance of the data set $\{88, 72, 61, 90, 97, 68, 88, 79, 86, 93, 97, 71, 80, 84, 89\}$ is:

$$\sigma^2 = 10.81^2 = 116.86$$

Percentile and Quartile

Percentiles and quartiles are other methods of describing data within a set. **Percentiles** tell what percentage of the data in the set fall below a specific point. For example, achievement test scores are often given in percentiles. A score at the 80th percentile is one which is equal to or higher than 80 percent of the scores in the set. In other words, 80 percent of the scores were lower than that score.

Quartiles are percentile groups that make up quarter sections of the data set. The first quartile is the 25th percentile. The second quartile is the 50th percentile; this is also the median of the dataset. The third quartile is the 75th percentile.

For the ordered data set $\{61, 68, 71, 72, 79, 80, 84, 86, 88, 88, 89, 90, 93, 97, 97\}$:

25th percentile = first quartile	72
50th percentile = second quartile = (median)	86
75th percentile = third quartile	90

DISPLAYING INFORMATION

Charts and tables are ways of organizing information into separate rows and columns that are labeled to identify and explain the data contained in them. Some charts and tables are organized horizontally, with row lengths giving the details about the labeled information. Other charts and tables are organized vertically, with column heights giving the details about the labeled information.

FREQUENCY TABLES

Frequency tables show how frequently each unique value appears in a set. A **relative frequency table** is one that shows the proportions of each unique value compared to the entire set. Relative frequencies are given as percentages; however, the total percent for a relative frequency table will not necessarily equal 100 percent due to rounding. An example of a frequency table with relative frequencies is below.

Favorite Color	Frequency	Relative Frequency
Blue	4	13%
Red	7	22%
Green	3	9%
Purple	6	19%
Cyan	12	38%

Review Video: Data Interpretation of Graphs
Visit mometrix.com/academy and enter code: 200439

BAR GRAPHS

A **bar graph** is one of the few graphs that can be drawn correctly in two different configurations – both horizontally and vertically. A bar graph is similar to a line plot in the way the data is organized on the graph. Both axes must have their categories defined for the graph to be useful. Rather than placing a single dot to mark the point of the data's value, a bar, or thick line, is drawn from zero to the exact value of the data, whether it is a number, percentage, or other numerical value. Longer bar lengths correspond to greater data values. To read a bar graph, read the labels for the axes to find the units being reported. Then look where the bars end in relation to the scale given on the corresponding axis and determine the associated value.

The bar chart below represents the responses from our favorite color survey.

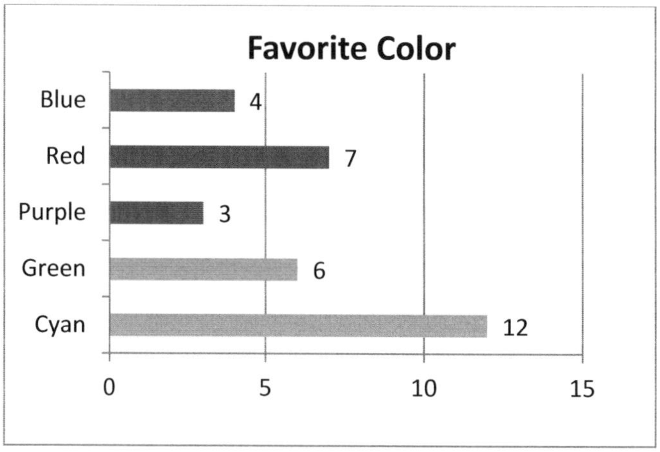

CIRCLE GRAPHS

Circle graphs, also known as *pie charts*, provide a visual depiction of the relationship of each type of data compared to the whole set of data. The circle graph is divided into sections by drawing radii to create central angles whose percentage of the circle is equal to the individual data's percentage of the whole set. Each 1% of data is equal to 3.6° in the circle graph. Therefore, data represented by a 90° section of the circle graph makes up 25% of the whole. When complete, a circle graph often looks like a pie cut into uneven wedges.

The pie chart below shows the the responses from our favorite color survey.

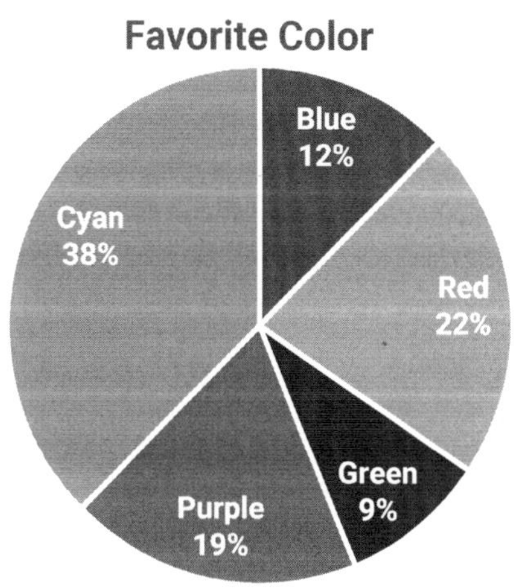

PICTOGRAPHS

A **pictograph** is a graph, generally in the horizontal orientation, that uses pictures or symbols to represent the data. Each pictograph must have a key that defines the picture or symbol and gives the quantity each picture or symbol represents. Pictures or symbols on a pictograph are not always shown as whole elements. In this case, the fraction of the picture or symbol shown represents the same fraction of the quantity a whole picture or symbol stands for. For example, each symbol in the following graph represents 1 person:

Review Video: Pictographs
Visit mometrix.com/academy and enter code: 147860

Line Graphs

Line graphs have one or more lines of varying styles (solid or broken) to show the different values for a set of data. The individual data are represented as ordered pairs, much like on a Cartesian plane. In this case, the x- and y-axes are defined in terms of their units, such as dollars or time. The individual plotted points are joined by line segments to show whether the value of the data is increasing (line sloping upward), decreasing (line sloping downward) or staying the same (horizontal line). Multiple sets of data can be graphed on the same line graph to give an easy visual comparison. An example of this would be graphing achievement test scores for different groups of students over the same time period to see which group had the greatest increase or decrease in performance from year-to-year (as shown below).

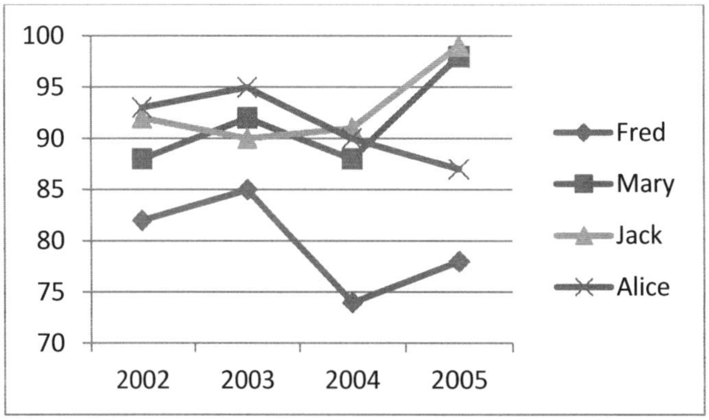

Review Video: How to Create a Line Graph
Visit mometrix.com/academy and enter code: 480147

LINE PLOTS

A **line plot**, also known as a *dot plot*, has plotted points that are not connected by line segments. In this graph, the horizontal axis lists the different possible values for the data, and the vertical axis lists the number of times the individual value occurs. A single dot is graphed for each value to show the number of times it occurs. This graph is more closely related to a bar graph than a line graph. Do not connect the dots in a line plot or it will misrepresent the data.

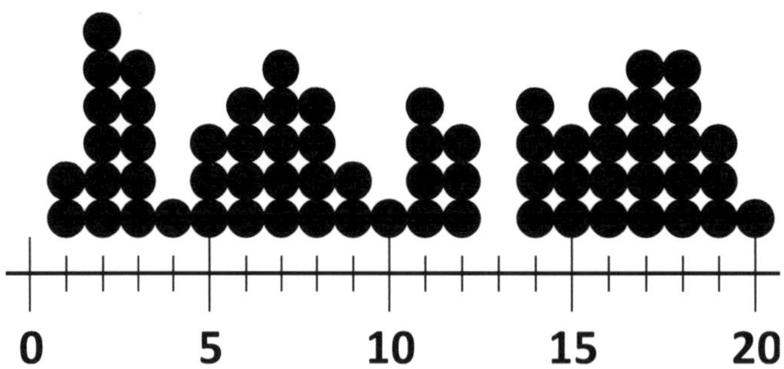

Review Video: Line Plot
Visit mometrix.com/academy and enter code: 754610

STEM AND LEAF PLOTS

A **stem and leaf plot** is useful for depicting groups of data that fall into a range of values. Each piece of data is separated into two parts: the first, or left, part is called the stem; the second, or right, part is called the leaf. Each stem is listed in a column from smallest to largest. Each leaf that has the common stem is listed in that stem's row from smallest to largest. For example, in a set of two-digit numbers, the digit in the tens place is the stem, and the digit in the ones place is the leaf. With a stem and leaf plot, you can easily see which subset of numbers (10s, 20s, 30s, etc.) is the largest. This information is also readily available by looking at a histogram, but a stem and leaf plot also allows you to look closer and see exactly which values fall in that range. Using a sample set of test scores (82, 88, 92, 93, 85, 90, 92, 95, 74, 88, 90, 91, 78, 87, 98, 99), we can assemble a stem and leaf plot like the one below.

Test Scores	
7	4 8
8	2 5 7 8 8
9	0 0 1 2 2 3 5 8 9

Review Video: Stem-and-Leaf Plots
Visit mometrix.com/academy and enter code: 302339

Histograms

At first glance, a **histogram** looks like a vertical bar graph. The difference is that a bar graph has a separate bar for each piece of data and a histogram has one continuous bar for each *range* of data. For example, a histogram may have one bar for the range 0–9, one bar for 10–19, etc. While a bar graph has numerical values on one axis, a histogram has numerical values on both axes. Each range is of equal size, and they are ordered left to right from lowest to highest. The height of each column on a histogram represents the number of data values within that range. Like a stem and leaf plot, a histogram makes it easy to glance at the graph and quickly determine which range has the greatest quantity of values. A simple example of a histogram is below.

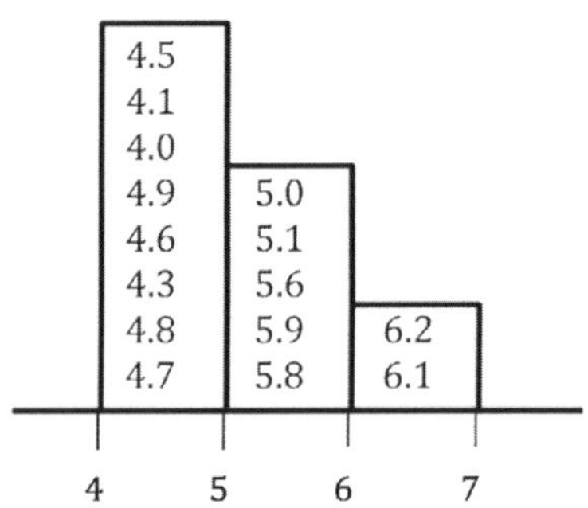

5-Number Summary and Box and Whisker Plots

The **5-number summary** of a set of data gives a very informative picture of the set. The five numbers in the summary include the minimum value, maximum value, and the three quartiles. This information gives the reader the range and median of the set, as well as an indication of how the data is spread about the median.

A **box-and-whisker plot** is a graphical representation of the 5-number summary. To draw a box-and-whiskers plot, plot the points of the 5-number summary on a number line. Draw a box whose ends are through the points for the first and third quartiles. Draw a vertical line in the box through the median to divide the box in half. Draw a line segment from the first quartile point to the minimum value, and from the third quartile point to the maximum value.

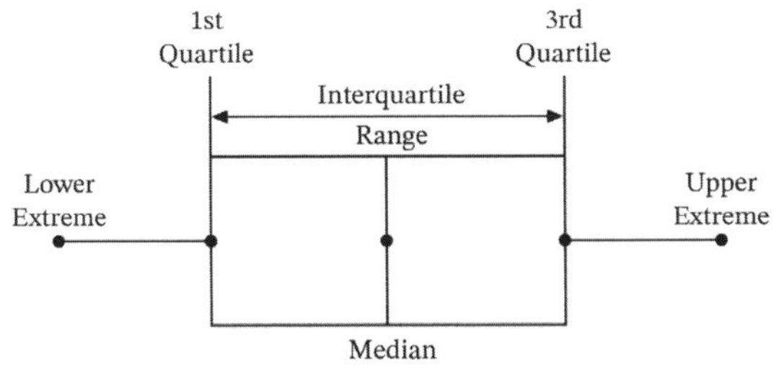

Review Video: <u>Box and Whisker Plots</u>
Visit mometrix.com/academy and enter code: 810817

DSST Practice Test

1. Determine the number of diagonals of a dodecagon.

a. 12
b. 24
c. 54
d. 108

2. A circular bracelet contains 5 charms, A, B, C, D, and E, attached at specific points around the bracelet, with the clasp located between charms A and B. The bracelet is unclasped and stretched out into a straight line. On the resulting linear bracelet, charm C is between charms A and B, charm D is between charms A and C, and charm E is between charms C and D. Which of these statements is (are) necessarily true?

I. The distance between charms B and E is greater than the distance between charms A and D.
II. Charm E is between charms B and D.
III. The distance between charms D and E is less than the distance of bracelet between charms A and C.

a. I, II, and III
b. II and III
c. II only
d. None of these is necessarily true.

3. In a town of 35,638 people, about a quarter of the population is under the age of 35. Of those, just over a third attend local K-12 schools. If the number of students in each grade is about the same, how many fourth graders likely reside in the town?

a. Fewer than 100
b. Between 200 and 300
c. Between 300 and 400
d. More than 400

4. Identical rugs are offered for sale at two local shops and one online retailer, designated Stores A, B, and C, respectively. The rug's regular sales price is $296 at Store A, $220 at Store B, and $198.00 at Store C. Stores A and B collect 8% in sales tax on any after-discount price, while Store C collects no tax but charges a $35 shipping fee. A buyer has a 30% off coupon for Store A and a $10 off coupon for Store B. Which of these lists the stores in order of lowest to highest final sales price after all discounts, taxes, and fees are applied?

a. Store A, Store B, Store C
b. Store B, Store A, Store C
c. Store B, Store C, Store A
d. Store C, Store B, Store B

5. Two companies offer monthly cell phone plans, both of which include free text messaging. Company A charges a $25 monthly fee plus five cents per minute of phone conversation, while Company B charges a $50 monthly fee and offers unlimited calling. Both companies charge the same amount when the total duration of monthly calls is

a. 500 hours.
b. 8 hours and 33 minutes.
c. 8 hours and 20 minutes.
d. 5 hours.

6. A dress is marked down by 20% and placed on a clearance rack, on which is posted a sign reading, "Take an extra 25% off already reduced merchandise." What fraction of the original price is the final sale price of the dress?

a. $\frac{1}{4}$
b. $\frac{2}{5}$
c. $\frac{3}{5}$
d. $\frac{9}{20}$

7. On a floor plan drawn at a scale of 1:100, the area of a rectangular room is 30 cm^2. What is the actual area of the room?

a. 30,000 cm^2
b. 3,000 cm^2
c. 3,000 m^2
d. 30 m^2

8. The ratio of employee wages and benefits to all other operational costs of a business is 2:3. If a business's total expenses are $130,000 per month, how much money does the company spend on employee wages and benefits?

a. $43,333.33
b. $86,666.67
c. $52,000.00
d. $78,000.00

9. Zeke drove from his house to a furniture store in Atlanta and then back home along the same route. It took Zeke three hours to drive to the store. By driving an average of 20 mph faster on his return trip, Zeke was able to save an hour of diving time. What was Zeke's average driving speed on his round trip?

a. 24 mph
b. 48 mph
c. 50 mph
d. 60 mph

10. Complete the analogy: x^3 is to $\sqrt[3]{y}$ as ...

a. $x + a$ is to $x - y$.
b. e^x is to $\ln y, y > 0$.
c. $\frac{1}{x}$ is to $y, x, y \neq 0$.
d. $\sin x$ is to $\cos y$.

11. Which of these statements is (are) true for deductive reasoning?

I. A general conclusion is drawn from specific instances.
II. If the premises are true and proper reasoning is applied, the conclusion must be true.

a. Statement I is true
b. Statement II is true
c. Both statements are true
d. Neither statement is true

12. Given that premises "all *a* are *b*," "all *b* are *d*," and "no *b* are *c*" are true and that premise "all *b* are *e*" is false, determine the validity and soundness of the following arguments:

Argument I: All *a* are *b*. No *b* are *c*. Therefore, no *a* are *c*.
Argument II: All *a* are *b*. All *d* are *b*. Therefore, all *d* are *a*.
Argument III: All *a* are *b*. All *b* are *e*. Therefore, all *a* are *e*.

a.

	Invalid	Valid	Sound
Argument I		X	X
Argument II	X		
Argument III		X	

b.

	Invalid	Valid	Sound
Argument I	X		
Argument II		X	X
Argument III	X		

c.

	Invalid	Valid	Sound
Argument I		X	X
Argument II		X	X
Argument III	X		

d.

	Invalid	Valid	Sound
Argument I		X	X
Argument II	X		
Argument III	X		

13. Given statements *p* and *q*, which of the following is the truth table for the statement:

$$q \leftrightarrow \neg(p \wedge q)$$

a.

p	q	$q \leftrightarrow \neg(p \wedge q)$
T	T	F
T	F	T
F	T	T
F	F	T

b.

p	q	$q \leftrightarrow \neg(p \wedge q)$
T	T	T
T	F	T
F	T	T
F	F	F

c.

p	q	$q \leftrightarrow \neg(p \wedge q)$
T	T	F
T	F	F
F	T	F
F	F	T

d.

p	q	$q \leftrightarrow \neg(p \wedge q)$
T	T	F
T	F	F
F	T	T
F	F	F

14. If $p \rightarrow q$ is true, which of these is also necessarily true?

a. $q \rightarrow p$
b. $\neg p \rightarrow \neg q$
c. $\neg q \rightarrow \neg p$
d. None of these

15. Which of the following is the truth table for logic circuit shown below? (0 = False; 1 = True)

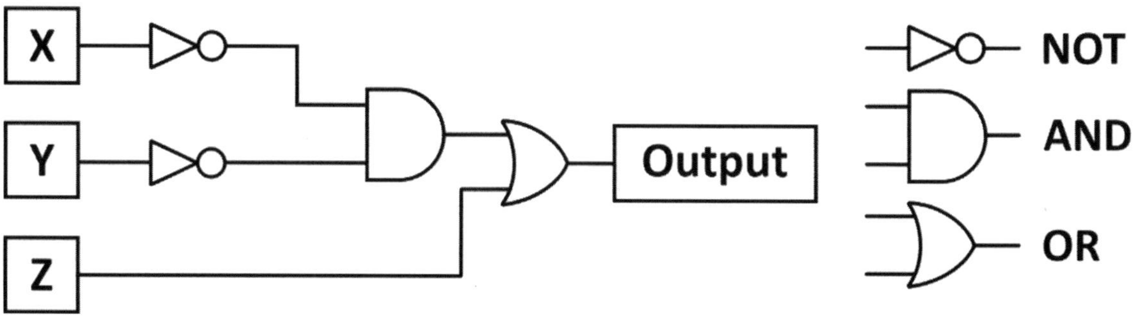

a.

X	Y	Z	Output
0	0	0	1
0	0	1	0
0	1	0	0
0	1	1	0
1	0	0	0
1	0	1	0
1	1	0	0
1	1	1	1

b.

X	Y	Z	Output
0	0	0	0
0	0	1	1
0	1	0	1
0	1	1	1
1	0	0	1
1	0	1	1
1	1	0	1
1	1	1	1

c.

X	Y	Z	Output
0	0	0	0
0	0	1	0
0	1	0	0
0	1	1	1
1	0	0	1
1	0	1	1
1	1	0	1
1	1	1	0

d.

X	Y	Z	Output
0	0	0	0
0	0	1	0
0	1	0	0
0	1	1	0
1	0	0	1
1	0	1	1
1	1	0	1
1	1	1	0

16. Which of these demonstrates the relationship between the sets of prime numbers, real numbers, natural numbers, complex numbers, rational numbers, and integers?

$\mathbb{P}$ – Prime; $\mathbb{R}$ – Real; $\mathbb{N}$ – Natural; $\mathbb{C}$ – Complex; $\mathbb{Q}$ – Rational; $\mathbb{Z}$ – Integer

a. $\mathbb{P} \subseteq \mathbb{Q} \subseteq \mathbb{R} \subseteq \mathbb{Z} \subseteq \mathbb{C} \subseteq \mathbb{N}$
b. $\mathbb{P} \subseteq \mathbb{N} \subseteq \mathbb{Z} \subseteq \mathbb{Q} \subseteq \mathbb{R} \subseteq \mathbb{C}$
c. $\mathbb{C} \subseteq \mathbb{R} \subseteq \mathbb{Q} \subseteq \mathbb{Z} \subseteq \mathbb{N} \subseteq \mathbb{P}$
d. None of these

17. To which of the following sets of numbers does -4 NOT belong?

a. The set of whole numbers
b. The set of rational numbers
c. The set of integers
d. The set of real numbers

18. Consider three sets, of which one contains the set of even integers, one contains the factors of twelve, and one contains elements 1, 2, 4, and 9. If each set is assigned the name A, B, or C, and $A \cap B \subseteq B \cap C$, which of these must be set C?

a. The set of even integers
b. The set of factors of 12
c. The set $\{1, 2, 4, 9\}$
d. The answer cannot be determined from the given information.

19. Given that x is a prime number and that the greatest common factor of x and y is greater than 1, compare the two quantities.

Quantity A	Quantity B
y	the least common multiple of x and y

a. Quantity A is greater.
b. Quantity B is greater.
c. The two quantities are the same.
d. The relationship cannot be determined from the given information.

20. Given the partial table of values for $f(x)$ and $g(x)$, find $f(g(-4))$. (Assume that $f(x)$ and $g(x)$ are the simplest polynomials that fit the data.)

x	$f(x)$	$g(x)$
-2	8	1
-1	2	3
0	0	5
1	2	7
2	8	9

a. 69
b. 31
c. 18
d. 9

21. Find $[g \circ f]x$ when $f(x) = 2x + 4$ and $g(x) = x^2 - 3x + 2$.

a. $4x^2 + 10x + 6$
b. $2x^2 - 6x + 8$
c. $4x^2 + 13x + 18$
d. $2x^2 - 3x + 6$

22. If $f(x)$ and $g(x)$ are inverse functions, which of these is the value of x when $f(g(x)) = 4$?

a. -4
b. $\frac{1}{4}$
c. 2
d. 4

23. Determine which pair of equations are NOT inverses.

a. $y = x + 6; y = x - 6$
b. $y = 2x + 3; y = 2x - 3$
c. $y = \frac{2x+3}{x-1}; y = \frac{x+3}{x-2}$
d. $y = \frac{x-1}{2}; y = 2x + 1$

24. Which of these statements is (are) true for function $g(x)$?

$$g(x) = \begin{cases} 2x - 1 & x \geq 2 \\ -x + 3 & x < 2 \end{cases}$$

I. $g(3) = 0$
II. The graph of $g(x)$ is discontinuous at $x = 2$.
III. The range of $g(x)$ is all real numbers.

a. II
b. III
c. I, II
d. II, III

25. Which of the following could be the graph of $y = a(x + b)(x + c)^2$ if $a > 0$?

a. 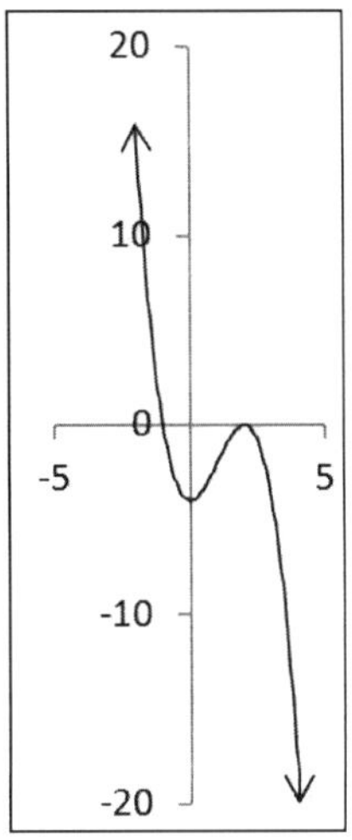

b. 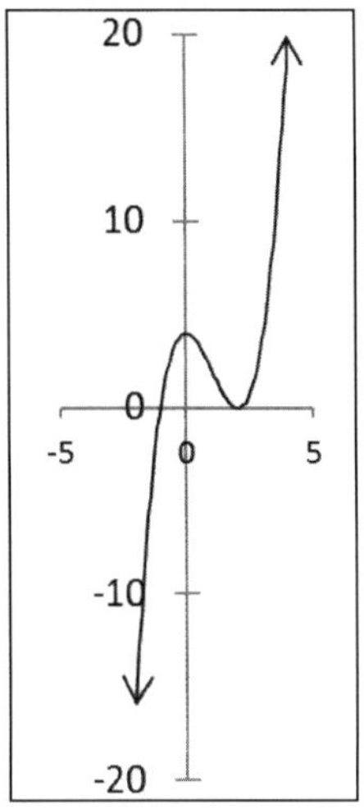

c. 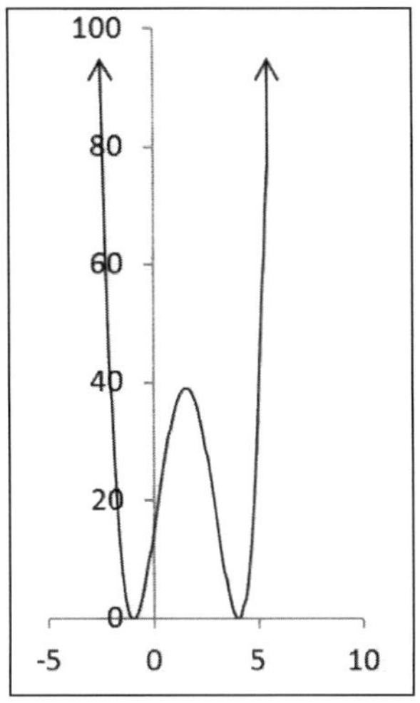

d. 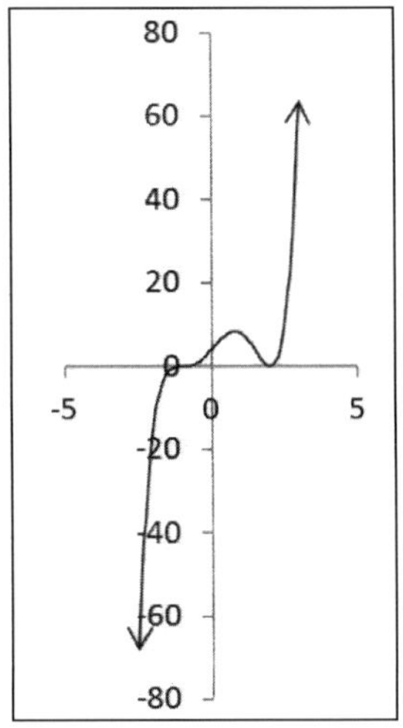

26. A school is selling tickets to its production of *Annie Get Your Gun*. Student tickets cost \$3 each, and non-student tickets are \$5 each. In order to offset the costs of the production, the school must earn at least \$300 in ticket sales. Which graph shows the number of tickets the school must sell to offset production costs?

a. 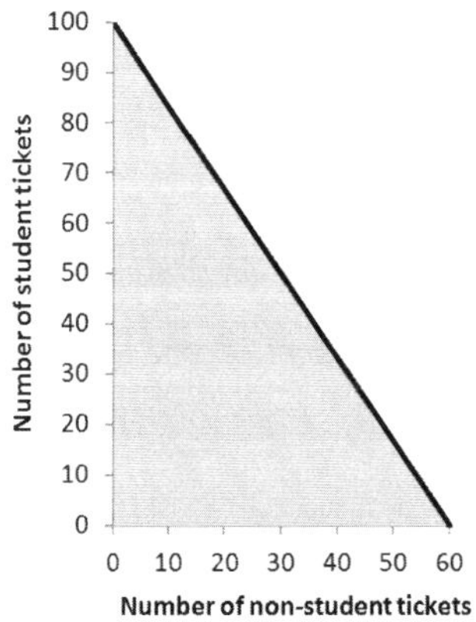

b. 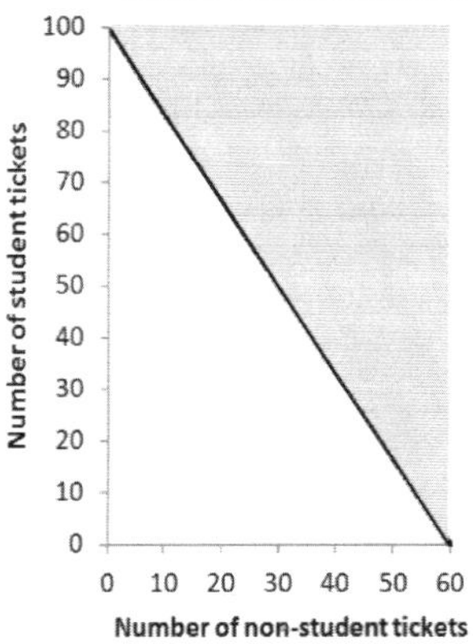

c. 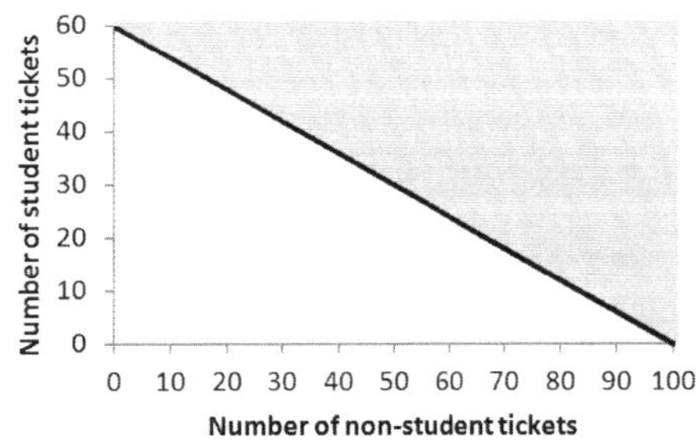

d. 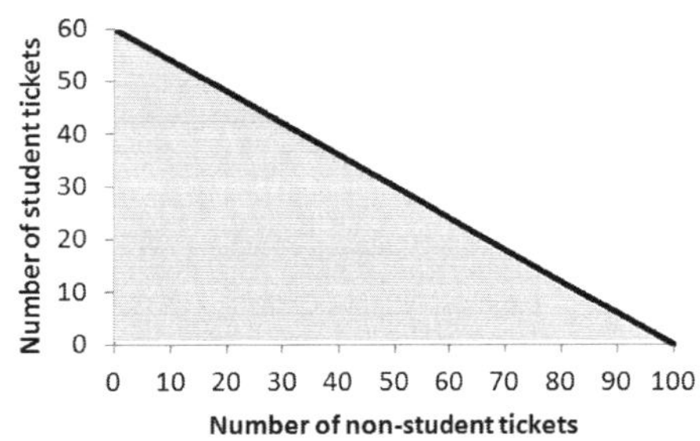

27. Which of these is the equation graphed below?

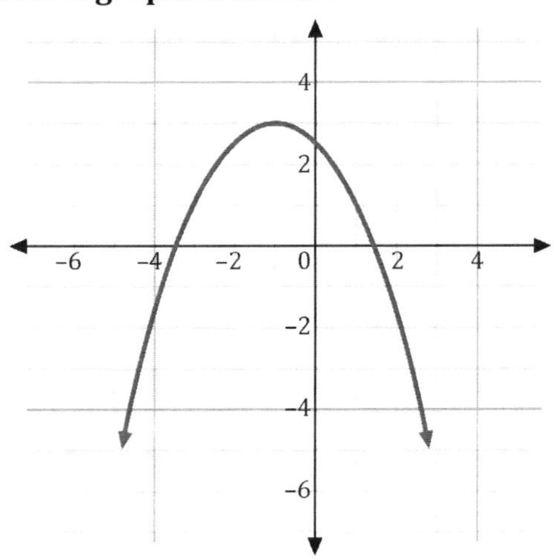

a. $y = -2x^2 - 4x + 1$
b. $y = -x^2 - 2x + 5$
c. $y = -x^2 - 2x + 2$
d. $y = -\frac{1}{2}x^2 - x + \frac{5}{2}$

28. Solve the system of equations: $\begin{array}{r} \mathbf{3x + 4y = 2} \\ \mathbf{2x + 6y = -2} \end{array}$

a. $\left(0, \frac{1}{2}\right)$
b. $\left(\frac{2}{5}, \frac{1}{5}\right)$
c. $(2, -1)$
d. $\left(-1, \frac{5}{4}\right)$

29. Which system of linear inequalities has no solution?

a. $\begin{cases} x - y < 3 \\ x - y \geq -3 \end{cases}$
b. $\begin{cases} y \leq 6 - 2x \\ \frac{1}{3}y + \frac{2}{3}x \geq 2 \end{cases}$
c. $\begin{cases} 6x + 2y \leq 12 \\ 3x \geq 8 - y \end{cases}$
d. $\begin{cases} x + 4y \leq -8 \\ y + 4x > -8 \end{cases}$

30. Solve the system of equations.

$$\begin{aligned} 2x - 4y + z &= 10 \\ -3x + 2y - 4z &= -7 \\ x + y - 3z &= -1 \end{aligned}$$

a. $(-1, -3, 0)$
b. $(1, -2, 0)$
c. $\left(-\frac{3}{4}, -\frac{21}{8}, -1\right)$
d. No solution

31. Solve $3x^3y^2 - 45x^2y = 15x^3y - 9x^2y^2$ for x and y.

a. $x = \{0, -3\},\ y = \{0, 5\}$
b. $x = \{0\},\ y = \{0\}$
c. $x = \{0, -3\},\ y = \{0\}$
d. $x = \{0\},\ y = \{0, 5\}$

32. Which of these statements is true for functions $f(x)$, $g(x)$, and $h(x)$?

$$\begin{aligned} f(x) &= 2x - 2 \\ g(x) &= 2x^2 - 2 \\ h(x) &= 2x^3 - 2 \end{aligned}$$

a. The degree of each polynomial function is 2.
b. The leading coefficient of each function is -2.
c. Each function has exactly one real zero at $x = 1$.
d. None of these is true for functions $f(x)$, $g(x)$, and $h(x)$.

33. Which of these can be modeled by a quadratic function?

a. The path of a sound wave
b. The path of a bullet
c. The distance an object travels over time when the rate is constant
d. Radioactive decay

34. Which of these is equivalent to $\log_y 256$ if $2\log_4 y + \log_4 16 = 3$ if y is positive?

a. 16
b. 8
c. 4
d. 2

35. Simplify $\frac{(x^2y)(2xy^{-2})^3}{16x^5y^2} + \frac{3}{xy}$

a. $\frac{3x+24y^6}{8xy^7}$
b. $\frac{x+6y^6}{2xy^7}$
c. $\frac{x+24y^5}{8xy^6}$
d. $\frac{x+6y^5}{2xy^6}$

36. Given: $f(x) = 10^x$. If $f(x) = 5$, which of these approximates x?

a. 100,000
b. 0.00001
c. 0.7
d. 1.6

37. Which of these statements is NOT necessarily true when $f(x) = \log_b x$ and $b > 1$?

a. The x-intercept of the graph of $f(x)$ is 1.
b. The graph of $f(x)$ passes through $(b, 1)$
c. $f(x) < 0$ when $x < 1$
d. If $g(x) = b^x$, the graph of $f(x)$ is symmetric to the graph of $g(x)$ with respect to $y = x$.

38. Last year, Jenny tutored students in math, in chemistry, and for the ACT. She tutored ten students in math, eight students in chemistry, and seven students for the ACT. She tutored five students in both math and chemistry, and she tutored four students both in chemistry and for the ACT, and five students both in math and for the ACT. She tutored three students in all three subjects. How many students did Jenny tutor last year?

a. 34
b. 25
c. 23
d. 14

39. Which of these could be the equation of the function graphed below?

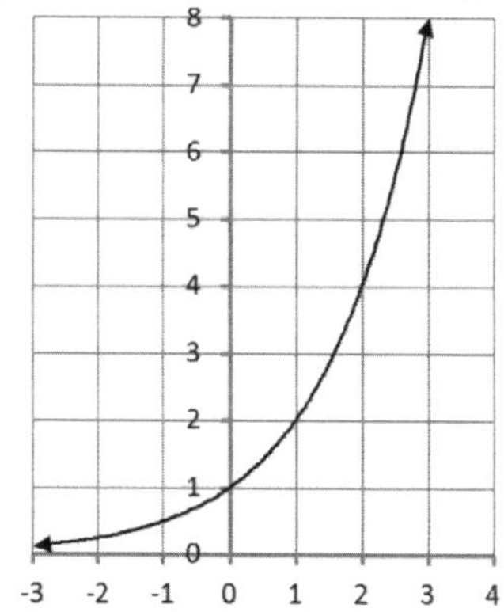

a. $f(x) = x^2$
b. $f(x) = \sqrt{x}$
c. $f(x) = 2^x$
d. $f(x) = log_2 x$

40. A colony of *Escherichia coli* is inoculated from a Petri dish into a test tube containing 50 mL of nutrient broth. The test tube is placed in a 37°C incubator/shaker; after one hour, the number of bacteria in the test tube is determined to be 8×10^6. Given that the doubling time of *E. coli* is 20 minutes with agitation at 37°C, approximately how many bacteria should the test tube contain after eight hours of growth?

a. 2.56×10^8
b. 2.05×10^9
c. 1.7×10^{14}
d. 1.7×10^{13}

41. The strength of an aqueous acid solution is measured by pH. $\text{pH} = -\log_{10}[\text{H}^+]$, where $[\text{H}^+]$ is the molar concentration of hydronium ions in the solution. A solution is acidic if its pH is less than 7. The lower the pH, the stronger the acid; for example, gastric acid, which has a pH of about 1, is a much stronger acid than urine, which has a pH of about 6. How many times stronger is an acid with a pH of 3 than an acid with pH of 5?

a. 2
b. 20
c. 100
d. 1000

42. Which of these does NOT have a solution set of $\{x: -1 \leq x \leq 1\}$?

a. $-4 \leq 2 + 3(x-1) \leq 2$
b. $-2x^2 + 2 \geq x^2 - 1$
c. $\frac{11-|3x|}{7} \geq 2$
d. $3|2x| + 4 \leq 10$

43. Solve the equation $2 - \sqrt{x} = \sqrt{x - 20}$.

a. $x = 6$
b. $x = 36$
c. $x = 144$
d. No solution

44. Solve $\frac{x-2}{x-1} = \frac{x-1}{x+1} + \frac{2}{x-1}$.

a. $x = 2$
b. $x = -5$
c. $x = 1$
d. No solution

45. Which of these functions includes 1 as an element of the domain and 2 as an element of the range?

a. $y = \frac{1}{x-1} + 1$
b. $y = -\sqrt{x+2} - 1$
c. $y = |x+2| - 3$
d. $y = \begin{cases} x & x < -1 \\ -x-3 & x \geq -1 \end{cases}$

46. Which of the following statements is (are) true when $f(x) = \frac{x^2-x-6}{x^3+2x^2-x-2}$?

I. The graph $f(x)$ has vertical asymptotes at $x = -2$, $x = -1$, and $x = 1$.
II. The x- and y-intercepts of the graph of $f(x)$ are both 3.

a. I
b. II
c. I and II
d. Neither statement is true.

47. At today's visit to her doctor, Josephine was prescribed a liquid medication with instructions to take 25 cc's every four hours. She filled the prescription on her way to work, but when it came time to take the medicine, she realized that the pharmacist did not include a measuring cup. Josephine estimated that the plastic spoon in her desk drawer was about the same size as a teaspoon and decided to use it to measure the approximate dosage. She recalled that one cubic centimeter (cc) is equal to one milliliter (mL) but was not sure how many milliliters were in a teaspoon. So, she noted that a two-liter bottle of soda contains about the same amount as a half-gallon container of milk and applied her knowledge of the customary system of measurement to determine how many teaspoons of medicine to take. Which of these calculations might she have used to approximate her dosage?

a. $\frac{25\times2\times16\times48}{1000\times(0.5)} \approx 77$
b. $\frac{25\times(0.5)\times16\times4\times12}{100\times2} \approx 48$
c. $\frac{100\times(0.5)\times16\times4\times12}{25\times2} \approx 768$
d. $\frac{25\times16\times48}{1000\times4} \approx 5$

48. If 1 inch on a map represents 60 feet, how many yards apart are two points if the distance between the points on the map is 10 inches?

a. 1,800 yards
b. 600 yards
c. 200 yards
d. 2 yards

49. Roxana walks x meters west and $x + 20$ meters south to get to her friend's house. On a neighborhood map which has a scale of 1cm:10 m, the distance between Roxana's house and her friend's house is 10 cm. How far did Roxana walk to her friend's house?

a. 60 m
b. 80 m
c. 100 m
d. 140 m

50. For ΔABC, what is AB?

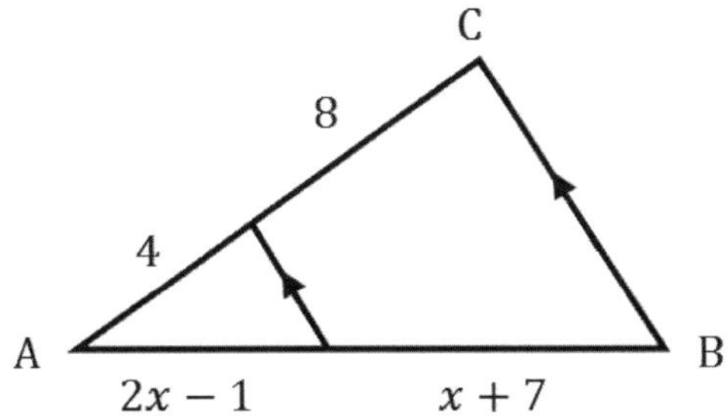

a. 3
b. 10
c. 12
d. 15

51. To test the accuracy and precision of two scales, a student repeatedly measured the mass of a 10g standard and recorded these results.

	Trial 1	Trial 2	Trial 3	Trial 4
Scale 1	9.99 g	9.98 g	10.02g	10.01g
Scale 2	10.206 g	10.209 g	10.210 g	10.208 g

Which of these conclusions about the scales is true?

a. Scale 1 has an average percent error of 0.15%, and Scale 2 has an average percent error of 2.08%. Scale 1 is more accurate and precise than Scale 2.
b. Scale 1 has an average percent error of 0.15%, and Scale 2 has an average percent error of 2.08%. Scale 1 is more accurate than Scale 2; however, Scale 2 is more precise.
c. Scale 1 has an average percent error of 0%, and Scale 2 has an average percent error of 2.08%. Scale 1 is more accurate and precise than Scale 2.
d. Scale 1 has an average percent error of 0%, and Scale 2 has an average percent error of 2.08%. Scale 1 is more accurate than Scale 2; however, Scale 2 is more precise.

52. A developer decides to build a fence around a neighborhood park, which is positioned on a rectangular lot. Rather than fencing along the lot line, he fences x feet from each of the lot's boundaries. By fencing a rectangular space 141 yd^2 smaller than the lot, the developer saves \$432 in fencing materials, which cost \$12 per linear foot. How much does he spend?

a. \$160
b. \$456
c. \$3,168
d. The answer cannot be determined from the given information.

53. Natasha designs a square pyramidal tent for her children. Each of the sides of the square base measures x ft, and the tent's height is h feet. If Natasha were to increase by 1 ft the length of each side of the base, how much more interior space would the tent have?

a. $\frac{h(x^2+2x+1)}{3}$ ft^3
b. $\frac{h(2x+1)}{3}$ ft^3
c. $\frac{x^2h+3}{3}$ ft^3
d. 1 ft^3

54. A rainbow pattern is designed from semi-circles as shown below.

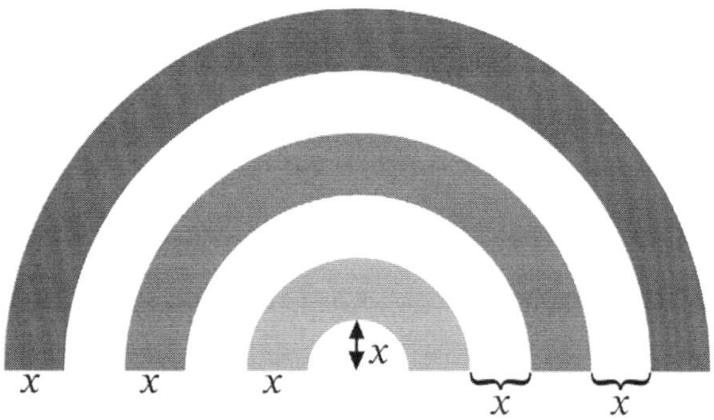

Which of the following gives the area A of the shaded region as a function of x?

a. $A = \frac{21x^2\pi}{2}$
b. $A = 21x^2\pi$
c. $A = 42x^2\pi$
d. $A = 82x^2\pi$

55. As shown below, four congruent isosceles trapezoids are positioned such that they form an arch. Find x for the indicated angle.

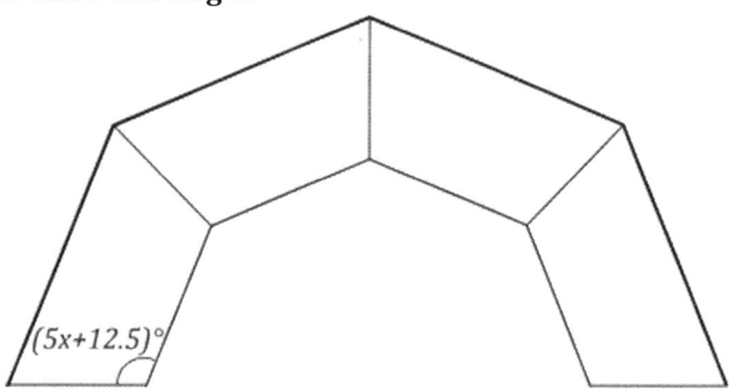

a. $x = 11$
b. $x = 20$
c. $x = 24.5$
d. The value of x cannot be determined from the information given.

56. Which of the following expressions gives the area A of the triangle below as a function of sides a and b?

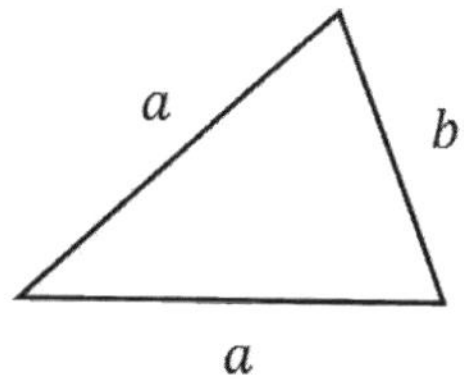

a. $\frac{2a^2-b^2}{4}$
b. $\frac{ab-a^2}{2}$
c. $\frac{b\sqrt{a^2-b^2}}{2}$
d. $\frac{b\sqrt{4a^2-b^2}}{4}$

57. Given the figure and the following information, find DE to the nearest tenth.

$\overline{AD}$ is an altitude of ΔABC
$\overline{DE}$ is an altitude of triangle ΔADC
$\overline{BD} \cong \overline{DC}$
$\overline{BC} = 24$; $\overline{AD} = 5$

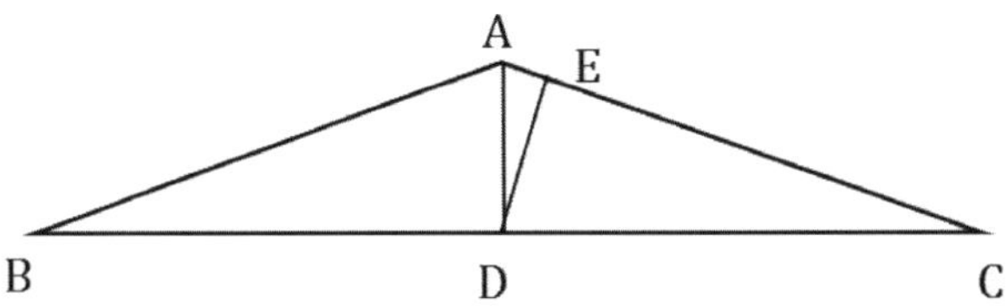

a. 4.2
b. 4.6
c. 4.9
d. 5.4

58. A cube inscribed in a sphere has a volume of 64 cubic units. What is the volume of the sphere in cubic units?

a. $4\pi\sqrt{3}$
b. $8\pi\sqrt{3}$
c. $32\pi\sqrt{3}$
d. $256\pi\sqrt{3}$

59. Which of these is NOT a net of a cube?

a.
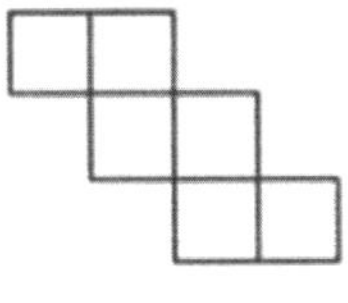

b.
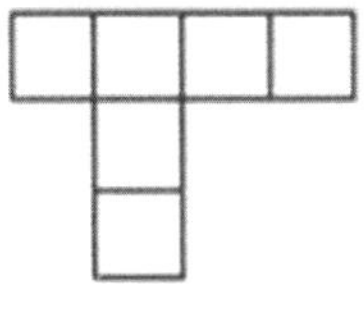

c.
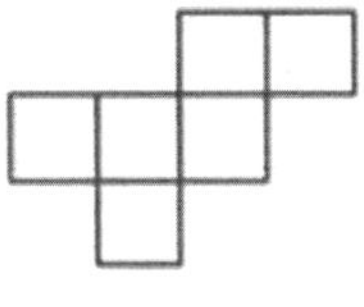

d.
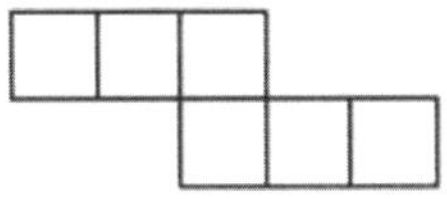

60. Identify the cross-section polygon formed by a plane containing the given points on the cube.

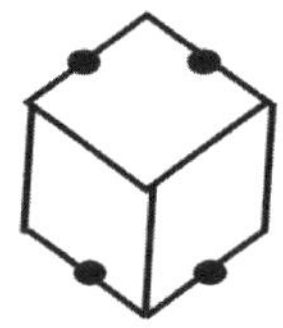

a. Rectangle
b. Trapezoid
c. Pentagon
d. Hexagon

61. Which of these represents the equation of a sphere which is centered in the xyz-space at the point $(1, 0, -2)$ and which has a volume of 36π cubic units?

a. $x^2 + y^2 + z^2 - 2x + 4z = 4$
b. $x^2 + y^2 + z^2 + 2x - 4z = 4$
c. $x^2 + y^2 + z^2 - 2x + 4z = -2$
d. $x^2 + y^2 + z^2 + 2x - 4z = 2$

62. A triangle has vertices $(0, 0, 0)$, $(0, 0, 4)$, and $(0, 3, 0)$ in the xyz-space. In cubic units, what is the difference in the volume of the solid formed by rotating the triangle about the z-axis and the solid formed by rotating the triangle about the y-axis?

a. 0
b. 4π
c. 5π
d. 25

63. If the midpoint of a line segment graphed on the xy-coordinate plane is $(3, -1)$ and the slope of the line segment is -2, which of these is a possible endpoint of the line segment?

a. $(-1,1)$
b. $(0,-5)$
c. $(7,1)$
d. $(5,-5)$

64. The vertices of a polygon are $(2, 3)$, $(8, 1)$, $(6, -5)$, and $(0, -3)$. Which of the following describes the polygon most specifically?

a. Parallelogram
b. Rhombus
c. Rectangle
d. Square

65. What is the radius of the circle defined by the equation $x^2 + y^2 - 10x + 8y + 29 = 0$?

a. $2\sqrt{3}$
b. $2\sqrt{5}$
c. $\sqrt{29}$
d. 12

66. Which of these describes the graph of the equation $2x^2 - 3y^2 - 12x + 6y - 15 = 0$?

a. Circular
b. Elliptical
c. Parabolic
d. Hyperbolic

67. A triangle with vertices $A(-4, 2), B(-1, 3)$, and $C(-5, 7)$ is reflected across $y = x + 2$ to give $\Delta A'B'C'$, which is subsequently reflected across the y-axis to give $\Delta A''B''C''$. Which of these statements is true?

a. A 90° rotation of ΔABC about (−2,0) gives ΔA″B″C″.
b. A reflection of ΔABC about the x-axis gives ΔA″B″C″.
c. A 270° rotation of ΔABC about (0,2) gives ΔA″B″C″.
d. A translation of ΔABC two units down gives ΔA″B″C″.

68. For which of these does a rotation of 120° about the center of the polygon map the polygon onto itself?

a. Square
b. Regular hexagon
c. Regular octagon
d. Regular decagon

69. Line segment $\overline{PQ}$ has endpoints (a, b) and (c, b). If $\overline{P'Q'}$ is the translation of $\overline{PQ}$ along a diagonal line such that P' is located at point (c, d), what is the area of quadrilateral $PP'Q'Q$?

a. $|a - c| \times |b - d|$
b. $|a - b| \times |c - d|$
c. $|a - d| \times |b - c|$
d. $(a - c)^2$

70. Which of these tables properly displays the measures of central tendency which can be used for nominal, interval, and ordinal data?

a.

	Mean	Median	Mode
Nominal			x
Interval	x	x	x
Ordinal		x	x

b.

	Mean	Median	Mode
Nominal			x
Interval	x	x	x
Ordinal	x	x	x

c.

	Mean	Median	Mode
Nominal	x	x	x
Interval	x	x	x
Ordinal	x	x	x

d.

	Mean	Median	Mode
Nominal			x
Interval	x	x	
Ordinal	x	x	x

71. Which of these would best illustrate change over time?

a. Pie chart
b. Line graph
c. Box-and-whisker plot
d. Venn diagram

Use the following data to answer questions 72-74:

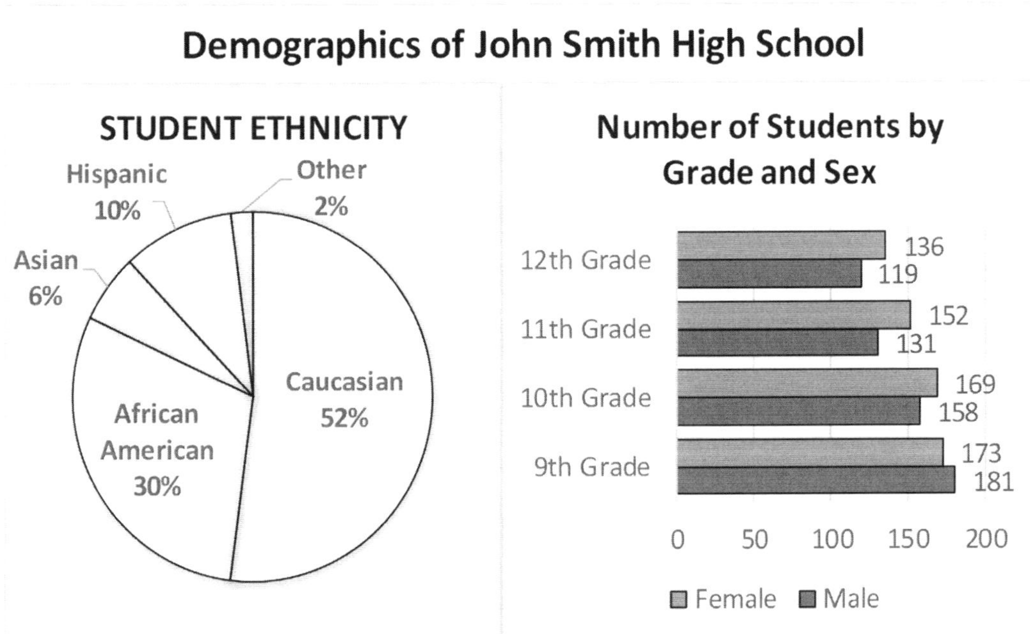

72. Which of these is the greatest quantity?

a. The average number of male students per grade in the 11th and 12th grades
b. The number of Hispanic students at the school
c. The difference in the number of male and female students at the school
d. The difference in the number of 9th and 12th grade students at the school

73. Compare the two quantities.

Quantity A	**Quantity B**
The percentage of Caucasian students	The percentage of female students, rounded to the nearest whole number

a. Quantity A is greater.
b. Quantity B is greater.
c. The two quantities are the same.
d. The relationship cannot be determined from the given information.

74. An eleventh grader is chosen at random to represent the school at a conference. What is the approximate probability that the student is male?

a. 0.03
b. 0.11
c. 0.22
d. 0.46

The box-and-whisker plot displays student test scores by class period. Use the data to answer questions 75 and 76:

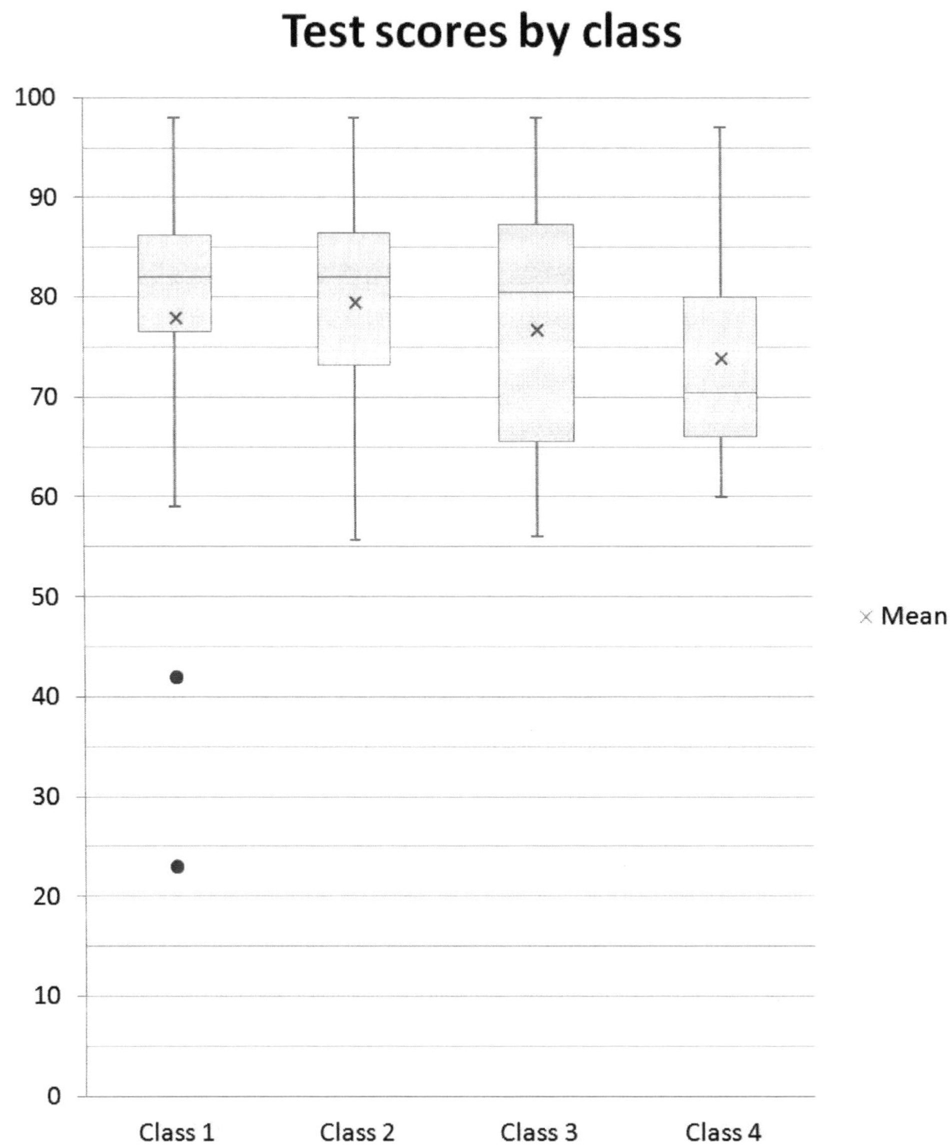

75. Which class has the greatest range of test scores?

a. Class 1
b. Class 2
c. Class 3
d. Class 4

76. What is the probability that a student chosen at random from class 2 made above a 73 on this test?

a. 0.25
b. 0.5
c. 0.6
d. 0.75

Use the information below to answer questions 77 and 78:

Each day for 100 days, a student tossed a single misshapen coin three times in succession and recorded the number of times the coin landed on heads. The results of his experiment are shown below.

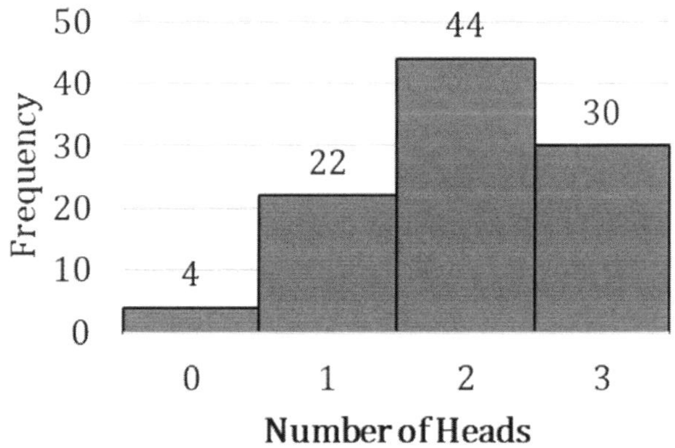

77. Given these experimental data, which of these approximates P(heads) for a single flip of this coin.

a. 0.22
b. 0.5
c. 0.67
d. 0.74

78. Which of these shows the graphs of the probability distributions from ten flips of this misshapen coin and ten flips of a fair coin?

a.

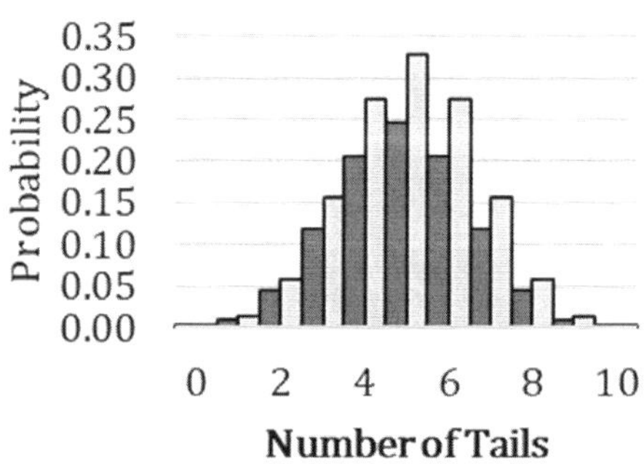

c.

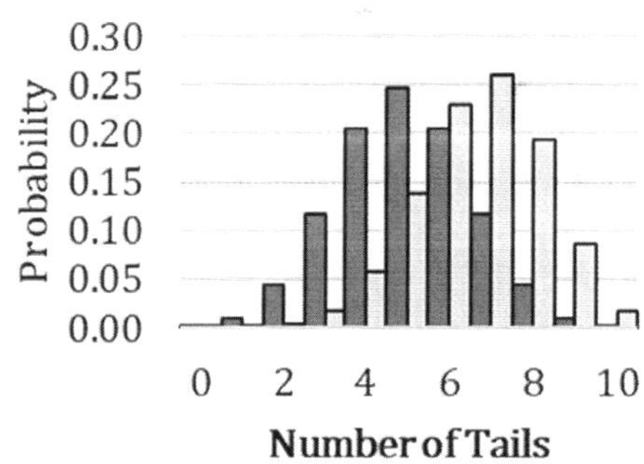

b.

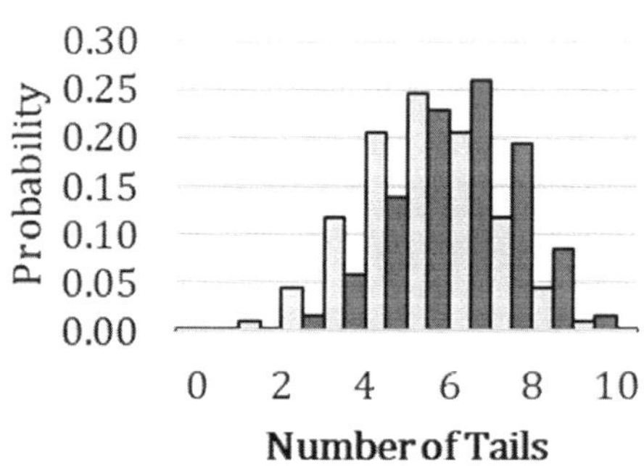

d.

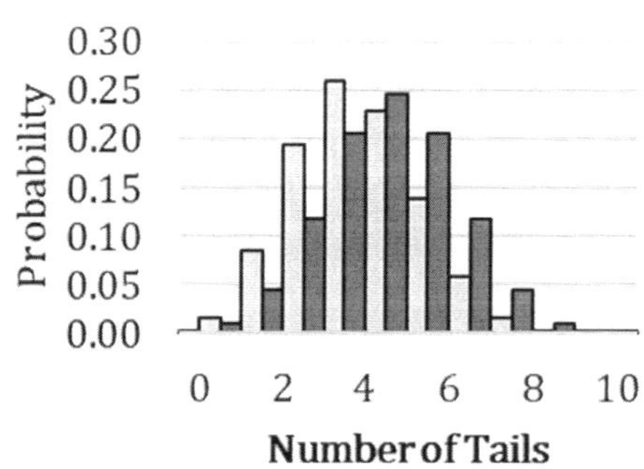

79. Attending a summer camp are 12 six-year-olds, 15 seven-year-olds, 14 eight-year-olds, 12 nine-year-olds, and 10 ten-year-olds. If a camper is randomly selected to participate in a special event, what is the probability that he or she is at least eight years old?

a. $\frac{2}{9}$
b. $\frac{22}{63}$
c. $\frac{4}{7}$
d. $\frac{3}{7}$

80. A small company is divided into three departments as shown. Two individuals are chosen at random to attend a conference. What is the approximate probability that two women from the same department will be chosen?

	Department 1	Department 2	Department 3
Women	12	28	16
Men	18	14	15

a. 8.6%
b. 10.7%
c. 11.2%
d. 13.8%

Answer Key and Explanations

1. C: One strategy is to draw polygons with fewer sides and look for a pattern in the number of the polygons' diagonals.

Polygon	Sides	Diagonals	Δ Diagonals
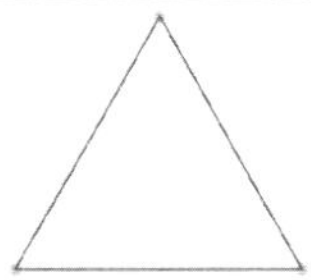	3	0	-
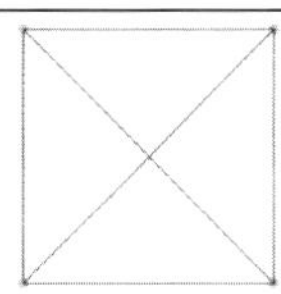	4	2	2
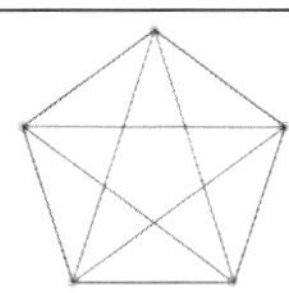	5	5	3
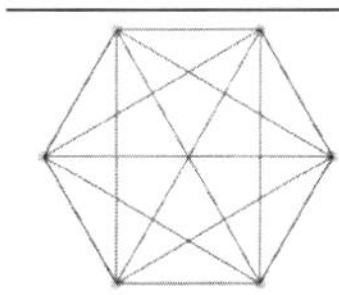	6	9	4

A quadrilateral has two more diagonals than a triangle, a pentagon has three more diagonals than a quadrilateral, and a hexagon has four more diagonals than a pentagon. Continue this pattern to find that a dodecagon has 54 diagonals.

2. B: The problem does not give any information about the size of the bracelet or the spacing between any of the charms. Nevertheless, creating a simple illustration which shows the order of the charms will help when approaching this problem. For example, the circle below represents the bracelet, and the dotted line between A and B represents the clasp. On the right, the line shows the stretched-out bracelet and possible positions of charms C, D, and E based on the parameters.

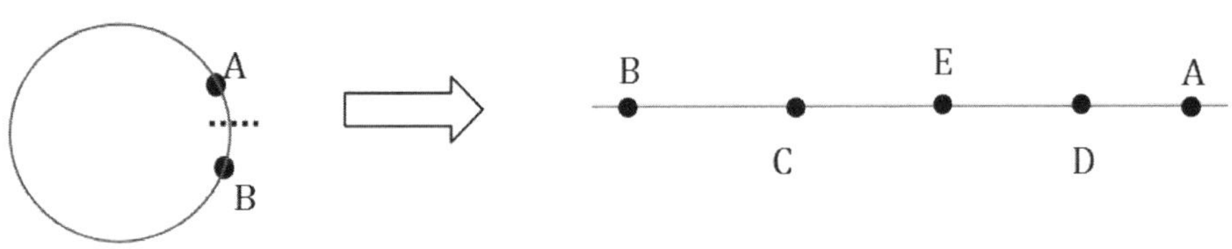

From the drawing above, it appears that statement I is true, but it is not necessarily so. The alternative drawing below also shows the charms ordered correctly, but the distance between B and E is now less than that between D and A.

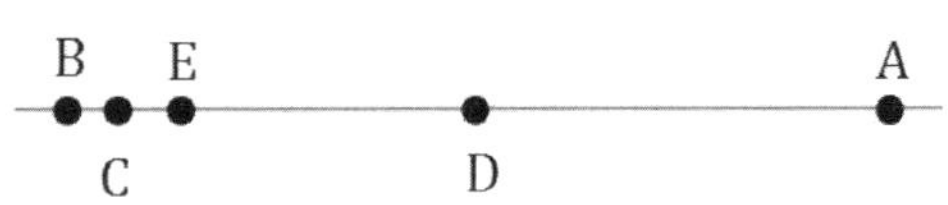

Statement II must be true: charm E must lie between B and D. Statement III must also be true: the distance between charms E and D must be less than that between C and A, which includes charms E and D in the space between them.

3. B: The population is approximately 36,000, so one quarter of the population consists of about 9,000 individuals under age 35. A third of 9,000 is 3,000, the approximate number of students in grades K-12. Since there are thirteen grades, there are about 230 students in each grade. So, the number of fourth graders is between 200 and 300.

4. A: Calculate the final sales price of the rug at each store. Please note that the explanation below uses 1.08 instead of 0.08 for tax in order to avoid having to perform addition later. If 0.08 were to be used, only the amount of tax charged would result instead of the total cost of the product with tax included. Thus, 1.08 is used to make sure 108% of the product price is calculated.

$$1.08(0.7 \times \$296) = \$223.78 \text{ at Store A}$$
$$1.08(\$220 - \$10) = \$226.80 \text{ at Store B}$$
$$\$198 + \$35 = \$233 \text{ at Store C}$$

Therefore, the stores in order of lowest to highest prices are Store A, Store B, Store C.

5. C: The expression representing the monthly charge for Company A is $\$25 + \$0.05m$, where m is the time in minutes spent talking on the phone. Set this expression equal to the monthly charge for Company B, which is $50. Solve for m to find the number of minutes for which the two companies charge the same amount:

$$\$25 + \$0.05m = \$50$$
$$\$0.05m = \$25$$
$$m = 500$$

Notice that the answer choices are given in hours, not in minutes. Since there are 60 minutes in an hour, $m = \frac{500}{60}$ hours $= 8\frac{1}{3}$ hours. $\frac{1}{3}$ of an hour is twenty minutes, so $m = 8$ hours and 20 minutes.

6. C: When the dress is marked down by 20%, the cost of the dress is 80% of its original price. Since a percentage can be written as a fraction by placing the percentage over 100, the reduced price of the dress can be written as $\frac{80}{100}x$, or $\frac{4}{5}x$, where x is the original price. When discounted an extra 25%, the dress costs 75% of the reduced price. This results in the expression $\frac{75}{100}\left(\frac{4}{5}x\right)$, which can be simplified to $\frac{3}{4}\left(\frac{4}{5}x\right)$, or $\frac{3}{5}x$. So the final price of the dress is three-fifths of the original price.

7. D: Since there are 100 cm in a meter, on a 1:100 scale drawing, each centimeter represents one meter. Therefore, an area of one square centimeter on the drawing represents one square meter in actuality. Since the area of the room in the scale drawing is 30 cm^2, the room's actual area is 30 m^2.

Another way to determine the area of the room is to write and solve an equation, such as this one: $\frac{l}{100} \times \frac{w}{100} = 30 \text{ cm}^2$, where l and w are the dimensions of the actual room. So, $\frac{lw}{10000} = 30 \text{ cm}^2$, which means Area $= 300{,}000 \text{ cm}^2$.

Convert cm^2 to m^2: $300{,}000 \text{ cm}^2 \times \frac{1 \text{ m}}{100 \text{ cm}} \times \frac{1 \text{ m}}{100 \text{ cm}} = 30 \text{ m}^2$.

8. C: Since the ratio of wages and benefits to other costs is 2:3, the amount of money spent on wages and benefits is $\frac{2}{(2+3)} = \frac{2}{5}$ of the business's total expenditure. $\left(\frac{2}{5}\right) \times \$130{,}000 = \$52{,}000$.

9. B: Since rate in mph $= \frac{\text{distance in miles}}{\text{time in hours}}$, Zeke's driving speed on the way to Atlanta and home from Atlanta in mph can be expressed as $d/3$ and $d/2$, respectively, when $d =$ distance between Zeke's house and his destination. Since Zeke drove 20 mph faster on his way home, $\frac{d}{2} - \frac{d}{3} = 20$.

$$6\left(\frac{d}{2} - \frac{d}{3}\right) = (20)6$$
$$3d - 2d = 120$$
$$d = 120$$

Since the distance between Zeke's house and the store in Atlanta is 120 miles, Zeke drove a total distance of 240 miles in five hours. Therefore, his average speed was $\frac{240 \text{ miles}}{5 \text{ hours}} = 48$ mph.

10. B: When $y = x^3$, $x = \sqrt[3]{y}$. Similarly, when $y = e^x$, $x = \ln y$ for $y > 0$. On the other hand, when $y = x + a$, $x = y - a$; when $y = 1/x$, $x = 1/y$ for $x, y \neq 0$; and when $y = \sin x$, $x = \sin^{-1} y$.

11. B: Deductive reasoning moves from one or more general statements to a specific, while inductive reasoning makes a general conclusion based on a series of specific instances or observations. Whenever the premises used in deductive reasoning are true, the conclusion drawn is necessarily true. In inductive reasoning, it is possible for the premises to be true and the conclusion to be false since there may exist an exception to the general conclusion drawn from the observations made.

12. A: The first argument's reasoning is valid, and since its premises are true, the argument is also sound. The second argument's reasoning is invalid; that the premises are true is irrelevant. (For example, consider the true premises "all cats are mammals" and "all dogs are mammals;" it cannot be logically concluded that all dogs are cats.) The third argument's reasoning is valid, but since one of its premises is false, the argument is not sound.

13. D: The symbol $\wedge$ is the logical conjunction symbol. In order for statement $(p \wedge q)$ to be true, both statements p and q must be true. The $\neg$ symbol means "not," so if $(p \wedge q)$ is true, then $\neg(p \wedge q)$ is false, and if $(p \wedge q)$ is false, then $\neg(p \wedge q)$ is true. The statement $q \leftrightarrow \neg(p \wedge q)$ is true when the value of q is the same as the value of $\neg(p \wedge q)$.

p	q	$(p \wedge q)$	$\neg(p \wedge q)$	$q \leftrightarrow \neg(p \wedge q)$
T	T	T	F	F
T	F	F	T	F
F	T	F	T	T
F	F	F	T	F

14. C: The logical representation $p \rightarrow q$ means that p implies q. In other words, if p, then q. Unlike the contrapositive (Choice C), neither the converse (choice A) nor the inverse (choice B) is necessarily true. For example, consider this statement: all cats are mammals. This can be written as an if/then statement: if an animal is a cat, then the animal is a mammal. The converse would read, "If an animal is a mammal, then the animal is a cat;" of course, this is not necessarily true since there are many mammals other than cats. The inverse statement, "If an animal is not a cat, then the animal is not a mammal," is false. The contrapositive, "If an animal is not a mammal, then the animal is not a cat" is true since there are no cats which are not mammals.

15. D: For the logical disjunction "or," the output value is true if either or both input values are true, else it is false. For the logical conjunction "and," the output value is true only if both input values are true. "Not A" is true when A is false and is false when A is true.

X	Y	Z	not Y	not Z	not Y or not Z	X and (not Y or not Z)
0	0	0	1	1	1	0
0	0	1	1	0	1	0
0	1	0	0	1	1	0
0	1	1	0	0	0	0
1	0	0	1	1	1	1
1	0	1	1	0	1	1
1	1	0	0	1	1	1
1	1	1	0	0	0	0

16. B: The notation $\mathbb{P} \subseteq \mathbb{N} \subseteq \mathbb{Z} \subseteq \mathbb{Q} \subseteq \mathbb{R} \subseteq \mathbb{C}$ means that the set of prime numbers is a subset of the set natural numbers, which is a subset of the set of integers, which is a subset of the set of rational numbers, which is a subset of the set real numbers, which is a subset of the set of complex numbers.

17. A: The set of whole numbers, $\{0, 1, 2, 3, \dots\}$, does not contain the number -4. Since -4 is an integer, it is also a rational number and a real number.

18. B: The table below shows the intersections of each set with each of the other sets.

Set	{2,4,6,8,10,12,...}	{1,2,3,4,6,12}	{1,2,4,9}
{2,4,6,8,10,12,... }	{2,4,6,8,10,12,...}	{2,4,6,12}	{2,4}
{1,2,3,4,6,12}	{2,4,6,12}	{1,2,3,4,6,12}	{1,2,4}
{1,2,4,9}	{2,4}	{1,2,4}	{1,2,4,9}

Notice that {2,4} is a subset of {2,4,6,12} and {1,2,4}. So, the intersection of {1,2,4,9} and the even integers is a subset of the intersection of the even integers and the factors of twelve, and the intersection of the set of even integers and {1,2,4,9} is a subset of the intersection of {1,2,4,9} and the factors of twelve. So, while it is not possible to determine which set is A and which is B, set C must be the set of factors of twelve: {1,2,3,4,6,12}.

19. C: If x is a prime number and that the greatest common factor of x and y is greater than 1, the greatest common factor of x and y must be x. The least common multiple of two numbers is equal to the product of those numbers divided by their greatest common factor. So, the least common multiple of x and y is $\frac{xy}{x} = y$. Therefore, the values in the two columns are the same.

20. C: Use the table of values to first write equations for $f(x)$ and $g(x)$: $f(x) = 2x^2$ and $g(x) = 2x + 5$. Then, use those equations to find $f(g(-4))$. Start by finding $g(-4)$.

$$g(-4) = 2(-4) + 5 = -8 + 5 = -3$$

From here, substitute $g(-4)$ into the function $f(x)$ to find $f(g(-4))$. Since $g(-4) = -3$, plug in -3 anywhere an x is found in $f(x)$.

$$f(-3) = 2(-3)^2 = 2(9) = 18$$

So, $f(g(-4)) = 18$.

21. A: Substitute and simplify:

$$\begin{aligned} [g \circ f\,]x &= g\big(f(x)\big) \\ &= g(2x + 4) \\ &= (2x + 4)^2 - 3(2x + 4) + 2 \\ &= 4x^2 + 16x + 16 - 6x - 12 + 2 \\ &= 4x^2 + 10x + 6 \end{aligned}$$

22. D: By definition, when $f(x)$ and $g(x)$ are inverse functions, $f(g(x)) = g(f(x)) = x$. So, $f(g(4)) = 4$.

23. B: To find the inverse of an equation, solve for x in terms of y; then, exchange the variables x and y. Or, to determine if two functions $f(x)$ and $g(x)$ are inverses, find $f(g(x))$ and $g(f(x))$; if both results are x, then $f(x)$ and $g(x)$ are inverse functions.

For example, to find the inverse of $y = x + 6$, rewrite the equation $x = y + 6$ and solve for y. Since $y = x - 6$, the two given equations given in Choice A are inverses. Likewise, to find the inverse of $y = \frac{2x+3}{x-1}$, rewrite the equation as $x = \frac{2y+3}{y-1}$ and solve for y:

$$\begin{aligned} xy - x &= 2y + 3 \\ xy - 2y &= x + 3 \\ y(x - 2) &= x + 3 \\ y &= \frac{x + 3}{x - 2} \end{aligned}$$

The two equations given in Choice C are inverses.

Choice B: $y = 2(2x + 3) - 3 = 4x + 6$. The two given equations are **NOT** inverses.

Choice D: $y = \frac{(2x+1)-1}{2} = \frac{2x}{2} = x$ and $y = 2\left(\frac{x-1}{2}\right) + 1 = x - 1 + 1 = x$, so the two given equations are inverses.

24. A: Below is the graph of $g(x)$.

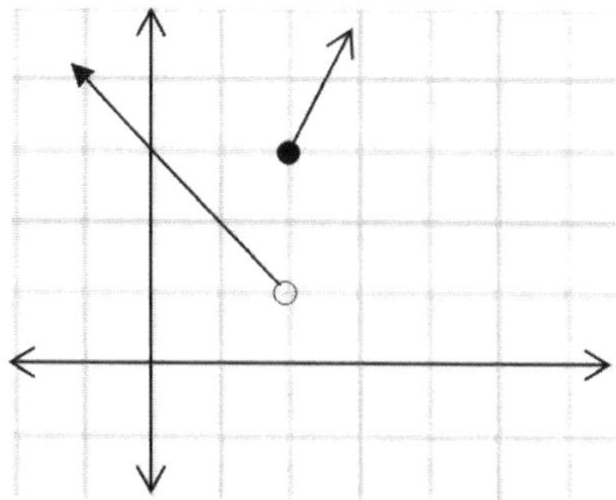

Statement II is true: the graph is indeed discontinuous at $x = 2$. Since $g(3) = 2(3) - 1 = 5$, Statement I is false, and since the range is $y > 1$, Statement III is also false.

25. B: If $y = a(x + b)(x + c)^2$, the degree of the polynomial is 3. Since the degree of the polynomial is odd and the leading coefficient is positive $(a > 0)$, the end behavior of the graph goes to (∞, ∞) and $(-\infty, -\infty)$. Therefore, neither Choice A nor Choice C can be a graph of $y = a(x + b)(x + c)^2$. The maximum number of critical points in the graph is at most one less than the degree of the polynomial, so Choice D, cannot be the graph of the function. Choice B displays the correct end behavior and has two bumps, so it is a possible graph of $y = a(x + b)(x + c)^2$.

26. B: $5n + 3s \geq 300$ where n is the number of non-student tickets which must be sold and s is the number of student tickets which must be sold. The intercepts of this linear inequality are $n = 60$ and $s = 100$. The solid line through the two intercepts represents the minimum number of each type of ticket which must be sold in order to offset production costs. All points above the line represent sales which result in a profit for the school.

27. D: The vertex form of a quadratic equation is $y = a(x - h)^2 + k$, where $x = h$ is the parabola's axis of symmetry and (h, k) is the parabola's vertex. The vertex of the graph is (-1,3), so the equation can be written as $y = a(x + 1)^2 + 3$. The parabola passes through point (1,1), so $1 = a(1 + 1)^2 + 3$. Solve for a:

$$\begin{aligned} 1 &= a(1+1)^2 + 3 \\ 1 &= a(2)^2 + 3 \\ 1 &= 4a + 3 \\ -2 &= 4a \\ -\frac{1}{2} &= a \end{aligned}$$

So, the vertex form of the parabola is $y = -\frac{1}{2}(x+1)^2 + 3$. Write the equation in the form $y = ax^2 + bx + c$.

$$\begin{aligned} y &= -\frac{1}{2}(x+1)^2 + 3 \\ &= -\frac{1}{2}(x^2 + 2x + 1) + 3 \\ &= -\frac{1}{2}x^2 - x - \frac{1}{2} + 3 \\ &= -\frac{1}{2}x^2 - x + \frac{5}{2} \end{aligned}$$

28. C: In order to eliminate x by linear combination, multiply the top equation by 2 and the bottom equation by -3 so that the coefficients of the x-terms will be additive inverses.

$$\begin{aligned} 2(3x + 4y) &= (2)2 \\ 6x + 8y &= 4 \end{aligned} \qquad \begin{aligned} -3(2x + 6y) &= (-2)(-3) \\ -6x - 18y &= 6 \end{aligned}$$

Then, add the two equations and solve for y.

$$\begin{array}{rrrcr} & 6x & +\ 8y & = & 4 \\ + & -6x & -18y & = & 6 \\ \hline & & -10y & = & 10 \\ & & y & = & -1 \end{array}$$

Substitute -1 for y in either of the given equations and solve for x.

$$\begin{aligned} 3x + 4(-1) &= 2 \\ 3x - 4 &= 2 \\ 3x &= 6 \\ x &= 2 \end{aligned}$$

The solution to the system of equations is $(2, -1)$.

29. C: The graph below shows that the lines are parallel and that the shaded regions do not overlap. There is no solution to the set of inequalities given in Choice C.

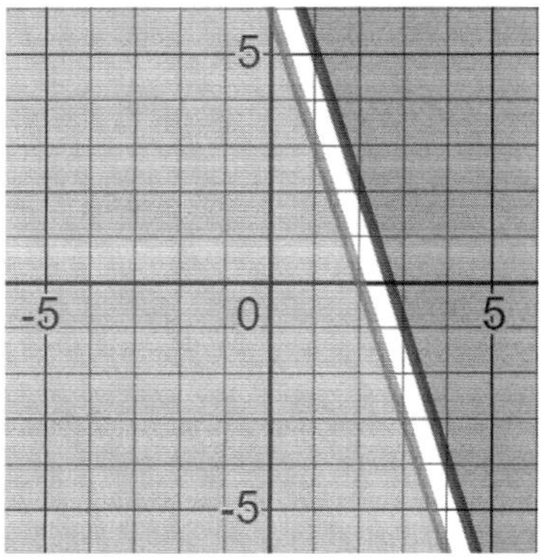

$$\begin{aligned} 6x + 2y &\le 12 \\ 2y &\le -6x + 12 \\ y &\le -3x + 6 \end{aligned}$$

$$\begin{aligned} 3x &\ge 8 - y \\ y &\ge -3x + 8 \end{aligned}$$

As in Choice C, the two lines given in Choice A are parallel; however, the shading overlaps between the lines, so that region represents the solution to the system of inequalities.

The shaded regions for the two lines in Choice B do not overlap except at the boundary, but since the boundary is same, the solution to the system of inequalities is the line $y = -2x + 6$.

Choice D contains a set of inequalities which have intersecting shaded regions; the intersection represents the solution to the system of inequalities.

30. B: Multiply the second equation by 2 and combine it with the first equation to eliminate y.

$$\begin{array}{rrrrcr} & 2x & -4y & +1z & = & 10 \\ + & -6x & +4y & -8z & = & -14 \\ \hline & -4x & & -7z & = & -4 \end{array}$$

Multiply the third equation by -2 and combine it with the original second equation to eliminate y.

$$\begin{array}{rrrrcr} & -3x & +2y & -4z & = & -7 \\ + & -2x & -2y & +6z & = & 2 \\ \hline & -5x & & +2z & = & -5 \end{array}$$

Multiply the equation from step one by 5 and the equation from step two by -4 and combine to eliminate x.

$$\begin{array}{rrrcr} & -20x & -35z & = & -20 \\ + & 20x & -\ 8z & = & 20 \\ \hline & & -43z & = & 0 \\ & & z & = & 0 \end{array}$$

Substitute 0 for z in the equation from step 2 to find x.

$$\begin{aligned} -5x + 2(0) &= -5 \\ -5x &= -5 \\ x &= 1 \end{aligned}$$

Substitute 0 for z and 1 for x into the first original equation to find y.

$$\begin{aligned} 2(1) - 4y + (0) &= 10 \\ 2 - 4y &= 10 \\ -4y &= 8 \\ y &= -2 \end{aligned}$$

31. A: First, set the equation equal to zero, then factor it.

$$\begin{aligned} 3x^3y^2 - 45x^2y &= 15x^3y - 9x^2y^2 \\ 3x^3y^2 - 15x^3y + 9x^2y^2 - 45x^2y &= 0 \\ 3x^2y(xy - 5x + 3y - 15) &= 0 \\ 3x^2y[x(y - 5) + 3(y - 5)] &= 0 \\ 3x^2y[(y - 5)(x + 3)] &= 0 \end{aligned}$$

Use the zero product property to find the solutions.

$$\begin{array}{ccc} 3x^2y = 0 & y - 5 = 0 & x + 3 = 0 \\ x = 0 & y = 5 & x = -3 \\ y = 0 & & \end{array}$$

So, the solutions are $x = \{0, -3\}$ and $y = \{0,5\}$.

32. D: The degree of $f(x)$ is 1, the degree of $g(x)$ is 2, and the degree of $h(x)$ is 3. The leading coefficient for each function is 2. Functions $f(x)$ and $h(x)$ have exactly one real zero ($x = 1$), while $g(x)$ has two real zeros ($x = \pm 1$):

$f(x) = 0$	$g(x) = 0$	$h(x) = 0$
$2x - 2 = 0$	$2x^2 - 2 = 0$	$2x^3 - 2 = 0$
$2x = 2$	$2x^2 = 2$	$2x^3 = 2$
$x = 1$	$x^2 = 1$	$x^3 = 1$
	$x = 1;\ x = -1$	$x = 1$

33. B: The path of a bullet is a parabola, which is the graph of a quadratic function. The path of a sound wave can be modeled by a sine or cosine function. The distance an object travels over time given a constant rate is a linear relationship, while radioactive decay is modeled by an exponential function.

34. B: First, use the properties of logarithms to solve for y.

$$\begin{aligned} 2\log_4 y + \log_4 16 &= 3 \\ \log_4 y^2 + \log_4 16 &= 3 \\ \log_4 16y^2 &= 3 \\ 16y^2 &= 4^3 \\ 16y^2 &= 64 \\ y^2 &= 4 \\ y &= \pm 2 \end{aligned}$$

Finally, since y is positive, substitute 2 for y in the expression $\log_y 256$ and simplify. $\log_2 256 = 8$ since $2^8 = 256$.

35. B: First, apply the laws of exponents to simplify the expression on the left. Then, add the two fractions:

$$\begin{aligned} \frac{(x^2y)(2xy^{-2})^3}{16x^5y^2} + \frac{3}{xy} &= \frac{(x^2y)(8x^3y^{-6})}{16x^5y^2} + \frac{3}{xy}\frac{8x^5y^{-5}}{16x^5y^2} + \frac{3}{xy} \\ &= \frac{1}{2y^7} + \frac{3}{xy} \\ &= \frac{1}{2y^7} \times \frac{x}{x} + \frac{3}{xy} \times \frac{2y^6}{2y^6} \\ &= \frac{x}{2xy^7} + \frac{6y^6}{2xy^7} \\ &= \frac{x + 6y^6}{2xy^7} \end{aligned}$$

36. C: If $f(x) = 10^x$ and $f(x) = 5$, then $5 = 10^x$. Since $\log_{10}x$ is the inverse of 10^x, $\log_{10}5 = \log_{10}(10^x) = x$. Therefore, $0.7 \approx x$.

37. C: The x-intercept is the point at which $f(x) = 0$. When $0 = \log_b x$, $b^0 = x$; since $b^0 = 1$, the x-intercept of $f(x) = \log_b x$ is always 1. If $f(x) = \log_b x$ and $x = b$, then $f(x) = \log_b b$, which is, by definition, 1. ($b^1 = b$.) If $g(x) = b^x$, then $f(x)$ and $g(x)$ are inverse functions and are therefore symmetric with respect to $y = x$. The statement choice C is not necessarily true since $x < 1$ includes numbers less than or equal to zero, the values for which the function is undefined. The statement $f(x) < 0$ is true only for x values between 0 and 1 $(0 < x < 1)$.

38. D: Use a Venn diagram to help organize the given information. Start by filling in the space where the three circles intersect: Jenny tutored three students in all three areas. Use that information to fill in the spaces where two circles intersect: for example, she tutored four students in chemistry and for the ACT, and three of those were students she tutored in all three areas, so one student was tutored in chemistry and for the ACT but not for math. Once the diagram is completed, add the number of students who were tutored in all areas to the number of students tutored in only two of the three areas to the number of students tutored in only one area. The total number of students tutored was $3 + 2 + 2 + 1 + 3 + 2 + 1 = 14$.

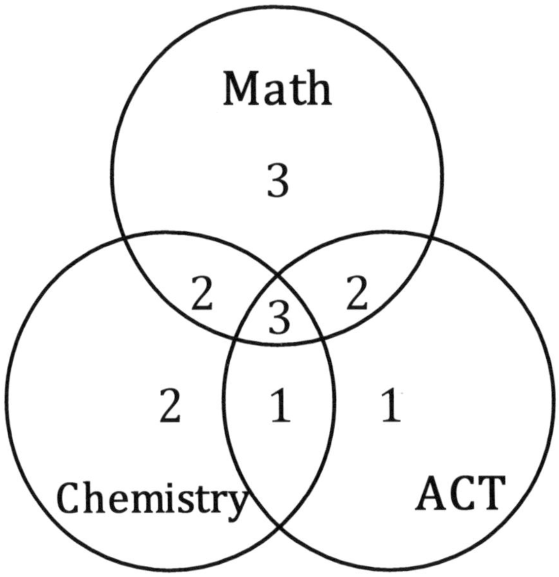

39. C: The graph shown is the exponential function $y = 2^x$. Notice that the graph passes through $(-2, 0.25)$, $(0,1)$, and $(2,4)$. A quick check of each option demonstrates the fit:

x	x^2	$\sqrt{x}$	2^x	$\log_2 x$
-2	4	undefined in $\mathbb{R}$	0.25	undefined
0	0	0	1	undefined
2	4	$\sqrt{2}$	4	1

40. D: Bacterial growth is exponential. Let x be the number of doubling times and a be the number of bacteria in the colony originally transferred into the broth and y be the number of bacteria in the broth after a doubling times. After 1 hour the population would have doubled three times:

$$a(2^3) = 8 \times 10^6$$
$$8a = 8 \times 10^6$$
$$a = 10^6$$

The equation for determining the number of bacteria is $y = (2^x) \times 10^6$. Since the bacteria double every twenty minutes, they go through three doubling times every hour. So, when the bacteria are allowed to grow for eight hours, they will have gone through 24 doubling times. When $x = 24$, $y = (2^{24}) \times 10^6 = 16777216 \times 10^6$, which is approximately 1.7×10^{13}.

41. C: Since the pH scale is a base–10 logarithmic scale, a difference in pH of 1 indicates a ratio between strengths of 10. So, an acid with a pH of 3 is 100 times stronger than an acid with a pH of 5.

42. C: Test each of the options:

$$-4 \le 2 + 3(x-1) \le 2$$
$$-6 \le 3(x-1) \le 0$$
$$-2 \le x - 1 \le 0$$
$$-1 \le x \le 1$$

$$-2x^2 + 2 \ge x^2 - 1$$
$$-3x^2 \ge -3$$
$$x^2 \le 1$$
$$-1 \le x \le 1$$

$$\frac{11 - |3x|}{7} \ge 2$$
$$11 - |3x| \ge 14$$
$$-|3x| \ge 3$$
$$|3x| \le -1$$
No solution

$$3|2x| + 4 \le 10$$
$$3|2x| \le 6$$
$$|2x| \le 2$$
$$-2 \le 2x \le 2$$
$$-1 \le x \le 1$$

43. D: To solve this equation, start by squaring both sides, then isolate the variable.

$$2 - \sqrt{x} = \sqrt{x - 20}$$
$$\left(2 - \sqrt{x}\right)^2 = \left(\sqrt{x - 20}\right)^2$$
$$\left(2 - \sqrt{x}\right)\left(2 - \sqrt{x}\right) = x - 20$$
$$4 - 4\sqrt{x} + x = x - 20$$
$$-4\sqrt{x} = -24$$
$$\sqrt{x} = 6$$
$$x = 36$$

When solving radical equations, check for extraneous solutions by substituting the found value into the original equation.

$$2 - \sqrt{x} = \sqrt{x - 20}$$

$$2 - \sqrt{36} = \sqrt{36 - 20}$$
$$2 - 6 = \sqrt{16}$$
$$-4 \ne 4$$

Since the solution results in an untrue statement, there is no solution. Alternatively, consider the graphs of the left and right side of the given equation. Notice the graphs $y = 2 - \sqrt{x}$ and $y = \sqrt{x - 20}$ do not intersect, which confirms there is no solution.

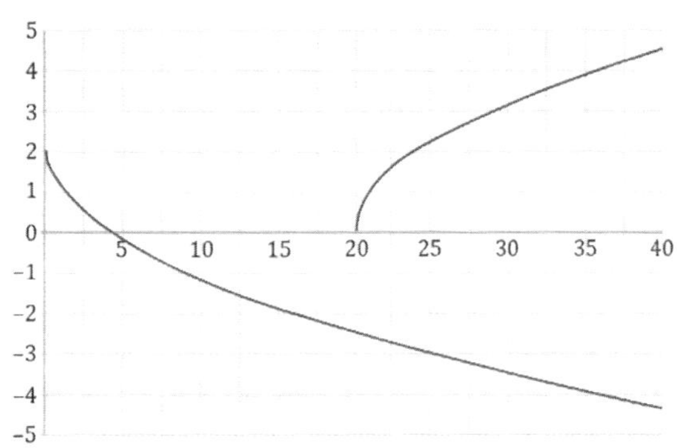

44. B: Notice that choice C cannot be correct since $x \neq 1$. ($x = 1$ results in a zero in the denominator.)

$$\frac{x-2}{x-1} = \frac{x-1}{x+1} + \frac{2}{x-1}$$
$$\frac{x-4}{x-1} = \frac{x-1}{x+1}$$
$$(x+1)(x-4) = (x-1)(x-1)$$
$$x^2 - 3x - 4 = x^2 - 2x + 1$$
$$-5 = x$$

45. C: The first function shifts the graph of $y = \frac{1}{x}$ to the right one unit and up one unit. The domain and range of $y = \frac{1}{x}$ are $\{x: x \neq 0\}$ and $\{y: y \neq 0\}$, so the domain and range of $y = \frac{1}{x-1} + 1$ are $\{x: x \neq 1\}$ and $\{y: y \neq 1\}$. The element 1 is not in its domain.

The second function inverts the graph of $y = \sqrt{x}$ and shifts it to the left two units and down one unit. The domain and range of $y = \sqrt{x}$ are $\{x: x \geq 0\}$ and $\{y: y \geq 0\}$, so the domain and range of $y = -\sqrt{x+2} - 1$ are $\{x: x \geq -2\}$ and $\{y: y \leq -1\}$. The range does not contain the element 2.

The third function shifts the graph of $y = |x|$ to the right one unit and up three units. The domain of $y = |x|$ the set of all real numbers and range is $\{y: y \geq 0\}$, so the domain of $y = |x+2| - 3$ is the set of all real numbers and the range is $\{y: y \geq -3\}$. The domain contains the element 1 and the range contains the element 2.

This is the graph of the fourth function. The domain of this piece-wise function is the set of all real numbers, and the range is $\{y: y < -1\}$. The range does not contain the element 2.

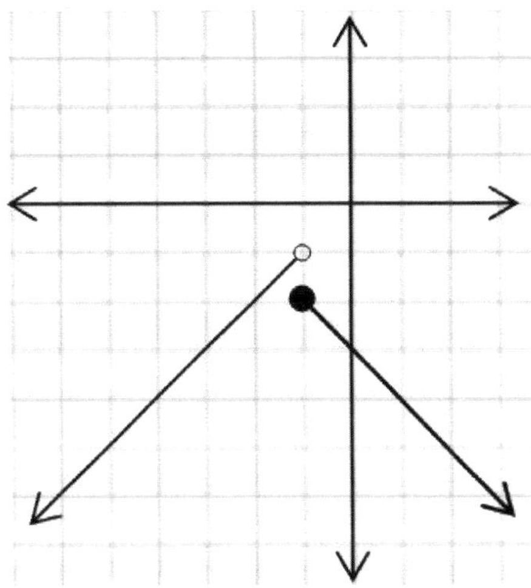

46. B: First, state the exclusions of the domain.

$$x^3 + 2x^2 - x - 2 \neq 0$$
$$(x+2)(x-1)(x+1) \neq 0$$

$$x + 2 \neq 0 \quad x - 1 \neq 0 \quad x + 1 \neq 0$$
$$x \neq -2 \quad x \neq 1 \quad x \neq -1$$

To determine whether there are asymptotes or holes at these values of x, simplify the expression:

$$\frac{x^2 - x - 6}{x^3 + 2x^2 - x - 2} = \frac{(x-3)(x+2)}{(x+2)(x-1)(x+1)} = \frac{x-3}{(x-1)(x+1)}$$

There are asymptotes at $x = 1$ and at $x = -1$ and a hole at $x = 2$. Statement I is false.

To find the x-intercept of $f(x)$, solve $f(x) = 0$. $f(x) = 0$ when the numerator is equal to zero. The numerator equals zero when $x = 2$ and $x = 3$; however, 2 is excluded from the domain of $f(x)$, so the x-intercept is 3. To find the y-intercept of $f(x)$, find $f(0)$.

$$\frac{0^2 - 0 - 6}{0^3 + 2(0)^2 - 0 - 2} = \frac{-6}{-2} = 3$$

The y-intercept is 3. Statement II is true.

47. D: There are many ways Josephine may have applied her knowledge to determine how to approximately measure her medicine using her plastic spoon. The only choice which correctly uses dimensional analysis is choice D: the dosage

$$\approx 25\text{ cc} \times \frac{1\text{ ml}}{1\text{ cc}} \times \frac{1\text{L}}{1000\text{ml}} \times \frac{0.5\text{ gal}}{2\text{L}} \times \frac{16\text{c}}{1\text{ gal}} \times \frac{48\text{t}}{1\text{c}} \times \frac{1\text{ spoonful}}{1\text{t}} \approx \frac{25 \times 16 \times 48}{1000 \times 4} \approx 5$$

48. C: Start by setting up a proportion to solve by cross multiplication: $\frac{1\text{ inch}}{60\text{ feet}} = \frac{10\text{ inches}}{x\text{ feet}}$. When the numbers are cross multiplied, you get $x = 600$ feet. Now we need to convert 600 feet to yards. There are 3 feet in 1 yard, so divide 600 by 3 to find the number of yards between the two points: $600 \div 3 = 200$. Therefore, the two points are 200 yards apart.

49. D: If the distance between the two houses is 10 cm on the map, then the actual distance between the houses is 100 m. To find x, use the Pythagorean Theorem:

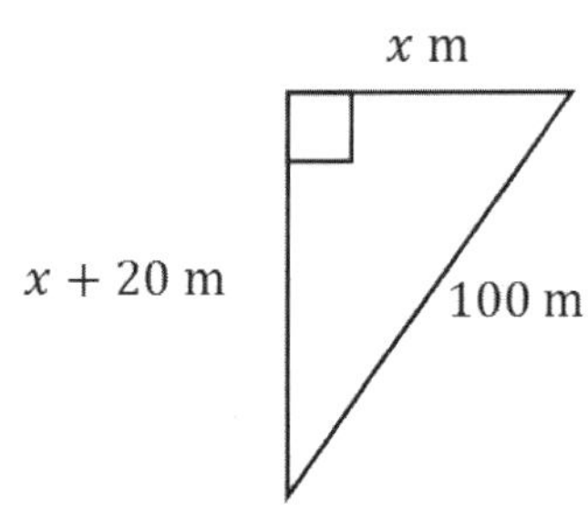

$$\begin{aligned} x^2 + (x+20)^2 &= (100)^2 \\ x^2 + x^2 + 40x + 400 &= 10000 \\ 2x^2 + 40x - 9600 &= 0 \\ 2(x^2 + 20x - 4800) &= 0 \\ 2(x-60)(x+80) &= 0 \end{aligned}$$

$$x = 60 \quad x = -80$$

Since x represents a distance, it cannot equal -80. Since $x = 60$, $x + 20 = 80$. Roxana walks a total of 140 m to get to her friend's house.

50. D: ΔABC is similar to the smaller triangle with which it shares vertex A. $\overline{AB} = (2x - 1) + (x + 7) = 3x + 6$. $AC = 4 + 8 = 12$. Set up a proportion and solve for x:

$$\frac{3x+6}{12} = \frac{2x-1}{4}$$
$$12x + 24 = 24x - 12$$
$$36 = 12x$$
$$3 = x$$

So, $\overline{AB} = 3x + 6 = 3(3) + 6 = 15$.

51. B: Percent error $= \frac{|\text{actual value} - \text{measured value}|}{\text{actual value}} \times 100\%$, and the average percent error is the sum of the percent errors for each trial divided by the number of trials.

	% error Trial 1	% error Trial 2	% error Trial 3	% error Trial 4	Average percent error
Scale 1	0.1%	0.2%	0.2%	0.1%	0.15%
Scale 2	2.06%	2.09%	2.10%	2.08%	2.08%

The percent error for Scale 1 is less than the percent error for Scale 2, so it is more accurate. The more precise scale is Scale 2 because its range of values, 10.210 g − 10.206 g = 0.004 g, is smaller than the Scale 2's range of values, 10.02 g − 9.98 g = 0.04 g.

52. C: If l and w represent the length and width of the enclosed area, its perimeter is equal to $2l + 2w$; since the fence is positioned x feet from the lot's edges on each side, the perimeter of the lot is $2(l + 2x) + 2(w + 2x)$. Since the amount of money saved by fencing the smaller are is $432, and since the fencing material costs $12 per linear foot, 36 fewer feet of material are used to fence around the playground than would have been used to fence around the lot. This can be expressed as the equation:

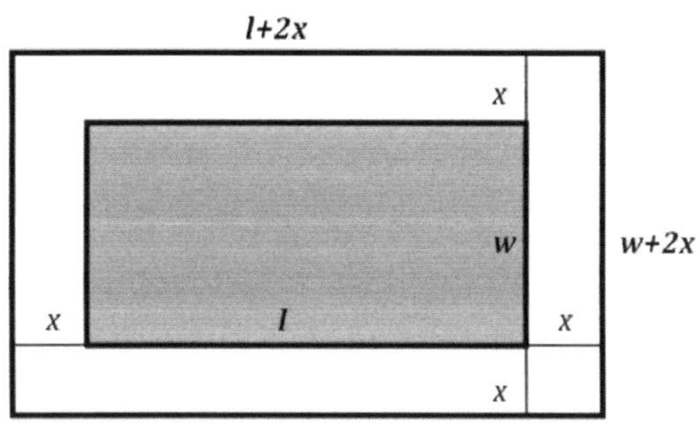

$$2(l + 2x) + 2(w + 2x) - (2l + 2w) = 36$$
$$2l + 4x + 2w + 4x - 2l - 2w = 36$$
$$8x = 36$$
$$x = 4.5 \text{ ft}$$

The difference in the area of the lot and the enclosed space is 141 yd^2, which is the same as 1269 ft^2. So, $(l + 2x)(w + 2x) - lw = 1269$. Substituting 4.5 for x,

$$(l + 9)(w + 9) - lw = 1269$$
$$lw + 9l + 9w + 81 - lw = 1269$$
$$9l + 9w = 1188$$
$$9(l + w) = 1188$$
$$l + w = 132 \text{ ft}$$

Therefore, the perimeter of the enclosed space, $2(l + w)$, is $2(132) = 264$ ft. The cost of 264 ft of fencing is $264 \times \$12 = \$3{,}168$.

53. B: The volume of a square pyramid can be calculated using the formula $V = \frac{Bh}{3}$, where B is the area of the base and h is the height of the pyramid. Therefore, the volume of Natasha's tent is $\frac{x^2h}{3}$. If she were to increase by 1 ft the length of each side of the square base, the tent's volume can be calculated by substituting $x + 1$ for x in the original tent volume formula.

$$\frac{(x+1)^2h}{3} = \frac{(x^2+2x+1)(h)}{3} = \frac{x^2h+2xh+h}{3} = \frac{x^2h}{3} + \frac{2xh+h}{3}$$

Notice this is the volume of Natasha's tent, $\frac{x^2h}{3}$, increased by $\frac{2xh+h}{3}$, or $\frac{h(2x+1)}{3}$. This is how much more interior space the tent would have.

54. A: The area of a circle is πr^2, so the area of a semicircle is $\frac{\pi r^2}{2}$. Illustrated below is a method which can be used to find the area of the shaded region.

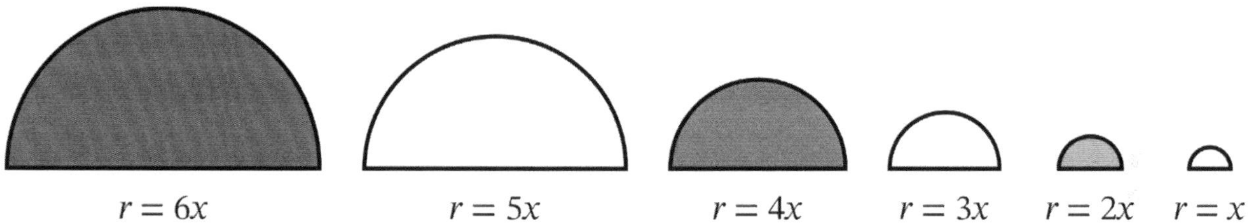

$$A = \frac{36\pi x^2}{2} - \frac{25\pi x^2}{2} + \frac{16\pi x^2}{2} - \frac{9\pi x^2}{2} + \frac{4\pi x^2}{2} - \frac{1\pi x^2}{2}$$
$$A = \frac{(36-25+16-9+4-1)\pi x^2}{2}$$
$$A = \frac{21\pi x^2}{2}$$

55. B: If the touching edges of the trapezoids are extended, they meet at a point on the horizontal. Using this information and the following geometric relationships, solve for x:

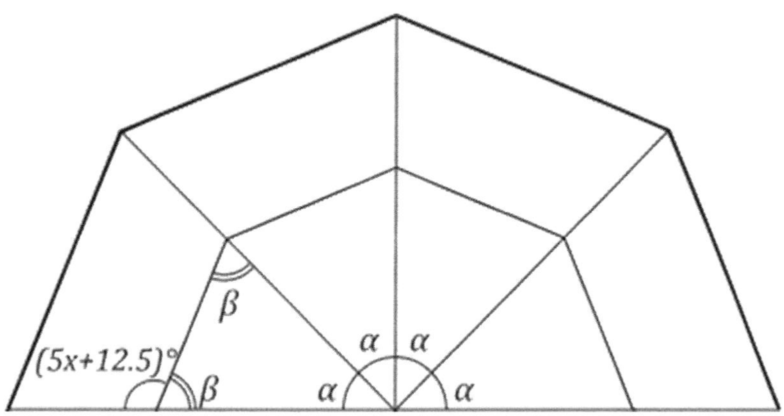

$$\begin{array}{ccc} 4\alpha = 180° & \alpha + 2\beta = 180° & (5x + 12.5)° + \beta = 180° \\ \alpha = 45° & \beta = \dfrac{135°}{2} & (5x + 12.5)° = 112.5° \\ & \beta = 67.5° & 5x = 100 \\ & & x = 20 \end{array}$$

56. D: Let b represent the base of the triangle. The height h of the triangle is the altitude drawn from the vertex opposite of b to side b.

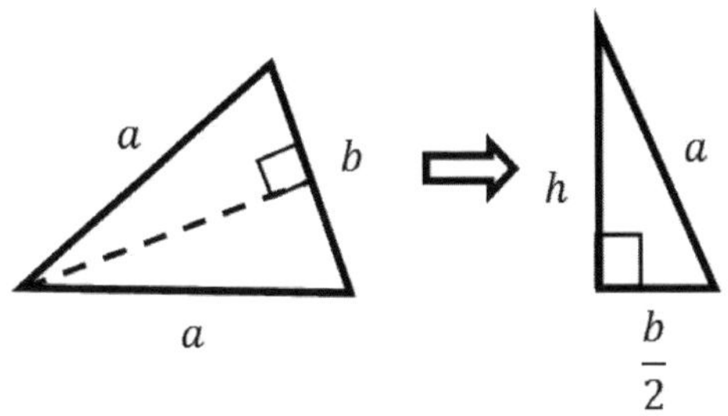

The height of the triangle can be found in terms of a and b by using the Pythagorean theorem:

$$h^2 + \left(\frac{b}{2}\right)^2 = a^2$$

$$h = \sqrt{a^2 - \frac{b^2}{4}}$$

$$= \sqrt{\frac{4a^2 - b^2}{4}}$$

$$= \frac{\sqrt{4a^2 - b^2}}{2}$$

The area of a triangle is $A = \frac{1}{2}bh, so\ A = \frac{1}{2}b\left(\frac{\sqrt{4a^2-b^2}}{2}\right) = \frac{b\sqrt{4a^2-b^2}}{4}$.

57. B: Since ΔADC is a right triangle with legs measuring 5 and 12, its hypotenuse measures 13. (5-12-13 is a Pythagorean triple.)

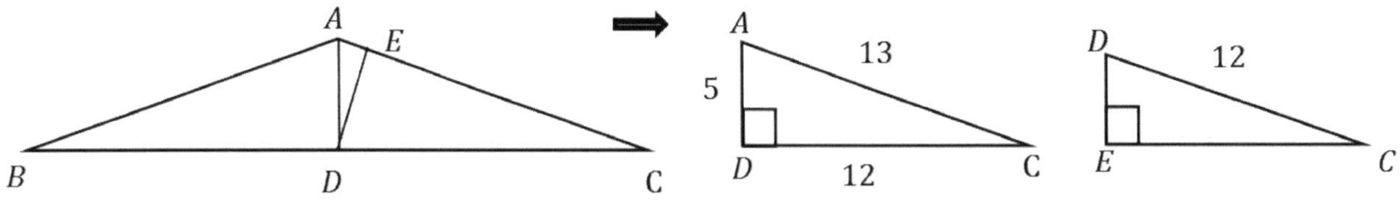

ΔADC and ΔDEC are both right triangles which share vertex C. By the AA similarity theorem $\Delta ADC \sim \Delta DEC$. Therefore, a proportion can be written and solved to find DE.

$$\frac{5}{DE} = \frac{13}{12}$$

$$DE = 4.6$$

58. C: The center of the sphere is shared by the center of the cube, and each of the corners of the cube touches the surface of the sphere. Therefore, the diameter of the sphere is the line which passes through the center of the cube and connects one corner of the cube to the opposite corner on the opposite face. Notice in the illustration below that the diameter d of the sphere can be represented as the hypotenuse of a right triangle with a short leg measuring 4 units. (Since the volume of the cube is 64 cubic units, each of its sides measures $\sqrt[3]{64} = 4$ units.) The long leg of the triangle is the diagonal of the base of the cube. Its length can be found using the Pythagorean theorem: $4^2 + 4^2 = x^2; x = \sqrt{32} = 4\sqrt{2}$.

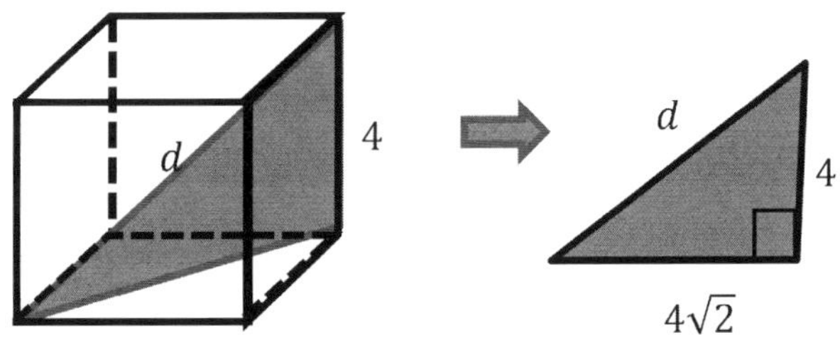

Use the Pythagorean theorem again to find d, the diameter of the sphere: $d^2 = \left(4\sqrt{2}\right)^2 + 4^2; d = \sqrt{48} = 4\sqrt{3}$. To find the volume of the sphere, use the formula $V = \frac{4}{3}\pi r^3$. Since the radius r of the sphere is half the diameter, $r = 2\sqrt{3}$, and $V = \frac{4}{3}\pi(2\sqrt{3})^3 = \frac{4}{3}\pi\left(24\sqrt{3}\right) = 32\pi\sqrt{3}$ cubic units.

59. B: A cube has six square faces. The arrangement of these faces in a two-dimensional figure is a net of a cube if the figure can be folded to form a cube. If this is folded, the bottom square in the second column will overlap the fourth square in the top row, so the figure does not represent a net of a cube. The other figures represent three of the eleven possible nets of a cube.

60. D: The cross-section is a hexagon.

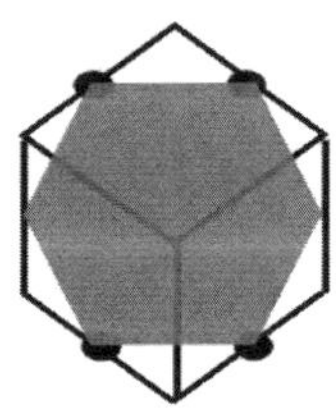

61. A: Use the formula for the volume of a sphere to find the radius of the sphere:

$$\begin{aligned} V &= \frac{4}{3}\pi r^3 \\ 36\pi &= \frac{4}{3}\pi r^3 \\ 36 &= \frac{4}{3}r^3 \\ 27 &= r^3 \\ 3 &= r \end{aligned}$$

Then, substitute the point $(h, k, l) = (1, 0, -2)$ and the radius $r = 3$ into the equation of a sphere:

$$(x-h)^2 + (y-k)^2 + (z-l)^2 = r^2$$
$$(x-1)^2 + y^2 + (z+2)^2 = 3^2$$
$$(x-1)^2 + y^2 + (z+2)^2 = 9$$
$$x^2 - 2x + 1 + y^2 + z^2 + 4z + 4 = 9$$
$$x^2 + y^2 + z^2 - 2x + 4z = 4$$

62. B: The triangle is a right triangle with legs 3 and 4 units long.

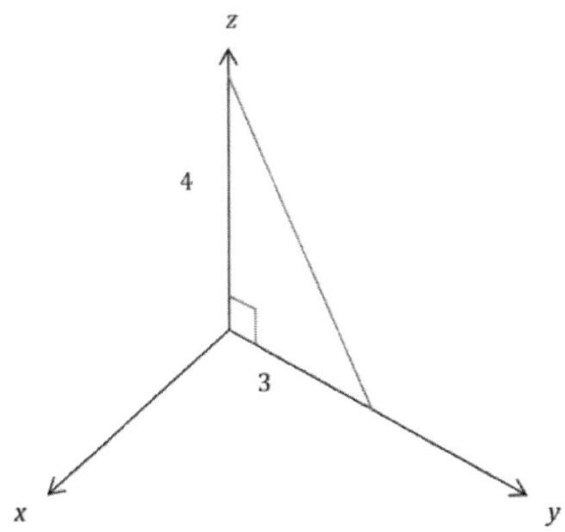

If the triangle is rotated about the z-axis, the solid formed is a cone with a height of 4 and a radius of 3. If the triangle is rotated about the y-axis, the solid formed is a cone with a height of 3 and a radius of 4.

$$V = \frac{1}{3}\pi r^2 h$$

$$V = \frac{1}{3}\pi(3^2)4 \quad V = \frac{1}{3}\pi(4^2)3$$
$$V = 12\pi \qquad V = 16\pi$$

The difference in the volumes of the two cones is $16\pi - 12\pi = 4\pi$ cubic units.

63. D: The point $(5, -5)$ lies on the line segment that has a slope of -2 and passes through $(3, -1)$. If $(5, -5)$ is one of the endpoints of the line segment, then the other would be $(1,3)$.

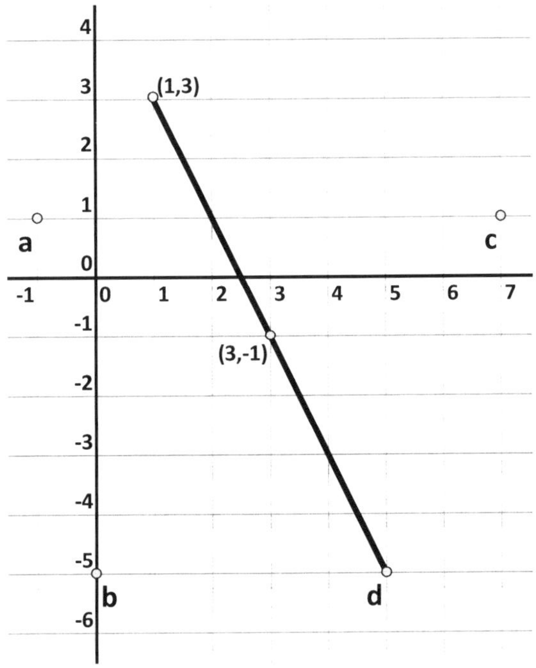

64. D: Since all of the answer choices are parallelograms, determine whether the parallelogram is also a rhombus, a rectangle, or both. One way to do this is by examining the parallelogram's diagonals. If the parallelogram's diagonals are perpendicular, then the parallelogram is a rhombus. If the parallelogram's diagonals are congruent, then the parallelogram is a rectangle. If a parallelogram is both a rhombus and a rectangle, then it is a square. A plot of the quadrilateral would be:

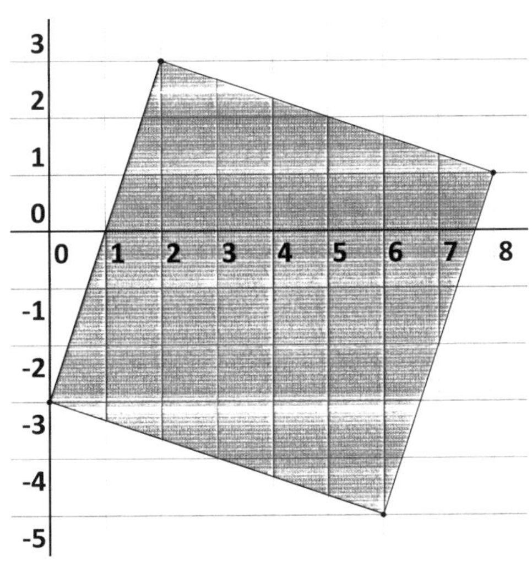

To determine whether the diagonals are perpendicular, find the slopes of the diagonals of the quadrilateral:

Diagonal 1: $\frac{6-2}{-5-3} = \frac{4}{-8} = -\frac{1}{2}$

Diagonal 2: $\frac{0-8}{-3-1} = -\frac{8}{-4} = 2$

The diagonals have opposite inverse slopes and are therefore perpendicular. Thus, the parallelogram is a rhombus.

To determine whether the diagonals are congruent, find the lengths of the diagonals of the quadrilateral:

Diagonal 1: $\sqrt{(6-2)^2 + (-5-3)^2} = \sqrt{(4)^2 + (-8)^2} = \sqrt{16+64} = \sqrt{80} = 4\sqrt{5}$

Diagonal 2: $\sqrt{(0-8)^2 + (-3-1)\text{^}2} = \sqrt{(-8)^2 + (-4)\text{^}2} = \sqrt{64+16} = \sqrt{80} = 4\sqrt{5}$

The diagonals are congruent, so the parallelogram is a rectangle.

Since the polygon is a rhombus and a rectangle, it is also a square.

65. A: The equation of the circle is given in general form. When the equation is written in the standard form $(x-h)^2 + (y-k)^2 = r^2$, where (h,k) is the center of the circle and r is the radius of the circle, the radius is easy to determine. Putting the equation into standard form requires completing the square for x and y:

$$x^2 - 10x + y^2 + 8y = -29$$
$$(x^2 - 10x + 25) + (y^2 + 8y + 16) = -29 + 25 + 16$$
$$(x-5)^2 + (y+4)^2 = 12$$

Since $r^2 = 12,$ and since r must be a positive number, $r = \sqrt{12} = 2\sqrt{3}.$

66. D: One way to determine whether the equation represents an ellipse, a circle, a parabola, or a hyperbola is to find the discriminant $b^2 - 4ac$ of the general equation form of a conic section, $ax^2 + bxy + cy^2 + dx + ey + f = 0,$ where $a, b, c, d, e,$ and f are constants. Given that the conic section is non-degenerate, if the discriminant is positive, then the equation is a hyperbola; if the discriminant is negative, then the equation is a circle (when $a = c$ and $b = 0$) or an ellipse; and if the discriminant is zero, then the equation is a parabola. For $2x^2 - 3y^2 - 12x + 6y - 15 = 0,$ $a = 2,\ b = 0,\ c = -3,\ d = -12,\ e = 6,$ and $f = -15.$ The discriminant $b^2 - 4ac$ is equal to $0^2 - 4(2)(-3) = 24.$ Since the discriminant is positive, the graph is hyperbolic.

67. C: When a figure is reflected twice over non-parallel lines, the resulting transformation is a rotation about the point of intersection of the two lines of reflection. The two lines of reflection $y = x + 2$ and $x = 0$ intersect at $(0,2)$. So, $\Delta A''B''C''$ represents a rotation of ΔABC about the point $(0,2)$. The angle of rotation is equal to twice the angle between the two lines of reflection when measured in a clockwise direction from the first to the second line of reflection. Since the angle between the lines or reflection measures 135°, the angle of rotation which is the composition of the two reflections measures 270°. All of these properties can be visualized by drawing ΔABC, $\Delta A'B'C'$, and $\Delta A''B''C''$.

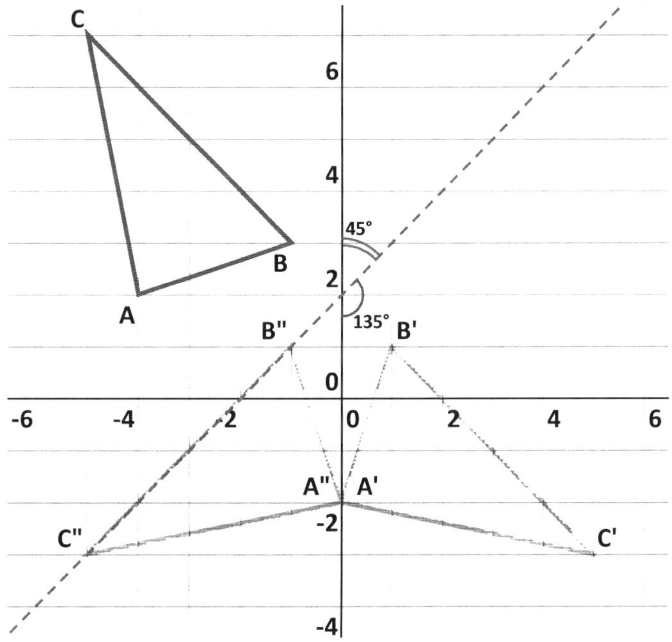

68. B: All regular polygons have rotational symmetry. The angle of rotation is the smallest angle by which the polygon can be rotated such that it maps onto itself; any multiple of this angle will also map the polygon onto itself. The angle of rotation for a regular polygon is the angle formed between two lines drawn from consecutives vertices to the center of the polygon. Since the vertices of a regular polygon lie on a circle, for a regular polygon with n sides, the angle of rotation measures $\frac{360°}{n}$.

Number of sides of regular polygon	Angle of rotation	Angles ≤ 360° which map the polygon onto itself
4	$\frac{360}{4} = 90°$	90°, 180°, 270°, 360°
6	$\frac{360}{6} = 60°$	60°, 120°, 180°, 240°, 300°, 360°
8	$\frac{360}{8} = 45°$	45°, 90°, 135°, 180°, 225°, 270°, 315°, 360°
10	$\frac{360}{10} = 36°$	36°, 72°, 108°, 144°, 180°, 216°, 252°, 288°, 324°, 360°

69. A: Since the y-coordinates of points P and Q are the same, line segment $\overline{PQ}$ is a horizontal line segment whose length is the difference in the x-coordinates a and c. Because the length of a line cannot be negative, and because it is unknown whether $a > c$ or $a < c$, $PQ = |a - c|$ or $|c - a|$. Since the x-coordinates of Q and Q' are the same, line segment $\overline{P'Q}$ is a vertical line segment whose length is $|d - b|$or $|b - d|$. The quadrilateral formed by the transformation of $\overline{PQ}$ to $\overline{P'Q'}$ is a parallelogram. If the base of the parallelogram is $\overline{PQ}$, then the height is $\overline{P'Q}$ since $\overline{PQ} \perp \overline{P'Q}$ For a parallelogram, $A = bh$, so $A = |a - c| \times |b - d|$.

70. A: Nominal data are data that are collected which have no intrinsic quantity or order. For instance, a survey might ask the respondent to identify his or her gender. While it is possible to compare the relative frequency of each response (for example, "most of the respondents are women"), it is not possible to calculate the mean, which requires data to be numeric, or median, which requires data to be ordered. Interval data are both numeric and ordered, so mean and median can be determined, as can the mode, the interval within which there are the most data. Ordinal data has an inherent order, but there is not a set interval between two points. For example, a survey might ask the respondents whether they were very dissatisfied, dissatisfied, neutral, satisfied, or very satisfied with the customer service received. Since the data are not numeric, the mean cannot be calculated, but since ordering the data is possible, the median has context.

71. B: A line graph is often used to show change over time. A Venn diagram shows the relationships among sets. A box-and-whisker plot displays how numeric data are distributed throughout the range. A pie chart shows the relationship of parts to a whole.

72. A: The average number of male students in 11th and 12th grade is 125 $\left(\text{calculated as } \frac{131 + 119}{2}\right)$. The number of Hispanic students at the school is 10% of 1219, which is 122 students (rounded up from 121.9). The difference in the number of male and female students at the school is $630 - 589 = 41$, and the difference in the number of 9th and 12th grade students at the school is $354 - 255 = 99$.

73. C: 52% of the student population is Caucasian. There are 630 female students at the school out of 1219 students, so the percentage of female students is $\frac{630}{1219} \times 100\% \approx 52\%$. The percentages rounded to the nearest whole number are the same.

74. D: 131 of 283 eleventh graders are male. Given that an 11th grader is chosen to attend the conference, the probability that a male is chosen is $\frac{\text{number of males}}{\text{number of 11th graders}} = \frac{131}{283} \approx 0.46$. Note that this is **NOT** the same question as one which asks for the probability of selecting at random from the school a student who is male and in eleventh grade, which has a probability of $\frac{131}{1219} \approx 0.11$.

75. A: The range is the spread of the data. It can be calculated for each class by subtracting the lowest test score from the highest, or it can be determined visually from the graph. The difference between the highest and lowest test scores in class A is $98 - 23 = 75$ points. The range for each of the other classes is much smaller.

76. D: 75% of the data in a set is above the first quartile. Since the first quartile for this set is 73, there is a 75% chance that a student chosen at random from class 2 scored above a 73.

77. C: Since each coin toss is an independent event, the probability of the compound event of flipping the coin three times is equal to the product of the probabilities of the individual events. For example, $P(HHH) = P(H) \times P(H) \times P(H)$, $P(HHT) = P(H) \times P(H) \times P(T)$, etc. When a coin is flipped three times, all of the possible outcomes are HHH, HHT, HTH, HTT, THH, THT, TTH, and TTT. Using the data from the all heads and all tails results, calculate an experimental probability $P(H)$:

$$P(three\ heads) = P(HHH) = P(H)P(H)P(H) = [P(H)]^3$$

$$[P(H)]^3 = \frac{30}{100}$$

$$[P(H)] = \sqrt[3]{0.3} \cong 0.67$$

$$P(no\ heads) = P(TTT) = P(T)P(T)P(T) = [P(T)]^3$$

$$[P(T)]^3 = \frac{4}{100}$$

$$[P(T)] = \sqrt[3]{0.04} \cong 0.34$$

$$P(H) = 1 - P(T) \cong 0.66$$

Notice that these calculated values of P(H) are approximately the same. Since 100 is a fairly large sample size for this kind of experiment, the approximation for $P(H)$ ought to be consistent for the compiled data set. Rather than calculating $P(H)$ using the data for one head and two heads, use the average calculated probability to confirm that the number of expected outcomes of one head and two head matches the number of actual outcomes.

$$P(one\ head) = P(HTT) + P(THT) + P(TTH) = 3P(H)P(T)P(T) = 3P(H)[P(T)]^2$$

$$P(two\ heads) = P(HHT) + P(HTH) + P(THH) = 3P(H)P(H)P(T) = 3[P(H)]^2P(T)$$

The number of expected outcomes of getting one head in three coin flips out of 100 trials $100\{3(0.665)[(1-0.665)^2]\} \approx 22$, and the expected outcome getting of two heads in three coin flips out of 100 trials three flips is $100\{3(0.665)^2(1-0.665)\} \approx 44$. Since 22 and 44 are, in fact, the data obtained, 0.665 is indeed a good approximation for P(H) when the coin used in this experiment is tossed.

78. D: A fair coin has a symmetrical binomial distribution which peaks in its center. Since choice B shows a skewed distribution for the fair coin, it cannot be the correct answer. From the frequency histogram given for the misshapen coin, it is evident that the misshapen coin is more likely to land on heads. Therefore, it is more likely that ten coin flips would result in fewer tails than ten coin flips of a fair coin; consequently, the probability distribution for the misshapen coin would be higher than the fair coin's distribution toward the smaller number of tails. Choice A shows a probability distribution which peaks at a value of 5 and which is symmetrical with respect to the peak, which verifies that it cannot be correct. (Furthermore, in choice A, the sum of the probabilities shown for each number of tails for the misshapen coin is not equal to 1.) The distribution for the misshapen coin in choice C is skewed in the wrong direction, favoring tails instead of heads, and must therefore also be incorrect. Choice D shows the correct binomial distribution for the fair coin and the appropriate shift for the misshapen coin.

Another way to approach this question is to use the answer from the previous problem to determine the probability of obtaining particular events, such as no tails and no heads, and then compare those probabilities to the graphs. For example, for the misshapen coin:

$$P(0\ tails) = P(10\ heads) \approx (0.665)^{10} \approx 0.017$$

$$P(10\ tails) \approx (0.335)^{10} \approx 0.000018$$

For a fair coin:

$$P(0\ tails) = P(10\ heads) = P(10\ tails) = P(0\ heads) = (0.5)^{10} \approx 0.001$$

To find values other than these, it is helpful to use the binomial distribution formula $({}_n\mathrm{C}_r)p^r q^{n-r}$, where n is the number of trials, r is the number of successes, p is the probability of success, and q is the probability of failure. For this problem, obtaining tails is a success, and the probability of obtaining tails is $p = 0.33$ for the misshapen coin and $p = 0.5$ for the fair coin; so, $q = 0.67$ for the misshapen coin and $q = 0.5$ for the fair coin. To find the probability of, say, getting three tails for ten flips of the misshapen coin, find:

$$({}_n\mathrm{C}_r)p^r q^{n-r} = ({}_{10}\mathrm{C}_3)(0.335)^3(0.665)^7 = \frac{10!}{3!\,7!}(0.335)^3(0.665)^7 \approx 0.259$$

The calculated probabilities match those shown in choice D.

79. C: The probability of an event is the number of possible occurrences of that event divided by the number of all possible outcomes. A camper who is at least eight years old can be eight, nine, or ten years old, so the probability of randomly selecting a camper at least eight years old is

$$\frac{\text{number of eight-, nine-, and ten-year old campers}}{\text{total number of campers}} = \frac{14 + 12 + 10}{12 + 15 + 14 + 12 + 10} = \frac{36}{63} = \frac{4}{7}$$

80. B: There are three ways in which two women from the same department can be selected: two women can be selected from the first department, or two women can be selected from the second department, or two women can be selected from the third department.

Department 1	**Department 2**	**Department 3**
$\frac{12}{103} \times \frac{11}{102} = \frac{132}{10506}$	$\frac{28}{103} \times \frac{27}{102} = \frac{756}{10506}$	$\frac{16}{103} \times \frac{15}{102} = \frac{240}{10506}$

Since any of these is a distinct possible outcome, the probability that two women will be selected from the same department is the sum of these outcomes:

$$\frac{132}{10506} + \frac{756}{10506} + \frac{240}{10506} = \frac{1128}{10506} \approx 0.107\text{, or } 10.7\%$$

How to Overcome Test Anxiety

Just the thought of taking a test is enough to make most people a little nervous. A test is an important event that can have a long-term impact on your future, so it's important to take it seriously and it's natural to feel anxious about performing well. But just because anxiety is normal, that doesn't mean that it's helpful in test taking, or that you should simply accept it as part of your life. Anxiety can have a variety of effects. These effects can be mild, like making you feel slightly nervous, or severe, like blocking your ability to focus or remember even a simple detail.

If you experience test anxiety—whether severe or mild—it's important to know how to beat it. To discover this, first you need to understand what causes test anxiety.

Causes of Test Anxiety

While we often think of anxiety as an uncontrollable emotional state, it can actually be caused by simple, practical things. One of the most common causes of test anxiety is that a person does not feel adequately prepared for their test. This feeling can be the result of many different issues such as poor study habits or lack of organization, but the most common culprit is time management. Starting to study too late, failing to organize your study time to cover all of the material, or being distracted while you study will mean that you're not well prepared for the test. This may lead to cramming the night before, which will cause you to be physically and mentally exhausted for the test. Poor time management also contributes to feelings of stress, fear, and hopelessness as you realize you are not well prepared but don't know what to do about it.

Other times, test anxiety is not related to your preparation for the test but comes from unresolved fear. This may be a past failure on a test, or poor performance on tests in general. It may come from comparing yourself to others who seem to be performing better or from the stress of living up to expectations. Anxiety may be driven by fears of the future—how failure on this test would affect your educational and career goals. These fears are often completely irrational, but they can still negatively impact your test performance.

Elements of Test Anxiety

As mentioned earlier, test anxiety is considered to be an emotional state, but it has physical and mental components as well. Sometimes you may not even realize that you are suffering from test anxiety until you notice the physical symptoms. These can include trembling hands, rapid heartbeat, sweating, nausea, and tense muscles. Extreme anxiety may lead to fainting or vomiting. Obviously, any of these symptoms can have a negative impact on testing. It is important to recognize them as soon as they begin to occur so that you can address the problem before it damages your performance.

The mental components of test anxiety include trouble focusing and inability to remember learned information. During a test, your mind is on high alert, which can help you recall information and stay focused for an extended period of time. However, anxiety interferes with your mind's natural processes, causing you to blank out, even on the questions you know well. The strain of testing during anxiety makes it difficult to stay focused, especially on a test that may take several hours. Extreme anxiety can take a huge mental toll, making it difficult not only to recall test information but even to understand the test questions or pull your thoughts together.

Effects of Test Anxiety

Test anxiety is like a disease—if left untreated, it will get progressively worse. Anxiety leads to poor performance, and this reinforces the feelings of fear and failure, which in turn lead to poor performances on subsequent tests. It can grow from a mild nervousness to a crippling condition. If allowed to progress, test anxiety can have a big impact on your schooling, and consequently on your future.

Test anxiety can spread to other parts of your life. Anxiety on tests can become anxiety in any stressful situation, and blanking on a test can turn into panicking in a job situation. But fortunately, you don't have to let anxiety rule your testing and determine your grades. There are a number of relatively simple steps you can take to move past anxiety and function normally on a test and in the rest of life.

Physical Steps for Beating Test Anxiety

While test anxiety is a serious problem, the good news is that it can be overcome. It doesn't have to control your ability to think and remember information. While it may take time, you can begin taking steps today to beat anxiety.

Just as your first hint that you may be struggling with anxiety comes from the physical symptoms, the first step to treating it is also physical. Rest is crucial for having a clear, strong mind. If you are tired, it is much easier to give in to anxiety. But if you establish good sleep habits, your body and mind will be ready to perform optimally, without the strain of exhaustion. Additionally, sleeping well helps you to retain information better, so you're more likely to recall the answers when you see the test questions.

Getting good sleep means more than going to bed on time. It's important to allow your brain time to relax. Take study breaks from time to time so it doesn't get overworked, and don't study right before bed. Take time to rest your mind before trying to rest your body, or you may find it difficult to fall asleep.

Along with sleep, other aspects of physical health are important in preparing for a test. Good nutrition is vital for good brain function. Sugary foods and drinks may give a burst of energy but this burst is followed by a crash, both physically and emotionally. Instead, fuel your body with protein and vitamin-rich foods.

Also, drink plenty of water. Dehydration can lead to headaches and exhaustion, especially if your brain is already under stress from the rigors of the test. Particularly if your test is a long one, drink water during the breaks. And if possible, take an energy-boosting snack to eat between sections.

Along with sleep and diet, a third important part of physical health is exercise. Maintaining a steady workout schedule is helpful, but even taking 5-minute study breaks to walk can help get your blood pumping faster and clear your head. Exercise also releases endorphins, which contribute to a positive feeling and can help combat test anxiety.

When you nurture your physical health, you are also contributing to your mental health. If your body is healthy, your mind is much more likely to be healthy as well. So take time to rest, nourish your body with healthy food and water, and get moving as much as possible. Taking these physical steps will make you stronger and more able to take the mental steps necessary to overcome test anxiety.

Mental Steps for Beating Test Anxiety

Working on the mental side of test anxiety can be more challenging, but as with the physical side, there are clear steps you can take to overcome it. As mentioned earlier, test anxiety often stems from lack of preparation, so the obvious solution is to prepare for the test. Effective studying may be the most important weapon you have for beating test anxiety, but you can and should employ several other mental tools to combat fear.

First, boost your confidence by reminding yourself of past success—tests or projects that you aced. If you're putting as much effort into preparing for this test as you did for those, there's no reason you should expect to fail here. Work hard to prepare; then trust your preparation.

Second, surround yourself with encouraging people. It can be helpful to find a study group, but be sure that the people you're around will encourage a positive attitude. If you spend time with others who are anxious or cynical, this will only contribute to your own anxiety. Look for others who are motivated to study hard from a desire to succeed, not from a fear of failure.

Third, reward yourself. A test is physically and mentally tiring, even without anxiety, and it can be helpful to have something to look forward to. Plan an activity following the test, regardless of the outcome, such as going to a movie or getting ice cream.

When you are taking the test, if you find yourself beginning to feel anxious, remind yourself that you know the material. Visualize successfully completing the test. Then take a few deep, relaxing breaths and return to it. Work through the questions carefully but with confidence, knowing that you are capable of succeeding.

Developing a healthy mental approach to test taking will also aid in other areas of life. Test anxiety affects more than just the actual test—it can be damaging to your mental health and even contribute to depression. It's important to beat test anxiety before it becomes a problem for more than testing.

Study Strategy

Being prepared for the test is necessary to combat anxiety, but what does being prepared look like? You may study for hours on end and still not feel prepared. What you need is a strategy for test prep. The next few pages outline our recommended steps to help you plan out and conquer the challenge of preparation.

Step 1: Scope Out the Test

Learn everything you can about the format (multiple choice, essay, etc.) and what will be on the test. Gather any study materials, course outlines, or sample exams that may be available. Not only will this help you to prepare, but knowing what to expect can help to alleviate test anxiety.

Step 2: Map Out the Material

Look through the textbook or study guide and make note of how many chapters or sections it has. Then divide these over the time you have. For example, if a book has 15 chapters and you have five days to study, you need to cover three chapters each day. Even better, if you have the time, leave an extra day at the end for overall review after you have gone through the material in depth.

If time is limited, you may need to prioritize the material. Look through it and make note of which sections you think you already have a good grasp on, and which need review. While you are studying, skim quickly through the familiar sections and take more time on the challenging parts.

Write out your plan so you don't get lost as you go. Having a written plan also helps you feel more in control of the study, so anxiety is less likely to arise from feeling overwhelmed at the amount to cover.

Step 3: Gather Your Tools

Decide what study method works best for you. Do you prefer to highlight in the book as you study and then go back over the highlighted portions? Or do you type out notes of the important information? Or is it helpful to make flashcards that you can carry with you? Assemble the pens, index cards, highlighters, post-it notes, and any other materials you may need so you won't be distracted by getting up to find things while you study.

If you're having a hard time retaining the information or organizing your notes, experiment with different methods. For example, try color-coding by subject with colored pens, highlighters, or post-it notes. If you learn better by hearing, try recording yourself reading your notes so you can listen while in the car, working out, or simply sitting at your desk. Ask a friend to quiz you from your flashcards, or try teaching someone the material to solidify it in your mind.

Step 4: Create Your Environment

It's important to avoid distractions while you study. This includes both the obvious distractions like visitors and the subtle distractions like an uncomfortable chair (or a too-comfortable couch that makes you want to fall asleep). Set up the best study environment possible: good lighting and a comfortable work area. If background music helps you focus, you may want to turn it on, but otherwise keep the room quiet. If you are using a computer to take notes, be sure you don't have any other windows open, especially applications like social media, games, or anything else that could distract you. Silence your phone and turn off notifications. Be sure to keep water close by so you stay hydrated while you study (but avoid unhealthy drinks and snacks).

Also, take into account the best time of day to study. Are you freshest first thing in the morning? Try to set aside some time then to work through the material. Is your mind clearer in the afternoon or evening? Schedule your study session then. Another method is to study at the same time of day that you will take the test, so that your brain gets used to working on the material at that time and will be ready to focus at test time.

Step 5: Study!

Once you have done all the study preparation, it's time to settle into the actual studying. Sit down, take a few moments to settle your mind so you can focus, and begin to follow your study plan. Don't give in to distractions or let yourself procrastinate. This is your time to prepare so you'll be ready to fearlessly approach the test. Make the most of the time and stay focused.

Of course, you don't want to burn out. If you study too long you may find that you're not retaining the information very well. Take regular study breaks. For example, taking five minutes out of every hour to walk briskly, breathing deeply and swinging your arms, can help your mind stay fresh.

As you get to the end of each chapter or section, it's a good idea to do a quick review. Remind yourself of what you learned and work on any difficult parts. When you feel that you've mastered the material, move on to the next part. At the end of your study session, briefly skim through your notes again.

But while review is helpful, cramming last minute is NOT. If at all possible, work ahead so that you won't need to fit all your study into the last day. Cramming overloads your brain with more information than it can process and retain, and your tired mind may struggle to recall even previously learned information when it is overwhelmed with last-minute study. Also, the urgent nature of cramming and the stress placed on your brain contribute to anxiety. You'll be more likely to go to the test feeling unprepared and having trouble thinking clearly.

So don't cram, and don't stay up late before the test, even just to review your notes at a leisurely pace. Your brain needs rest more than it needs to go over the information again. In fact, plan to finish your studies by noon or early afternoon the day before the test. Give your brain the rest of the day to relax or focus on other things, and get a good night's sleep. Then you will be fresh for the test and better able to recall what you've studied.

Step 6: Take a Practice Test

Many courses offer sample tests, either online or in the study materials. This is an excellent resource to check whether you have mastered the material, as well as to prepare for the test format and environment.

Check the test format ahead of time: the number of questions, the type (multiple choice, free response, etc.), and the time limit. Then create a plan for working through them. For example, if you have 30 minutes to take a 60-question test, your limit is 30 seconds per question. Spend less time on the questions you know well so that you can take more time on the difficult ones.

If you have time to take several practice tests, take the first one open book, with no time limit. Work through the questions at your own pace and make sure you fully understand them. Gradually work up to taking a test under test conditions: sit at a desk with all study materials put away and set a timer. Pace yourself to make sure you finish the test with time to spare and go back to check your answers if you have time.

After each test, check your answers. On the questions you missed, be sure you understand why you missed them. Did you misread the question (tests can use tricky wording)? Did you forget the information? Or was it something you hadn't learned? Go back and study any shaky areas that the practice tests reveal.

Taking these tests not only helps with your grade, but also aids in combating test anxiety. If you're already used to the test conditions, you're less likely to worry about it, and working through tests until you're scoring well gives you a confidence boost. Go through the practice tests until you feel comfortable, and then you can go into the test knowing that you're ready for it.

Test Tips

On test day, you should be confident, knowing that you've prepared well and are ready to answer the questions. But aside from preparation, there are several test day strategies you can employ to maximize your performance.

First, as stated before, get a good night's sleep the night before the test (and for several nights before that, if possible). Go into the test with a fresh, alert mind rather than staying up late to study.

Try not to change too much about your normal routine on the day of the test. It's important to eat a nutritious breakfast, but if you normally don't eat breakfast at all, consider eating just a protein bar. If you're a coffee drinker, go ahead and have your normal coffee. Just make sure you time it so that the caffeine doesn't wear off right in the middle of your test. Avoid sugary beverages, and drink enough water to stay hydrated but not so much that you need a restroom break 10 minutes into the test. If your test isn't first thing in the morning, consider going for a walk or doing a light workout before the test to get your blood flowing.

Allow yourself enough time to get ready, and leave for the test with plenty of time to spare so you won't have the anxiety of scrambling to arrive in time. Another reason to be early is to select a good seat. It's helpful to sit away from doors and windows, which can be distracting. Find a good seat, get out your supplies, and settle your mind before the test begins.

When the test begins, start by going over the instructions carefully, even if you already know what to expect. Make sure you avoid any careless mistakes by following the directions.

Then begin working through the questions, pacing yourself as you've practiced. If you're not sure on an answer, don't spend too much time on it, and don't let it shake your confidence. Either skip it and come back later, or eliminate as many wrong answers as possible and guess among the remaining ones. Don't dwell on these questions as you continue—put them out of your mind and focus on what lies ahead.

Be sure to read all of the answer choices, even if you're sure the first one is the right answer. Sometimes you'll find a better one if you keep reading. But don't second-guess yourself if you do immediately know the answer. Your gut instinct is usually right. Don't let test anxiety rob you of the information you know.

If you have time at the end of the test (and if the test format allows), go back and review your answers. Be cautious about changing any, since your first instinct tends to be correct, but make sure you didn't misread any of the questions or accidentally mark the wrong answer choice. Look over any you skipped and make an educated guess.

At the end, leave the test feeling confident. You've done your best, so don't waste time worrying about your performance or wishing you could change anything. Instead, celebrate the successful completion of this test. And finally, use this test to learn how to deal with anxiety even better next time.

Review Video: Test Anxiety
Visit mometrix.com/academy and enter code: 100340

Important Qualification

Not all anxiety is created equal. If your test anxiety is causing major issues in your life beyond the classroom or testing center, or if you are experiencing troubling physical symptoms related to your anxiety, it may be a sign of a serious physiological or psychological condition. If this sounds like your situation, we strongly encourage you to seek professional help.

Online Resources

Due to our efforts to try to keep this book to a manageable length, we've created a link that will give you access to all of your online resources:

mometrix.com/resources719/dsstmathla

It's Your Moment, Let's Celebrate It!

Share your story @mometrixtestpreparation